INDIAN MYTHOLOGY

INDIAN MYTHOLOGY

Veronica Ions

PAUL HAMLYN
LONDON · NEW YORK · SYDNEY · TORONTO

Contents

11 Religion and history

13 Early deities

14 Vedic deities
14 Varuna 15 Prithivi and Dyaus - Indra
17 The Maruts - Vayu - Tvashtri 18 The Ribhus -
Agni 19 Soma 20 Chandra - Aditi and the Adityas -
Vivasvat - Savitri 21 Surya - Ushas 22 Ratri -
The Aswins - Rudra 23 Vishnu

23 Developments of the Brahmanic age

24 Time and the creation of the universe

32 Creation of man and of death

38 Pantheism and polytheism

40 Hindu mythology

40 The Hindu triad
41 Brahma 42 Shiva 46 Vishnu 48 Vishnu's avatars: Matsya -
Kurma - Varaha 50 Narasinha 51 Vamana - Parasurama
54 Ramachandra (Rama) 61 Krishna 72 Buddha - Kalki

73 The Vedic gods in Hinduism
73 Indra 77 Yama 78 Varuna 79 Agni - Surya
80 Vayu 81 Soma

84 New gods
84 Kubera - Karttikeya 88 Visvakarma - Dharma -
Kama

89 Goddesses
89 Sarasvati 90 Lakshmi 91 Devi 94 The triad of
goddesses - Aditi 95 Saranyu - Prithivi 96 Rati -
Diti 97 Manasa - Shasti and Shitala

100 Animal deities
100 Ganesa 101 Garuda 102 Hanuman

105 Other mythological animals
105 Jambavan 108 Sugriva - Bali - The Nagas

109 Mountains, rivers and pools as deities
109 Mountains - Rivers 110 Holy pools

111 Enemies of the gods

115 Enemies of men

117 Other spirits

118 Troops of minor deities

THE HAMLYN PUBLISHING GROUP LIMITED · LONDON · NEW YORK · SYDNEY · TORONTO
Hamlyn House, Feltham, Middlesex, England
First edition 1967   Third impression 1973   Copyright © 1967 Veronica Ions   ISBN 0 600 02369 9
Manufactured in the United States of America

118 Demi-gods and rishis

119 The Mahabharata

126 Buddhist mythology
126 Buddha's previous lives 128 Buddha's birth -
Boyhood 129 Marriage - The four signs -
The search for enlightenment 132 Enlightenment
133 Preaching 134 The opposition to Buddha -
The desire for death

135 Buddhist cosmology and the Buddhist pantheon

136 Jain mythology
138 The Jain universal cycle - The Jain universe

140 Further reading list

140 Acknowledgments

140 Index

Colour plates

6 The tower of the Parthasarathi Temple at Triplicane

26 Two primitive deities

27 The face of Shiva at Elephanta

30 Shiva Nataraja, Lord of the Dance

31 Shiva and his family at the burning ground

34 Harihara, the composite form of Vishnu and Shiva

35 Vishnu as Varaha, the boar avatar

49 Vishnu and his avatars

52 The Rajarani Temple at Bhubaneswar

53 Ravana rallies his demons

56 Krishna and Radha

57 Krishna and the serpent

74 Surya, the sun god

75 Durga destroys Mahisha

82 The ceiling of the temple at Dilwara

83 The goddess Sarasvati

98 Kama, god of love

99 Garuda, king of the birds

103 The Horse Court at Srirangam

106 Arjuna propitiates the gods

107 The north gate at Sanchi

127 Manjusri, Buddhist god of wisdom

130 Buddha sits meditating

131 Sakra commands the exchange of babies

Religion and history

India's recorded civilisation is one of the longest in the course of world history and its mythology spans the whole of that time and more. Furthermore the mythology is distinguished from that of most other lands, and certainly from those of the West, by the fact that it is still part of the living culture—and not merely of the uneducated masses but of every level of society. As we shall see, the Indians have always tended to retain their early beliefs and mould them—sometimes perhaps to distort them—in such a way as to mirror new social conditions or to fit into a new philosophical scheme. Deities and the myths attached to them have thus multiplied despite recurrent attempts on the part of priests and philosophers to impose a pantheistic or monotheistic scheme on the existing polytheism.

The influence wielded by the priesthood in India has always been great and at times has succeeded, at least among the educated, in transforming the very pattern of beliefs. In some cases the changes advocated only foreshadowed the natural evolution of India's mythology as a consequence of historical circumstances: dynastic changes, invasions, economic conditions and the resultant social setting of the Indian peoples. Such changes were particularly apt to alter mythological beliefs, for Indian myths as well as the religions around which they have grown up are closely tied to the social structure. It may be said that this is true of all mythologies, but Indian mythology, through its persistence beyond the primitive levels of civilisation and into a highly developed and stratified culture, has been able, for instance, to reinforce the doctrines of caste, so that even government disapproval cannot oust it from the hearts of the people, educated or not. Others of the priests' innovations were inspired by philosophical developments understood only by the few—in general only the priests themselves—but affecting all. Just as in Egypt, where mythology first sought to explain natural phenomena, then served to bolster the status of the monarch, and finally became a symbolic language expressing the ideas of philosophers, so in India the esoteric cults treated the great body of accumulated myths as a source of symbols with which to express philosophical ideas. Inevitably the myths themselves were sometimes moulded to conform to the ideas that they were made to represent.

Changes in the social and philosophical backgrounds were not the only factors at play—these may be termed the natural causes of evolution. Factors less openly admitted but of equal importance were the various efforts on the part of the priests, or Brahmins, to maintain their

Mohenjodaro. Part of the excavated remains of one of the great cities of the pre-Aryan civilisation, c. 2000 B.C. Elaborate town planning and domestic architecture testify to the advanced level of life. The ruins of a Buddhist stupa, built 2000 years ago, can be seen in the distance.

Below: *Goddess standing between the parted branches of a sacred pipal tree (the tree of Buddha's enlightenment). Half-kneeling before her is a suppliant god, leading a mythical animal, part human, part bull and part ram, apparently to be sacrificed. The horned crowns worn by goddess and suppliant indicate their divine nature. In the foreground are seven maidservants. Seal found at Harappa. c. 2000 B.C.*

Above: *A symbol of fortune, bringer of good luck. The swastika, whose arms could be turned in either direction, became associated in Hinduism with the sun and also with Ganesa, the pathfinder whose image is often found where two roads cross. Harappa, second millennium B.C. British Museum*

own power and influence with the masses by accepting their more primitive beliefs and deities and weaving them into the new system by means of myth. By maintaining the allegiance of the people during periods of foreign domination, especially from about 300 B.C. to A.D. 1000, the Brahmins consolidated their own position of trust with the rulers.

That none of these trends was completely dominant is attested by the extreme complexity of Hindu mythology as it exists today, and even more by the numerous contradictions and inconsistencies which exist in the stories concerning practically every deity in the Indian pantheon, and the thread of anti-Brahminism which runs through some myths. Some of these contradictions and in part the great differences which today exist between the beliefs held by the educated and the peasants may be traced to the overcomplicated systems thus evolved. The philosophical preoccupations of the Brahmins and the growing intricacies of their rituals led to the exclusion of the common people, who were thus often thrown back on earlier beliefs, whose attendant mythology had more bearing on their own preoccupations. Still more often they accepted the new beliefs only on condition that they should be able to identify the new gods with the old in an attempt to reconcile all beliefs. In this they were certainly helped by the developing ideas of the priests. The idea of reincarnation, which was unknown to the Aryan invaders and is never mentioned in the Vedas, was developed to the point where any deity, hero, spirit or human being might be an incarnation of any other. By applying this principle to the old and the new gods it became possible to claim that the priests were really worshipping the same deity as the common people under another name and in another incarnation or avatar.

Despite this apparent confusion and variety, one of the remarkable features of India's mythology is precisely its homogeneity over the whole country, with the exception of myths current among the few isolated hill tribes which still exist. The beliefs of these are roughly at the stage of the earliest pre-Aryan, largely Dravidian peoples whose contribution to the body of Indian mythology was made earlier than 2000 B.C. but whose beliefs were later to be revived to some extent. The myth of the civilised peoples of India follows social and particularly educational strata rather than geographic or ethnic distribution. In terms of religion the common people are at least one step behind the educated; sometimes indeed their beliefs have even regressed. But because of the various factors outlined above, the complexity of the pantheon is common to all. However strictly attached the sectarian Hindu may be to one particular god, he has always felt the need to fit the others into his own system. Hence the continued growth of mythology, which it is best to approach historically.

A bull standing before a censer. The most common symbol on Indus civilisation seals, it suggests the connection with Iranian religion. Mohenjodaro, 2000 B.C.

An idealised representation of the bull of the Indus Valley civilisation, with the as yet undeciphered characters which date back over 4,000 years. From Harappa.

Left: *Female bust in terracotta, probably a votive offering or amulet invoking the protection of a fertility goddes. c. 150 B.C. from Mathura. Victoria and Albert Museum*

EARLY DEITIES

The Dravidian peoples, who spread into almost every part of India and Ceylon, were a mixture of the native populations of India and the dominating Proto-Dravidians, who seem to have entered India in waves from about 4000 B.C. to 2500 B.C. The seat of what was evidently an advanced civilisation was the Indus Valley, where the chief cities were Harappa and Mohenjodaro. Though no literature has so far been discovered, archaeological remains tell us something about the religious cults of the Dravidians, and tend to support the theory, evolved on the basis of later developments in Indian deities and cults, that the pre-Aryan deities were of Mesopotamian origin and more exactly of Iranian provenance; and that their resurgence was one of the reasons for the decline of the Aryan gods.

An agricultural people, the Dravidians worshipped gods connected in one way or another with fertility. There were two main elements in this: phallic worship typified in the seals found at Harappa, which show a god seated with legs crossed and wearing bull's horns (the bull being a universal symbol of male fertility); and the cult of mother-goddesses, most plainly depicted on seals which show plants growing from the womb of a female deity, or which show a naked goddess before whom a human sacrifice is being performed. Such figures are accompanied by animal ministrants, the goddess by what appears to be half-bull, half-ram, and the god by deer, an elephant, a tiger, a rhinoceros and a buffalo—or in other cases by votive serpents.

Shiva and his consort, Hindu deities, resembled these figures in many particulars, Shiva often being depicted in a crosslegged yogic posture with the bull as his symbol, and his consort being associated with human sacrifice.

Varuna, universal monarch, sustainer of creation and guardian of the cosmic law. He is ever-watchful for men's transgressions, and fetters sinners with the rope he carries about his shoulders. Stone sculpture, eleventh century.

VEDIC DEITIES

Towards 1700 B.C. a new wave of conquest destroyed the Indus Valley civilisation, and the invaders brought with them their own religion, which for perhaps a thousand years dominated the Indian scene. These Aryans were at the time of their arrival in India a warrior people of relatively low culture. They were light-skinned, hard-drinking folk, whose mastery of horses and chariots and whose use of swords brought them swift victory over the Dravidians, whom they accordingly despised as 'Dasyus', or dark-skinned. Unlike the conquered Dravidians, the Aryans had previously never settled for long; their gods were connected less with the soil on which they lived than with the universal elements. Our direct knowledge of these gods stems from the Vedas, collections of hymns which seem to have been completed by about 800 B.C. By this time, however, the Aryan pantheon had acquired

considerably more sophistication despite its retention of the earlier elements, and the accompanying mythology reflected moral preoccupations and a divine hierarchy.

Varuna

There are relatively few of the Vedic hymns addressed to Varuna, though he is the guardian of the cosmic law and the universal monarch, the object of greater veneration than the more obviously Aryan deities. Varuna is the Prime Mover of the universe. He is pictured first as creating the universe, standing in the air and, by exercise of his creative will, or maya, and using the sun as his instrument, measuring out the three worlds and forming them: the heavens, the earth, and the air between them. But Varuna's creative activity is continuous: again by exercise of his maya, he causes rain to fall and rivers to flow and thus sustains his creatures. His breath is the wind. In a sense he is embodied in his creation, or at least omnipresent in it, for he surveys it continuously with the sun as his eye, and he himself props up the heavens. Alternatively he is thought to be seated majestically in his thousand-columned, thousand-doored gold palace in the sky surrounded by his ever-watchful spies, one of whom is the sun itself which daily rises to Varuna's mansion at the zenith and reports on what it sees. Varuna's function is thus moral even more than it is creative: his maya is equally the principle of truth or justice and the god thus has the priest-like function of judging his creatures. He evaluates their actions against *rta*, laws which are unknowable to men. Varuna nevertheless punishes men for transgressing these laws, and for this purpose he carries a rope with which to tie them up, symbolic of the sins with which they fetter themselves in their ignorance. Men cannot know how they come to find themselves guilty, for Varuna's ordinances are inscrutable; they have to fall back on fear, the hope of forgiveness, and extreme circumspection in all their dealings with the god.

Varuna retained his elevated position for a relatively short time; one by one the attributes for which the great 'universal encompasser' was revered passed to other gods. Two distinct stages of this development had already occurred by the close of the Vedic age. The first change was introduced when Varuna became one of what was perhaps the first of India's long series of divine triads. This triad was composed of Varuna, Mitra and Aryaman. Mitra was in most ways similar to Varuna and like him could bind mortals with their sins, petitions to the two gods being man's sole hope of forgiveness; but Varuna's realm of jurisdiction was split, Mitra becoming guardian of the day, while Varuna's part was reduced to the guardianship of the night. Aryaman's functions are ill-defined but he must also have been a god of the heavens for the triad was known as the Adityas, or Celestial Deities, who, like Varuna alone, were credited with being the source of all heavenly gifts, the regulators of sun and moon, winds and waters, and of the seasons. Mitra in particular was therefore considered as a corn god or fertility god.

The second change in Varuna's status came when the Adityas, until then apparently a group of gods of Iranian origin, were joined by three or by nine gods of the Aryan tradition. The changed membership of the group brought a change in function, and the Adityas became no more than minor gods representing the sun in its twelve annual phases. Meanwhile the idea of a divine triad was perpetuated with figures from the Aryan pantheon: Vayu (wind), Agni (fire) and Surya (the sun); or Indra, Agni and Surya.

Prithivi and Dyaus

Prithivi, the earth, and Dyaus, the sky or heaven, were symbolised as cow and bull. They were early deities, worshipped as fertility gods and thought to have engendered all the other gods and men. Their importance diminished, however, and though they survived into later pantheons their progeny was much reduced. Ushas, the dawn, was their daughter and Agni, fire, their son. But their greatest claim to fame is through Indra. Prithivi was the 'heroic female' and Dyaus the 'vigorous god' who were Indra's parents. At the time of Indra's birth from Prithivi's side the heavens, earth and mountains began to shake and all the gods were afraid. Prithivi herself was fearful and hid her son and gave him no attention. None of the gods would come to the infant's aid for they all felt, as was indeed the case, that this child was the herald of great changes in the divine order and possibly of their own doom. As we shall see, he lost no time in justifying their fears.

Indra

Indra is a storm god, wielder of the thunderbolt, Vajra, a weapon which he carries in his right hand. Like an Aryan warrior-king, he is fair-complexioned with ruddy or golden skin and rides a horse, or alternatively rides in a golden chariot drawn by two tawny horses with flowing manes and tails. He has a violent nature, an insatiable thirst for soma, an intoxicating drink which gives him his strength, and is a steadfast defender of gods and men against Vritra, a demon who typifies the harsh aspect of nature, especially drought. As bringer of rain to a parched Indian countryside Indra was the most frequently invoked of the Vedic gods and the deity on which most of the early myths centred. The stories about his birth and his exploits as an infant make this devotion clear and explain in mythological terms Indra's rivalry to Varuna (which may be understood in terms of rivalry between the Brahmin priest caste and the Kshatriya warrior caste), his gradual assumption of many of Varuna's functions and virtues, and his eventual ousting of Varuna as chief of the gods.

Prithivi's attempts to conceal the birth of her son were ill-fated, for immediately the golden child Indra began to display that energy and impulsiveness which characterise him. At the time of his birth men were imploring the gods to come to their aid against the demon Vritra who had imprisoned the cloud-cattle, thus reducing men to starvation through drought. Hearing the men crying out, 'Who will come to our aid?', Indra seized from Tvashtri the soma which they were offering to the gods and drank a huge quantity of it, worth a hundred cows. This drink fortified him to such an extent that he filled the two worlds. Seizing the thunderbolt that had belonged to his father, Indra set off in a chariot drawn by two horses to do battle against Vritra, accompanied by attendants and followers. Vritra roared as Indra approached, heaven shook and the gods retreated. Prithivi grew fearful for her son; but Indra was inspired by the great draught of soma and by the hymns of the priests on earth and was strengthened by men's sacrifices; above all he possessed the thunderbolt, Vajra. He stormed and took Vritra's ninety-nine fortresses and then faced the demon himself. Though Vritra thought himself invulnerable, Indra soon discovered his weak points and laid him low with the thunderbolt. Therewith the cloud-cattle were released and torrents of water flowed down to earth. According to some versions Indra repeats this heroic act at the end of every summer drought and thus re-establishes his strength in the eyes of men and gods.

But Indra hardly paused to hear the praises of the priests and of his fellow-gods. Scarcely born, he had seized the initiative as bringer of rain. In this act he had supplanted Varuna—though it must be admitted that he required much more effort to supply water than did Varuna. His next act was to turn on his father (who is sometimes identified with Varuna). Seizing him by the ankle, he dashed him to the ground and killed him. His mother's plaints were of no avail: Indra had achieved his victory with the aid of his father's weapon so that in a sense his father performed the deed through him. But by killing Dyaus Indra set the seal on his independence and full stature as a god; his murder of his father established his succession to him, just as his defeat of Vritra in part established his right of succession to Varuna's position of supremacy. By his first heroic acts Indra became king of the three worlds. Having acquired the air of life and the strength of soma, he gave them to others. He thus stands for the power of personal intervention, for the activity of the warrior, whereas Varuna stands for the inevitability of the cosmic order. While Varuna's strength is based on law and magic power, the source of Indra's strength is quite clear: it depends on the might of the god himself, supported by the offerings of men. Men cannot understand the ways of Varuna, but by transferring allegiance to Indra they can hope to affect or even to direct the flow of divine benefits.

Indra is tireless in his opposition to demons. He repeatedly subdues Vritra, under whose leadership the Danavas were able to upset the eternal equipoise established between gods and demons, devas and asuras, good and evil, light and dark, and forces the Danavas to retreat to the ocean darkness. He also defends men and animals against the machinations of other demons. As bringer of rain, Indra already had some claim to worship as god of fertility; the following myth explains how he definitively captured that function from the other gods. At one point during the long struggle with the god, the demons, counting on the fact that the gods derived much of their strength from the sacrifices of men, decided to debilitate the gods by using poison and magic spells to defile the plants used by men and beasts. They were so successful that men ceased to

Indrani, chosen as the wife of Indra. A later tradition says that she was carried off forcibly by him. Stone sculpture, eighth century.

eat and the beasts stopped grazing, and famine brought them near to death. But the gods were equal to this challenge; they offered sacrifices and succeeded in ridding the plants of the poison. A great ceremony was held to celebrate this victory, at which offerings were to be made of the first plants to grow after the poison had been dispersed. However, a dispute arose as to which of the gods should be the first to receive this offering. It was decided that the matter should be settled by running a race. Indra and Agni won the race, and ever after Indra was regarded as a source of fertility—a role for which his parents, a bull and a cow, well fitted him.

Indra gradually took over some of Varuna's other functions, and his role as fertility god extended to a new role as creator god. Like other Indian conceptions of the creator, however, Indra did not form the universe from the void but rather rearranged it, after taking possession. Thus, like Varuna, he used the sun as his instrument and measured out space; the six broad spaces which he noted included every existing thing. He then proceeded to build the universe like a house: he set up four corner posts and between them built the walls of the world; he thatched the house with the cloudy sky. The house had two large doors: the eastern was opened wide every morning to admit the sun; the western briefly every evening so that Indra could fling the sun out into the surrounding darkness. These doors were also used by the gods when they came to partake of sacrifices and libations. Indra maintained his creation by propping up the heavens, by maintaining the two worlds and the atmosphere, and by holding up the earth and stretching it. He was also the source of the major rivers.

Fortified with soma, Indra has the energy to regulate the heavens and the days, the months and the seasons. His love for and dependence upon soma are increasingly dwelt upon in the Vedas, but it is not until much later that this is regarded in any way as a weakness. In the Vedic age Indra is unquestionably the greatest of the gods, even though he may not be the object of such awe or fear as Varuna inspired at the time of his former glory. In the latter part of the Vedic period Indra became a more dignified, less active sovereign. He is pictured reigning in his heaven, Swarga, flanked by his queen, Indrani, and his advisers, the Vasus. Though still accompanied by a hunting dog (the dog was later to become an unclean animal), he has given up his horses, and his mount is a great white elephant called Airavata, which has four tusks and whose huge snowy bulk is likened to Mount Kailasa, where Shiva's heaven was to be.

The Maruts

The Maruts, the spirits of tempest and thunder, were the sons of Rudra, and the constant companions of Indra. They were handsome young men, vigorous and courageous, who, according to the *Rig Veda*, numbered either twenty-seven or one hundred and eighty. They wore golden helmets and golden breastplates and they draped bright skins on their shoulders; they loved to scrub each other clean and to adorn their arms and ankles with golden bracelets. When they rode forth they 'rode on the whirlwind and directed the storm', and were conveyed on a golden-wheeled chariot sparkling in the lightning and drawn by three fleet-footed deer. They were strongly armed with bows and arrows and axes, and especially with gleaming spears. With these weapons they shattered the cloud-cattle and cleft cloud-rocks, so that torrents of rain fell to earth and the eye of the sun was covered. Like Indra, their leader, the Maruts were alternately gay youths and fearsome warriors and they were valuable allies to Indra when he attacked the demon Vritra, frightening his followers with their war-cries and adept at harrying the cloud-cattle.

Vayu

Vayu is the god of air or wind, and is sometimes said to have been born from the breath of Purusha. Though infrequently invoked in the Vedas, he was an important early god, a member of one of the first triads together with Agni and Surya, being supplanted in this triad by Indra after his rise. Despite Indra's ascendancy, Vayu maintained his individuality and survives to the present day. He is sometimes thought to be the father of the Maruts, and like them rides in a chariot drawn by deer. At other times he more closely resembles Indra, riding a chariot drawn by two red horses or, more often, riding with Indra as charioteer. This in a chariot made of gold which touches the sky and which is drawn by a thousand horses. Vayu's role is not only that of a nature deity: his breath gives life to all the gods and to men. Vayu became the son-in-law of the artisan god Tvashtri.

Tvashtri

Like Indra, Tvashtri was the son of Dyaus, but his power resided more in magic than in brute force and he never retained for long any sort of dominion over gods or men. From the first, however, he aided Indra and gave him strength. It was from Tvashtri that Indra snatched the soma that fortified him for the fight against Vritra; and it was Tvashtri who fashioned for the gods the wonderful bowl which constantly filled itself with soma, source of their strength. In some stories the most important use to which he put his miraculous powers was as an artisan, helping Indra to overcome Vritra by making for him the thunderbolt, Vajra, sometimes depicted as a club or hammer, sometimes as a discus-like weapon with a central hole. He also made Indra's other thunderbolts and weapons for the gods and he was revered as the archetype of the skilled workman. This role remained to him in later times, when he was known as Visvakarma.

In the early hymns, however, his powers are wider: he

not only fashions, but contains within him the archetype of all the forms of creation, to which he gives life. His influence continues beyond the initial creation, for he also bestows the generative power in men and grants them off-spring; he creates husband and wife for each other. He is even responsible for giving heaven and earth their shape and for producing water and nourishment for his worshippers. As nourisher and protector of all, he is the guardian also of sacrifice and is invoked in order to ensure the safe receipt of the sacrifice either directly by himself or by the other gods. He is thus the source of—or the potential obstacle to—all blessings, the possessor of wealth and the granter of prosperity. During this phase of his power, Tvashtri is sometimes considered to be in opposition to Indra. Indra showed his animosity to Tvashtri by killing his son Visvarupa ('Omniform').

The Ribhus

The Ribhus were artisan elves, sons of Indra by Saranyu, daughter of Tvashtri. They occasionally engaged in friendly competition with their grandfather, Tvashtri, but in some cases their activities amounted to serious rivalry, which may have mirrored the tension between Tvashtri and their father Indra. As rivals of Tvashtri they were credited with having shaped heavens and earth or with having helped Indra to do so, with supporting the sky, with having created a man called Vibhvan, and with having the power to rejuvenate aged and decrepit parents (with 'reuniting the old cow to the calf'), that is, with providing the generative function by which a man can obtain immortality through his sons.

As more or less friendly competitors of their grandfather, the Ribhus were supposed to have fashioned Indra's horses and chariot and those of the other gods, and to have improved on Tvashtri's creation of the self-filling soma cup by forming four similar cups out of it (these cups may represent phases of the moon). They also created the miraculous cow of plenty, which dwelt in Indra's heaven and which had the power to bestow all blessings. The Ribhus make grass and herbs and create the channels for streams. As a reward for their constant performance of good deeds and in particular for the creation of the four soma cups, the Ribhus were granted the boon of immortality. With the assumption of divinity they became entitled to praise and adoration. When regarded as creator, Indra himself is sometimes called a Ribhu.

Agni

Agni, the fire god, was another great deity of the early pantheon and a serious rival to Indra, who eventually won his support to the detriment of Varuna.

As the god of fire, Agni may well have been of Iranian origin and this would explain his early predominance and Indra's rivalry. Nevertheless Agni soon acquired a mythology that in many respects was similar to that of Indra. As

the product on earth of friction between an upper and a lower, a male and a female fire-stick, Fire is said to be the son of Earth and Heaven, Prithivi and Dyaus, and therefore the brother of Indra. Like Indra, Agni was born fully matured, and immediately began to feed upon his parents. After consuming them he sought another source of sustenance, and just as Indra fed upon soma, so Agni fed upon the offerings of clarified butter which were poured on to the sacrificial fire. In order to lick up the butter Agni had seven tongues, each of which had a special name. Like Indra, he used the power thus obtained to succour others: as Indra gave the air of life to men, so Agni symbolised the vital spark, the element of life in man, beast, and fish as well as in plants and trees. Though he consumed, this destruction was a necessary prelude to renewed creation. He was known as the ever youthful, even though, as originator of sacrificial rites, he can be considered the oldest of all priests. As son of heaven and of earth and as archetypal priest, Agni is the mediator between the gods and men: messenger of the gods, he visits men: and vehicle of men's sacrifices, he conducts the gods to the places of worship.

One myth about his birth alludes to the tradition that made him the presiding deity of earth, while Vayu or Indra presided over air and Surya over the sky; at the same time, however, it suggests that Agni encompassed all three worlds and their presiding gods. He is said to be thrice-born: that is, he was born—and is constantly reborn—in heaven as the sun, or sometimes more particularly as the flames of the sun; he was born a second time in the atmosphere, where he was kindled in the waters of the storm clouds and descends to earth in the shape of lightning; and he was born a third time on earth, where he is kindled by the hand not only of priests, when he becomes the sacrificial fire, but also by the hand of every man, whom he warms, protects and nourishes in the form of the hearth fire. The smoke from these earthly fires rises again to become the clouds of the atmosphere. Omnipresent in the universe, Agni also touches and observes every aspect, however mundane, of man's life and is accordingly invoked not only as a celestial or elemental deity but as a domestic spirit, whose great virtue is that he is also familiar with the abode of the gods.

Besides the creative, life-giving role, Agni shared other characteristics with his brother Indra. His demon-slaying aspect is increasingly brought to the fore. The best-known of such struggles was that with the Kravyads, rakshasas who were known as flesh-eaters. Even though Agni was in a sense himself a Kravyad, he was called upon, together with the rest of the gods, to destroy them. For this purpose he cast aside his usual appearance, which was that of a red man with three flaming heads, three legs and seven arms, wearing a garland of fruit, and assumed that of a Kravyad, a hideous being with tusks. Agni sharpened his two iron tusks and, roaring like a bull, charged among the Kravyads, piercing them with the tusks, and swallowing them.

Agni, god of fire, with his usual companion, a ram. Agni is the intermediary between the three worlds of the heavens, the atmosphere, and the earth and his two heads here represent domestic fire and the fire of sacrifice. South Indian wood carving.

Soma, god of sacrifice, whose importance to Indra enhanced his power so that he was considered as bestower of strength and riches and even as a warrior himself. In this south Indian wood carving he bears bow and arrow and is riding to battle.

Even though he was himself a consumer of flesh given in sacrifice, Agni enjoyed a special dispensation whereby he remained pure whatever he ate, and was even able to purify impure objects by consuming them. This dispensation was granted by the sage Bhrigu, who one day abducted a girl who was betrothed to an asura, or demon. The asura, knowing that Agni had access to all places, asked him where the girl was. Agni, renowned for his truthfulness, told the asura and thus enabled him to recover her. At this Bhrigu cursed Agni to eat everything, pure and impure. But Agni convinced him that as a god he had been obliged to speak the truth. Bhrigu then added the dispensation which guaranteed Agni's purity.

Another story is told of how Agni (fire) was brought to mankind by a demi-god, Matarisvan, the recipients of this long-sought gift being the Bhrigus, a priestly family descended from the sage Bhrigu, and of how they established the worship of Agni on earth.

Sometimes Agni is said to feed not upon clarified butter but, like Indra, upon soma. By association with Brihaspati,

Lord of Prayer, Agni was also deemed to have helped Indra in the creation of the universe. A further extension of his role came in the late Vedic period, at a time when Indra had nearly succeeded in absorbing him; during this time Agni was considered as a sky and storm god and, through smoke becoming cloud, as a provider of rain. Though this inflation of the fire god was not to last, his universality and the essential part he plays in the sacrifice assured him a continued place of importance in succeeding pantheons.

Soma

Soma was the milky fermented liquor produced from the soma plant, which was an integral part of Vedic sacrifices, where it was drunk by the priests in token of its acceptance by the gods. Like the sap in trees and the blood in animals, soma juice was considered to be the vital fluid in all beings, just as Agni was their vital spark. Its powers were soon personified in the god Soma. As the source of Indra's power as a warrior against the enemies of the gods, Soma too was thought to be a warrior, and his power increased in step with that of Indra. Indeed to some degree he *was* Indra, and borrowed many of that god's roles. Indra himself was said to have discovered soma in the Himalayas and to have brought it back to share its strength with the other gods, who were thereby enabled to resist the power of their enemies the demons. Consequently, as we shall see, the demons were unceasing in their efforts to obtain this source of strength and immortality. Another myth relates that the ṣoma plant originally belonged to the Gandharvas (celestial spirits), for it grew in the mountains where the Gandharvas dwelt; that it was given by them to the goddess Vach, one of Indra's wives, goddess of waters and called 'the melodious cow who milked forth sustenance and water'. Even though soma—or amrita (ambrosia) as it is often called—was frequently represented as the passive object of disputes between the gods and between gods and demons, its power was such that the god which personified it was sometimes elevated even above Indra, who without soma had no strength. Thus Soma became known as a primeval deity, all-powerful, healing all diseases, bestower of riches, and even the supreme god himself.

Because of this the ritual pressing of the soma juice assumed cosmic significance. The sieve through which the juice was pressed symbolised the sky, and the juice which passed through was the rain, so that Soma became lord of the waters. The yellow juice and the noise it made passing through the sieve were lightning and thunder. It warmed like the rays of the sun and as the milky liquor descended into the vat it was like a bull fertilising a herd of cows.

As in other mythologies, where the moon is associated with the regulation of waters and in general with fertility, so in India, the god which personified the water of life became linked with the moon. Soma was said to partake of the nature of the moon, while Agni partook of the nature of the sun. Agni's great love of soma was thus enshrined in the myth which tells of Soma's marriage with Surya, the maiden of the sun. Gradually the ritual use of soma as an intoxicant died out, and was explained by a myth which related that Brahma cursed intoxicants after drunkenly committing incest with his daughter; or that a sage, Sukra, cursed the beverage after mistakenly drinking the ashes of his disciple in a cup of wine. Soma's role as the moon nevertheless remained, the only vestige of his former associations being his aspect as lord of herbs and healing.

Chandra

Chandra was the god of the moon and source of fertility. The absorption of Chandra by Soma was no chance, according to late myths, for Chandra was produced during the churning of the milk ocean, the object of which was to produce amrita, or soma. It is thus only fitting that though Chandra was originally considered to be an independent god, he should eventually be another name of Soma. Every night Chandra rises anew from the ocean.

Aditi and the Adityas

Aditi, whose name means 'free' or 'boundless', was usually known in later times as the mother of the gods but was in fact mother of only some of them, in particular those of Iranian origin who were in early times known as the asuras (before the absolute supremacy of Indra and the other Aryan gods led to the term 'asura' being used only for demons). Aditi seems to represent the boundless heaven, and she is known as the supporter of the sky, sustainer of the earth and sovereign of this world. In the Vedas Aditi's husband was said to be Vishnu, but Vishnu is generally considered to be her son. There is equal confusion over the names of her children, the Adityas, though no dispute over who was the chief of them. This was Varuna, who is sometimes called simply the Aditya (eternal, celestial light). All the sons in some way represent the eternal forces which lie behind the celestial bodies, rather than those bodies themselves. Though their number was later increased to twelve, to represent the sun in the twelve months of the year, they originally numbered only seven. Beside Varuna, they were Mitra, Aryaman, Indra, Savitri, Bhaga and Ansa. The last two never attained any prominence, but Savitri was worshipped as the personification of the setting sun and, despite his mother, an eighth, unloved son became the personification of the mighty rising sun, Marttanda, more commonly known as Vivasvat. When the Adityas were born, Aditi cherished the first seven, but she felt no love for the eighth, who was born as a shapeless lump which she threw away. But it was taken up by the divine artificer and moulded into Vivasvat. The unused parts fell to earth and became elephants. For this reason elephants partake of the divine nature. One of the more important of the later Adityas was Pushan, who surveyed the universe, guarded cattle and all living creatures, aided in the revolution of day and night, nourished the world after its creation, and guided the souls of the deceased to the afterworld.

Vivasvat

Though as rising sun Vivasvat was a mighty deity, his career as a husband was scarcely more happy than as a son. He was married to the daughter of Tvashtri, Saranyu. Tvashtri prepared a great wedding feast for the pair and all the gods assembled, together with the whole world. But after the marriage, the bride disappeared, and another girl looking just like her had to be created for Vivasvat. From this marriage with a double wife were born two pairs of twins, the Aswins and Yama and Yami. As we shall see, elaborations of this myth were later ascribed to Surya, who surpassed him in importance.

Savitri

Savitri, a golden-haired deity, personified the sun in its morning and evening aspects. He was also known as the 'Generator' or the 'Stimulator', despite the fact that he is celebrated for his daily command to Night to approach, so that men may cease their labours, birds seek their nests and cattle their sheds. But just as Agni creates through destruction, so Savitri stimulates everything by putting it to rest. He is seen riding his golden car drawn by two brilliant horses between heaven and earth, and every day as he passes he banishes disease and dispels tribulation, bestowing longevity on men and immortality on the gods.

Surya

Surya was the chief sun god, and in time Savitri and Vivasvat were absorbed to become mere aspects of him. Surya has golden hair and arms and rides a golden chariot drawn by seven mares, or alternatively by a mare with seven heads. He became an honorary Aditya, for he was referred to as the eye of Varuna and Mitra, and in the Varuna and Indra versions of creation was used as the measuring instrument. In his Savitri aspect, Surya was revered as the Divine Vivifier, who stimulates the understanding of men, commands the waters and winds and exercises dominion over everything, moving and static, and even the other gods. Himself moving according to fixed laws, he gave permanence and stability to earth and heavens by fixing them with bonds. Like Indra and Agni, Surya is generally considered to be the son of Dyaus. These three sons of Dyaus were the most important gods of the Vedic period and at first were all of equal stature, forming the early Triad—indeed the concept of a triad is said to have sprung from the three aspects of the sun god—in which only Surya retained his place. There are few Vedic myths about him, perhaps because he was so firmly established as one of the great gods. One early myth relates that he was the father of the Aswins by a nymph who disguised herself as a mare and was therefore called Aswini. Soma or Chandra is sometimes said to be another son of Surya. According to this myth, Surya is the original source of amrita, which he passes to the moon, Soma, for distribution among gods, men, animals and plants. The sun thereby also nourishes the moon, enabling it to grow again when it begins to wane–almost devoured by the great draughts of soma consumed by the gods.

Ushas

Ushas, the dawn, was one of the most popular Vedic deities and inspired some of the most beautiful hymns. Clothed in crimson robes and veiled with gold, she was likened to a gentle bride, or to a wife whose beauties seem greater every morning when her husband beholds her. Though eternal she is ever young, and gives the breath of life to all living beings, waking sleepers from their seeming death, arousing birds from their nests and sending men out on their appointed tasks. Ushas brings wealth and light to all men, whether great or humble, and gives honour to all their dwellings. But though she remains young herself she brings age to men. Ushas is a daughter of Dyaus and sister of Agni. Like her brother, whose triple birth in the sea, in the sky and in the clouds she celebrates, Ushas is revered as the friend of man and the link between heaven and earth. Sometimes Ushas is said

Ushas, goddess of dawn and one of the most popular Vedic deities. The friend of man, her gentle expression is likened to that of a young wife, and she is ever-youthful. South Indian wood carving.

to be sister to the Adityas, sometimes wife of Surya. Her vehicle is similar to that of Surya: a shining chariot drawn by seven ruddy cows.

Ratri

Ratri, night, is the sister of Ushas and, like her, associated with Agni. She wears dark robes set off with gleaming stars. Her approach is welcomed as much as her sister's, for when she draws near men may rest, birds seek their nests and cattle lie down. A benevolent goddess, Ratri is invoked for protection against the perils of darkness, against robbers and fierce wolves, and people pray to her to be taken safely across her shadow. She herself is not to be feared, for she no sooner casts her dark shadow than she beckons her sister Ushas to return.

The Aswins

The Aswins, twin sons of Surya or of Vivasvat, were horsemen born of a nymph who changed herself into a mare. The Aswins were connected with celestial light, like their father, though there is some question as to their exact nature. As harbingers of Ushas, whom they preceded each morning in their golden car drawn by horses or birds, they were known as the twin gods of morning. But other interpretations make them day and night or, as sons of Dyaus, heaven and earth. In general, however, their connection with the early morning sun is quite clear. They are represented as young and handsome, agile and brilliant. They received perhaps even more enthusiastic worship than Ushas, for while like her they were ancient yet ever young, they differed from her in that they were capable of bestowing youth on men. They were known as the physicians of the gods in Swarga (Indra's heaven), in which function they were called Dasra and Nasatya. Many tales are told of their benevolence to men, but the most important is that concerning the sage Chyavana, which led to their admission to the ranks of the immortals. Chyavana had grown very old and decrepit; some boys, finding his hideous and shrivelled body lying by the wayside, pelted it with clods. Chyavana was enraged by this, but the boys' father managed to appease him by offering him his daughter as a wife.

The Aswins subsequently paid a visit to the old hermit's home and one of them commiserated with her over her old husband and tried to seduce her. But she resisted him, and prompted by her clever husband taunted them with being in some respect incomplete. The Aswins promised her that if she would tell them what she meant by this they would restore her husband to youth. Accordingly Chyavana bathed in a certain pool indicated by the Aswins and emerged with his youth restored, and Sukanya, his wife, informed the Aswins that they were incomplete in that they were not invited to drink soma with the gods at a feast then being celebrated. The Aswins hurried to the feast and asked to be allowed to drink the soma. But Indra

Vishnu striding through the universe. In the Vedas he is the manifestation of solar energy, and his three steps are manifestations of light—the sun, lightning and fire. The tradition of the three strides persisted and in later myths is part of the subjugation of Bali, shown here, in Vishnu's dwarf avatar. Relief from Mahabalipuram, seventh century.

refused; they had wandered among men as physicians and assumed all kinds of forms. Chyavana thereupon started to perform a sacrifice to the Aswins and Indra, enraged, rushed to attack him, with a mountain in one hand and his thunderbolt in the other. Chyavana retaliated by creating a monster, Mada, with enormous teeth and jaws so huge that one could enclose the earth and the other the heavens. When Mada was about to engulf the whole universe and the gods with it, Indra relented and allowed the Aswins to join the immortal soma-drinkers.

Rudra

Rudra, whose name means 'Howler', was a relatively unimportant Vedic deity of storms and winds, the father of Indra's companions the Maruts, who are also called Rudras. The Rudras are sometimes held to be personifications of the various aspects of Rudra, a strange mixture of fearsome and beneficent qualities—a characteristic which he shares with Shiva, the great Hindu god who developed out of him and who gives Rudra his importance. In his terrible aspect Rudra was depicted as a ruddy or swarthy man, of wild temper, murderous, spitting like a wild beast and riding a boar; he was a robber god and lord of thieves, and the divine archer who shoots the arrows of death and disease at gods, men and cattle. But like Agni, with whom he is sometimes identified, Rudra not only destroyed, but also healed or created. Thus he is known as lord of cattle and wild life, the intelligent, bountiful one, the lord of song and sacrifices and, as divine physician, renowned for his healing arts. In this aspect he was thought to be as brilliant as the sun, shining like gold, best and most beautiful of the gods. As lord of cattle he was represented as a bull. He was invoked for protection against the unknown sentences or enmity of Varuna and was himself considered a sort of judge, smiter of the workers of evil and nourisher of the virtuous.

In some of the Vedas Rudra's name is said to derive from the word for 'weeping'. He was the son of Ushas and the creator Prajapati, who one day found him weeping. He told his father that he wept because he had no name and because his evil had not been taken away. His father therefore named him Rudra, 'Weeper'. The later cult of Shiva associated this weeping with despair at the condition of eternal life, in turn linked with the pre-Aryan yogic Lord of the Beasts, prototype of Shiva and the yogi.

Vishnu

Vishnu was another deity of minor rank in the Vedas, whose character and status changed radically in later times. A manifestation of the sun's energy, who envelops all things with the dust of his beams, Vishnu's chief exploit in the Vedas is the taking of the famous three steps with which he strode through and measured the seven worlds. The three steps are said to represent the place of the sun's rising, its zenith and the place of its setting; or the manifestations of light in fire, lightning and the sun. Other versions suggest that they represented earth, air and heavens, for the first two steps were visible to men, whereas the third was hidden from them. By measuring the universe, Vishnu took part in its creation—either independently, as was thought in later times, or as an assistant to Indra, whom he also accompanied in battle against Vritra and other demons. Vishnu was sometimes thought of as an aspect of Agni, and he shared that deity's position as intermediary between gods and men; for as the 'kinsman' he welcomed faithful worshippers to heaven. His benevolent aspect was thus prominent in the Vedas, and he was already called 'the unconquerable preserver', a sign of his coming place in the Hindu triad.

Developments of the Brahmanic age

Many diverse trends were at work towards the end of the Vedic period. Gods which had begun as simple personifications of aspects of nature began to acquire increasingly elaborate mythologies which personalised or anthropomorphised them. At the same time, each of the gods was considered to encompass certain activities of others and the divisions between them became blurred.

So while many claimed to be creators or to exercise dominion over the universe, none really emerged as supreme lord. One of the great preoccupations of the Brahmanic age was the search for the identity of the supreme being or universal spirit which suffused all creation and all the other gods. There was much speculation about the hierarchy and about whether one of the Vedic gods should occupy the supreme position – and whether a new deity, Brahma, should be considered a manifestation of one of the old gods or whether he was truly a new figure.

This whole controversy was complicated by a further factor: through the course of the Vedic age—and perhaps because of the greatly confused hierarchy—the power of the priests, Brahmins, grew stronger and their essential function, the performance of sacrifice, developed accordingly. In the Brahmanic age the situation developed so far that sacrifice itself became the object of religious ritual, for sacrifice represented not so much reverence to the gods as the creation of powers which ensured the continuance of the universal cycles of time, which in turn regulated the existence of the gods within the universe and their cyclic death and rebirth.

TIME AND THE CREATION OF THE UNIVERSE

According to beliefs evolved during the Brahmanic period, universal time is a never-ending cycle of both creation and destruction, each complete cycle being represented by one hundred years in the life of Brahma. At the end of this period the entire universe, Brahma himself, gods, sages, demons, men, animals and matter are dissolved in the Great Cataclysm, Mahapralaya. This is followed by one hundred years of chaos, after which another Brahma is born and the cycle begins anew. Within this system are many divisions and sub-cycles. The most important of these is the Kalpa, one mere day in the life of Brahma but equivalent to 4,320 million years on earth. When Brahma wakes, the three worlds (heavens, middle and lower regions) are created, and when he sleeps they are reduced to chaos; all beings who have not obtained liberation are judged and must prepare for rebirth according to their

deserts when Brahma wakes on the new day. The Kalpa is divided into one thousand Great Ages (Mahayugas), and each of these is further divided into four ages or Yugas, called Krita, Treta, Dwapara and Kali.

The Kritayuga is a golden age lasting 1,728,000 years, in which Dharma, god of justice and duty, is said to walk on four legs. Men are contented, healthy and virtuous and they worship only one god, who is white.

The Tretayuga, which lasts 1,296,000 years, is a less happy age in which virtue falls short by one-quarter and in which Dharma is three-legged. In general men follow their duty, though they sometimes act from ulterior motives and are quarrelsome. Brahmins are more numerous than wrongdoers, and the deity is red in colour.

In the Dwaparayuga virtue is only half present and Dharma stands on only two legs. During this age, which lasts for 864,000 years, the deity is yellow and discontent, lying and quarrels abound. Nevertheless many tread the right path and Brahmins, Kshatriyas and Vaisyas are careful to perform their duties.

The Kaliyuga, or age of degeneration, is the one through which we are now passing. Dharma is one-legged and helpless, and all but one-quarter of virtue has vanished. In this age, lasting 432,000 years, during which the deity is black, the majority of men are Sudras, or slaves. They are wicked, quarrelsome and beggar-like and they are unlucky because they deserve no luck. They value what is degraded, eat voraciously and indiscriminately, and live in cities filled with thieves. They are dominated by their womenfolk, who are shallow, garrulous and lascivious, bearing too many children. They are oppressed by their kings and by the ravages of nature, famines and wars. Their miseries can only end with the coming of Kalki, the destroyer.

Destruction is preceded by the most terrible portents. After a drought lasting one hundred years, seven suns appear in the skies and drink up all the remaining water. Fire, swept by the wind, consumes the earth and then the underworld. Clouds looking like elephants garlanded with lightning then appear and, bursting suddenly, release rain that falls continuously for twelve years, submerging the whole world. Then Brahma, contained within a lotus floating on the waters, absorbs the winds and goes to sleep, until the time comes for his awakening and renewed creation. During this time gods and men are temporarily reabsorbed into *Brahman*, the Universal Spirit.

The creation to come will consist of a redeployment of the same elements. Geographically, the mythical world seems to change little. Our earth is shaped like a wheel and is the innermost of seven concentric continents. In the centre of the world is Mount Meru, whose summit, 84,000 leagues high, is the site of Brahma's heaven, which is encircled by the River Ganges and surrounded by the cities of Indra and other deities. The foothills of Mount Meru are the home of benevolent spirits such as Gandharvas, while the valleys are peopled by the demons. The whole world is supported by the hood of the great serpent Shesha, who is sometimes himself coiled upon the back of a tortoise floating on the primal waters; or the world is supported by four elephants; or it is held up by four giants,

Left: The prelude to creation according to Vishnuite belief. Vishnu is seen reclining on the serpent Ananta on the waters of Nara, watched by Shumi or Prithivi, goddess of the Earth. The lotus blossom from which Brahma will appear, to recreate the universe, is about to rise from Vishnu's navel. In the panel above are the coming divine hierarchy: Vishnu riding on Garuda, who is seen swallowing the serpent; Brahma; and Shiva. Rajasthani painting, late seventeenth century.

Kalki, Vishnu's tenth and last incarnation, which has yet to come. Vishnu himself will appear on earth at the close of the Kaliyuga, the present age, riding the white horse Kalki, and will destroy the world in preparation for a new creation. Polished sandstone, from Kompong Thom, tenth century.

Overleaf left: Two primitive deities. Left, a mother goddess with a child at her breast. Kond tribal bronze. The Kond tribes once practised human sacrifice, but in later times their female fertility deities lost their bloody associations. Right, a terracotta figurine of a fertility goddess of the second century B.C., Bengal. Such figures survived into the Vedic age and were to be revived in the Devi cults of the Hindus. It combines the symbols of abundance with the staring 'fish eyes' characteristic of a deity expecting sacrifice. Victoria and Albert Museum

Overleaf right: Shiva, the Great Lord. The central, outward looking aspect from the Mahesamurti carving in the rock temple at Elephanta. With its serene impassivity it represents the Absolute or Eternity. The masculine profile, symbolising his virility and will power, can be seen to the right. There is a third, out of view, which shows his feminine aspect. Early seventh century.

who cause earthquakes by shifting their burden from one shoulder to the other.

At the beginning of each cycle of creation the waters of the cataclysmic flood cover the universe. There are many myths to explain the sequence of the new creation. One of the most favoured Vedic versions relates that the golden cosmic egg, symbol of fire, was floating on the waters for a thousand years. At the end of this period the egg burst open to reveal the Lord of the Universe, who took the form of the first, eternal man, whose soul is identical with that of the Universal Spirit and who, because he was the first to destroy all sins by fire, was called Purusha. Though he had been entirely alone, communing with himself for so long, when he emerged from the egg and cast his eyes about him on the empty waters he felt afraid—and this is why men feel afraid when they are

alone. But he comforted himself with the thought that as he was the only being in the universe, he need feel no fear. On the other hand, he felt no delight—and this is why no one feels delight when alone. Then he felt desire for another, and so divided himself into two, one half male and the other female; but then he felt himself to be disunited, so he joined with his other half, Amvika or Viraj, who thus became his wife and bore offspring, mankind. Thereafter Purusha and Viraj assumed the forms of pairs of cattle, horses, asses, goats, sheep and all other creatures right down to ants, and each pair produced offspring.

Another one of these myths states that the creator was Narayana, who in some versions appears to be an aspect of Brahma and in others an aspect of Vishnu. Narayana lay for long ages on the primeval waters, Nara, floating on a banyan leaf while sucking his toe—a position symbolising eternity. After this self-communion, the universe was

formed by his will to create. Speech was born from his mouth, the Vedas from the humours of his body, amrita from his tongue; the very firmament rose from his nose, heaven and the sun from the pupils of his eyes, places of pilgrimage from his ears, clouds and rain from his hair, flashes of lightning from his beard, rocks from his nails, mountains from his bones.

An early myth, which originated about the time when sacrifice, and in particular human sacrifice, attained great importance, was perpetuated with some modification into modern times. This myth dispenses with the primal waters and thus is intermediate between myths which take the great cataclysm into account and those earlier ones which, without explanations, state that Indra, or Varuna, or Indra, Agni and the Maruts created the universe (though it should be noted that these early creations also appear to be more rearrangements of existing matter than creations *ex nihilo*). According to this, the gods performed a sacrifice with Purusha, the Universal Spirit which took the form of a giant and was the first man. Spring was the butter of this sacrifice, Summer was its fuel, and Autumn was its accompanying offering. From Purusha's head rose the sky, from his navel the air, and from his feet the earth. From his mind sprang the moon, from his eye the sun, from his ears the four quarters, from his mouth Indra and Agni, and from his breath Vayu. The four castes, whose symbolic colours are related to the colours of the four deities of the Yugas, also sprang from Purusha: the Brahmins from his mouth, the Kshatriyas from his arms, the Vaisyas from his thighs, and the Sudras from his feet. The myth was later adapted to Brahma, who was substituted for Purusha after becoming established as the one universal spirit. In this way Brahma too, though originally a philosophical, abstract conception—the world spirit, identification with which was the key to salvation or release—became a personalised deity. In later times Brahma was universally regarded as the fount of caste and its justification.

The later myths all refer in some way to Brahma as creator. Thus one relates that the lord of the universe brooded over the cosmic egg as it lay on the surface of the ocean for a thousand years. As he lay there in self-communion a lotus, bright as a thousand suns, rose from his navel and spread until it seemed as if it could contain the whole world. From this lotus sprang Brahma, self-created, but imbued with the powers of the lord of the universe. He set about his work of creation but he was not omniscient, and made several mistakes. At his first attempt he created ignorance, and threw her away; but she survived

The opening of the present age of degeneration, according to Brahmanic teaching, was heralded by the appearance of Buddha—as the ninth avatar of Vishnu. Seeking to minimise the effect of the new religion, they described him as the spirit of negation—one who denied the essential doctrines—rather than acknowledge the great teacher so lovingly depicted in this sandstone carving. Eleventh century, from Bayon.

and became Night and from her issued the Beings of Darkness. Brahma had still not succeeded in creating anything else, and these creatures in their hunger made to devour him. He defended himself, appealing to them not to eat their own father. But some of them would not listen to this appeal and wanted to eat him anyway; these became the rakshasas, enemies of men, while their less bloodthirsty brothers became the yakshas, who are sometimes enemies of men but mostly friendly. Brahma learnt from this experience, and thereafter he created a series of immortal beings and celestials. He also created the asuras from his hip, the earth from his feet, and all the other components of the world from other parts of his body.

Yet another version ends the story differently. According to this, Brahma became discouraged with his failures and created four sages or Munis to carry out the work for him. These sages were, however, less interested in the task of creation that in the worship of Vasudeva (the universal spirit, later a name of Krishna). Brahma became very angry at seeing the sages engaged in austerities instead of fulfilling the purpose for which they had been created, and from his anger sprang forth Rudra, who proceeded with and completed the work.

The version of creation given in the Laws of Manu combines many elements from the myths already discussed, but it introduces a new feature: Manu is a human being, a sage, who survives the destruction of one Mahayuga (Great Age) and lives to play a leading part in the creation of the next. This creation myth, imparted by Manu himself, hinges on the notion which became current in the Brahmanic period that sages, strengthened by knowledge and austerities, could acquire powers superior to those of the gods themselves, for they could become absorbed into the universal world spirit. Manu recounts that the self-existent spirit felt desire (this is sometimes personified as Kama, god of desire, who thus becomes the creative force). He wished to create all the living things from his own body, so he first created the waters, Nara, and threw a seed into them. From the seed grew a golden egg, bright as the sun. The self-existent spirit, who became known as Narayana after Nara, his first dwelling place, developed within the egg as Brahma, sometimes also called Purusha, the Male. After a year's contemplation in the egg, Brahma divided his body into two parts, one half male and the other female. Within the female part he implanted Viraj (a male), and Viraj in turn created Manu, who then created the world. Sometimes each age is said to have its own Manu, and it is not clear whether all the Manus are really one. The following elaboration of the myth suggests that the selfsame Manu existed in at least two ages. According to the sage Markandeya, Manu, who was a great rishi, or sage, himself escaped destruction in the general cataclysm at the end of the last age.

Manu had performed ten thousand years of austerities and had become equal to Brahma himself in glory. As he was meditating one day beside a stream a fish spoke to him from the water and besought his protection against another fish, which was chasing it. Manu took the fish and put it into a jar. But the fish grew too big for the jar, and asked to be taken to the Ganges. It outgrew the Ganges, and Manu had to take it to the ocean. There at last the fish was content and revealed to Manu that it was none other than Brahma himself. It further warned Manu of the approaching destruction of the world by flood, and instructed him to build an ark and to place in it the seven rishis and the seeds of everything recognised by the Brahmins. When Manu had done this the deluge began and gradually submerged everything but the ark which, tossed upon the surface of the waters, was drawn along by cables attached to the horns of the fish, until it came to rest upon the highest peak of the Himalayas, where Manu moored it to a tree. After many years the floodwaters began to recede, and Manu and his ark slowly descended into the valleys, where the sage took up the work of creation for the next great age. After worshipping the fish and engaging in austerities, Manu performed a sacrifice in which he offered up milk, clarified butter, curds and whey. After a year these offerings grew into a beautiful woman, who came to Manu and told him that she was his daughter and advised him that with her help at a sacrifice he would become rich in children and cattle and would obtain any blessing he desired. So Manu did as she instructed and they performed many austerities; in due time, as she had predicted, Manu begot the race of men and received many other blessings.

As Indian philosophy became more detached from worldly preoccupations and came to regard life with its series of incarnations as a source of misery, its influence affected the creation myth. Typical of this pessimistic school of thought is the story of Prajapati, or Brahma Prajapati, who himself was created by mind. When Prajapati arose from the primordial waters he looked about him and wept. From the tears that he wiped away arose the air; from the tears that fell into the waters arose the earth; and those tears which he wiped upwards became the sky. Then, by casting off the shells of his body, Prajapati created in turn the asuras, and darkness; men, and moonlight; the seasons, and twilight; the gods, and day; and finally, death.

Overleaf left: Shiva Nataraja, Lord of the Dance, dancing on the body of a dwarf demon. His victory over the spirit of evil is of cosmic significance, for the destruction of evil presages re-creation and the establishment of divine order. The surrounding halo both honours Shiva and represents the cycle of creation, destruction and rebirth. Tenth-century bronze, from Madras. Victoria and Albert Museum

Overleaf right: Shiva and his family. As Bhuteswara he is a haunter of cemeteries and places of cremation. At the burning ground his wife Parvati holds Karttikeya in her lap and watches while Ganesa and Shiva string together the skulls of the dead. Kangra painting, 1790. Victoria and Albert Museum

CREATION OF MAN AND OF DEATH

Yama and his twin sister Yami were said to be the first man and woman. They were the children of Vivasvat, the rising sun, and Saranyu, daughter of Tvashtri. At the entreaty of Yami, they founded the human race, despite Yama's doubts as to whether Varuna and Mitra really intended that they should be husband and wife.

When the human race had been established Yama became its pathfinder; he was the first to explore the hidden regions and discovered the road which became known as the 'path of the fathers'; this was the route which led the dead to heaven; Yama, having discovered it, became not only the first man to die but also became established as King of the Dead. At first, like Yama, the dead had to walk along this route, but later the path of the fathers (Manes or Pitris) was presided over by Agni, for when the dead were cremated his fire distinguished between the good and the evil in them. The ashes that remained on earth represented all that was evil and imperfect, while the fire carried aloft, intact, the skin and limbs of the deceased. There, brilliant like the gods and borne on wings or in a chariot, the purified soul rejoined its glorified body and was greeted by the forefathers, who lived a life of festivity in the kingdom of Yama. The afterlife was thus passed in a delectable abode, and was perfect in every way: all desires were fulfilled here, in the presence of the gods, and eternal time was spent in the pursuit of pleasure. Sometimes the abode of the gods was distinguished from that of the fathers, the kingdom of Yama; but the paths to both heavens were smoothed by Agni, their earthly entrances being the sacrificial fire and the funeral pyre.

Not all the dead were, however, permitted to remain in Yama's heaven. As a form of Mitra, and associated with

Varuna, Yama was a judge of the dead, known as Dharma-raja. Dharma, truth or righteousness, by which Yama judged mortals who approached his heaven, was a form of Varuna's *rta*, the inscrutable law. As Varuna formerly bound the guilty with their own sins against *rta*, so Yama consigned the wicked or unbelievers either to annihilation or to a realm of darkness called Put. He was assisted in the task of judgment by Varuna, who sat with him beneath a tree in the land of the fathers. Like a shepherd, Yama played his flute and drank soma with the other gods. As the dead approached him he gave the faithful draughts of the soma, thereby making them immortal. He was helped in this task by his messengers, a pigeon and an owl, as well as two brindled watch-dogs, each with four eyes. In later times his assistant was said to be Chitragupta, and he had other 'court recorders'.

At first, however, the emphasis was on the pleasures of Yama's heaven, a realm of light where life had no sorrows, nature was sweet and the air full of laughter and celestial music. The splendours of Yama's assembly house, built by Tvashtri from burnished gold, were equal to those of the sun. There Yama, as Pitripati (king of the fathers), was waited upon by servants who measured out the life span of mortals, and was surrounded and worshipped by rishis and Pitris, clad in white and decked with golden ornaments. The assembly house was filled with sweet sounds, perfumes and brilliant flowers.

Yama's heaven was not, however, without rivals, and in particular it was challenged by the splendours and delights of the heavens of Varuna and Indra. Varuna in his heaven was no longer judge of the dead, as he had been when seated beside Yama; he was already lord of the ocean. The heaven, which was constructed within the sea, by Tvashtri or Visvakarma, had walls and arches of pure white, surrounded by celestial trees made of brilliant jewels which always bore blossom and fruit; birds sang everywhere. In the white assembly house Varuna sat enthroned with his queen, both decked with jewels, ornaments of gold, and flowers. They were attended by the minor deities: the Adityas, the Nagas (serpents), by Daityas and Danavas (ocean demons), by the spirits of the rivers, seas and other waters, and by the personified forms of the cardinal points and the mountains.

Indra's heaven, also built by Tvashtri, was called Swarga and was situated on Mount Meru, but could be moved anywhere like a chariot. Like the other heavens it was adorned with celestial trees and filled with birdsong and the scent of flowers. Indra sat enthroned in glory in the assembly house, wearing white robes, garlanded with flowers and wearing gleaming bracelets and his crown.

He was accompanied by his queen, and attended by the Maruts, by the major gods and by sages and saints, whose pure souls without sin were resplendent as fire. This concept of Indra's heaven is the one still held today. In it there is no sorrow, suffering or fear, for it is inhabited by the spirits of prosperity, religion, joy, faith and intelligence. Also in Indra's heaven are found the spirits of the natural world: wind, thunder, fire, water, clouds, plants, stars and planets. Recreation is provided by the singing and dancing of the Apsaras and Gandharvas, celestial spirits; heroes or divine warriors perform feats of skill; and holy rites are performed. Divine messengers pass to and fro in their celestial chariots. The heaven presided over by the warrior god was thought to be especially the abode, permanent or temporary, of warriors. Thus in the *Mahabharata* Indra receives his son Arjuna, who is exceptionally skilled in military arts, and keeps him for several years on Mount Meru; and he welcomes the fallen heroes of both sides to his heaven, all those who have performed their warrior's duty being admitted. Some of those who enter receive special privileges, such as Bhishma, who resumed his place as one of the Vasus, Indra's advisers.

Yama's role changed with the growth of these other heavens and the idea that heaven was the reward for virtue, rather than a place where most of the dead were received unless they had the misfortune of having no children to perform the proper sacrifices for them. At first the idea of going to the abode of the fathers was simply less desirable than that of being received with special honours by the gods; later this developed into the notion that Yama's kingdom was not heaven but hell, where the tortures were pictured with growing elaboration, and Yama himself became a figure of terror. Opinions differ as to how many hells there are in his abode: some say hundreds of thousands, others say twenty-eight, or only seven. The tortures meted out are peculiarly suited to the sinner's offence. Thus cruel men are boiled in oil; those who are unnecessarily cruel to animals are consigned to a place where a monster tears them to pieces without ever killing them; those who kill Brahmins to a hell where the bottom is a furnace and the top a frying pan; oppressive kings are crushed between two rollers; those who kill mosquitoes are tortured by sleeplessness; the inhospitable are turned into worms and cast into a hell where they eat each other; those who marry outside their caste are forced

to embrace red-hot human forms; rulers and ministers who provoke religious dissension are thrown into a river full of the most horrible impurities where they are boiled and fed upon by aquatic animals.

These elaborate theories about the after-life developed in the face of the notions generally accepted by the more sophisticated philosophers in the Brahmanic period. Just as the vulgar had personalised the concept of Brahma as creator, so a growing belief in metempsychosis or transmigration of souls was the only element of the Brahmanic teaching on death and the after-life generally accepted by the masses, who misunderstood the idea of ultimate release from the eternal cycle of rebirths, samsara, by identification of the individual soul with the universal spirit.

The general belief was that the wicked went south to one of Yama's hells, or were reborn as worms, moths or biting serpents, while the good were sent either to the abode of the fathers on a path which passed south-east through the moon, or they went north-west, in the direction of the gods, to the sun. But distinctions were made between different sorts of the virtuous just as they were made among the wicked. Yama ceased to preside over the abode of the fathers and the gods no longer inhabited that region, having moved to one of the various heavens. Those who now followed the path to the abode of the fathers had dutifully obeyed their dharma—they had offered sacrifices, given alms generously and performed austerities —in other words they had followed tradition. Such men pass first into smoke, then into night, then arrive at the abode of the fathers, and finally pass on to the moon. There (by association of Soma, moon, and soma, ambrosia) they become the food of the gods; but they are given out from the gods into space, and from air pass successively into clouds, into rain, and so return to earth where, becoming food, they give rise to the principle of life in man and woman and so emerge into the world again. Akin to these beliefs were those that the stars were the souls of the dead (particularly of saints and heroes) or else that they were the souls of dead women.

Those virtuous deceased who were allowed to follow the 'path of the gods' were men who in their lifetime had faith – who, in other words, had attained fusion with the universal spirit and so won release from samsara. The stages of their journey into the after-life are as follows: the fire of their funeral pyre purifies their earthly natures, which then become flames themselves; they pass next into day, into the world of the gods and into lightning. They are then conducted by the supreme being into the realm of *Brahman*, the universal divine spirit which is without beginning or end and is without decay. From this realm there is no return, and here they achieve immortal bliss.

Among people clinging to ideas of an after-life spent in the presence of the Vedic gods, the so-called 'path of the gods' was easily misunderstood. Despite the general acceptance of the idea of metempsychosis, or rebirth according to karma (destiny created by actions in former lives), the older beliefs still crept in. Thus it was held that those who had led virtuous lives were permitted a break in the cycle of their rebirths by staying some time in Indra's heaven. Some still held to the old view that men were allowed to reap the benefit of their good actions in Indra's heaven before serving their allotted time in hell. Alternatively, like Yudhisthira in the *Mahabharata* and like all kings – who by nature of their calling cannot fail to commit some injustice, they are submitted to a vision of hell before being led to heaven.

Left: Rudra, the Vedic god who is both beneficent and terrible. He is an early form of the great god Shiva of the later Hindu trinity, and most resembles him in his form as Bhairava. But like Shiva he is many-faceted and also a healer. Sculpture from the Ellora cave temples, eighth century.

Right: Vishnu developed from a comparatively minor god in the Vedas into the Great Preserver of the Hindu trinity, the kind and compassionate god who stood with Brahma the Creator and Shiva the Destroyer. Pala sculpture, eighth century.

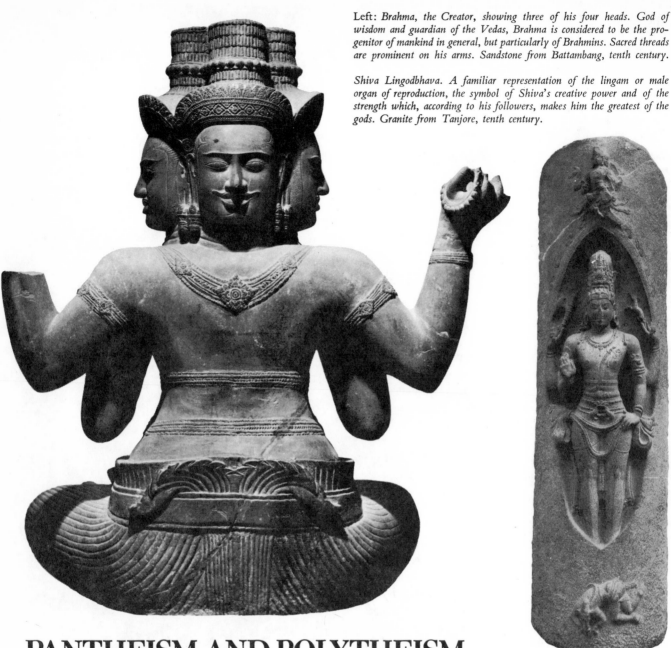

Left: *Brahma, the Creator, showing three of his four heads. God of wisdom and guardian of the Vedas, Brahma is considered to be the progenitor of mankind in general, but particularly of Brahmins. Sacred threads are prominent on his arms. Sandstone from Battambang, tenth century.*

Shiva Lingodbhava. A familiar representation of the lingam or male organ of reproduction, the symbol of Shiva's creative power and of the strength which, according to his followers, makes him the greatest of the gods. Granite from Tanjore, tenth century.

PANTHEISM AND POLYTHEISM

Paradoxically in an age preoccupied with systematising beliefs, the Brahmanic period and its aftermath was a time of religious confusion. New systems were constantly evolved while the old were retained, and myths had to be elaborated to explain both the trend to pantheism spearheaded by the priesthood's abstractions and the struggles for supremacy within the old Vedic pantheon of deities such as Varuna, Indra, Mitra, Agni and Soma. As a compromise between these trends Varuna was most often given the role of a pantheistic god, though Brahma was considered to be the All-god or universal spirit behind him. Thus Brahma the creator had become identical with *Brahman*—the world spirit. Other deities were subdivided and given special names for each of their functions, a process aided by the converse trend of absorption of lesser deities by the greater ones. For example, Surya was given

supplementary names meaning 'nourisher' (Savitri), 'the brilliant' (Vivasvat), 'light-maker', 'day-maker', 'lord of day', 'eye of the world', 'witness of the deeds of men', 'king of the constellations', 'possessed of rays', 'having a thousand rays', 'shorn of his beams' (a reference to a myth involving Visvakarma). A revival of early trends in the growth of Indian beliefs further complicated the pattern. Thus the early Iranian influences were brought to the fore, as is shown by the attention paid to Agni (though he was probably of Indian origin), and to the Sun and the Moon, as well as the significance attached to the opposition of light and dark, which symbolise gods and demons, heaven and hell. Dravidian trends can be discerned in the rise to importance of female deities as powers in their own right rather than as passive consorts to their divine husbands, and behind this the growing concern with sacrifice and fertility cults. Most important of all was the appearance of Shiva and the rise of Vishnu. While Shiva is partly a development from Rudra, he is equally reminiscent of the pre-Aryan, yogic Lord of the Beasts deity, while his consorts resemble the sacrifice-exacting mother-goddesses of the same period. Vishnu is less like his Vedic namesake than like another deity of non-Aryan origin, Varuna.

Popular and priestly ideas on all these deities differed widely. Confusion fostered the rampant growth of explanatory mythology, some of which seems to be scholarly and philosophical, though much of it must have sprung from the popular imagination.

Growth in the power of the priests and the increasing incomprehensibility of their ideas left the laity to work out their own beliefs to some extent and partly changed the notion of divinity. The popular expansion of myths and the resurgence of old cults was often tolerated by the Brahmins, whose chief concern at this time was to maintain their popularity among their own people so as to keep up their position of trust with the foreign conquerors then ruling in India. They further enhanced their status by the development of new ideas on the subject of sacrifice, of which of course they had the monopoly. Sacrifices, usually in the form of offerings of soma or, later, of milk or curds, were held to be essential for the maintenance of the gods' strength and for the continued progression of the universe on its appointed cycle. The priests therefore gained ascendancy over the gods, who depended upon them for their sustenance, and while they grew relatively weaker the priests grew in power until, finally, they were openly said to have greater eminence than the gods they served.

So the priests, with their mastery of sacrifice, were the first to emancipate themselves from the dominion of the gods. The sages carried this trend one stage further, for by austerities and the acquisition of knowledge they could become identified with the world soul even before death and, as we have seen with Manu, could survive even the periodic cataclysms and act as creator, thus surpassing even the reward of release from the pattern of rebirth.

Such developments occurred in religion as it was generally practised despite the fact that the esoteric faith, by its insistence on the unique value of knowledge, of uniting the individual soul with the Absolute, discounted the value of sacrifice. The emphasis on knowledge or the deeper philosophy was a stage on the road from belief in soma as the source of strength to belief in the strengthening virtues of austerities. The inconsistency between priestly cults and the beliefs of the philosophers was one of the factors leading to the growth of many heresies. Among these were the Jain movement, with its concentration on personal salvation through austerities and *ahimsa* (harmlessness), its belief that the gods of the old pantheon were unable to reach the spiritual heights attainable by holy men, and its rejection of the idea of a supreme deity in favour of an Absolute consisting of a plurality of souls. Buddhism, another heretical movement of the fifth century B.C., similarly rejected the priesthood (Buddha was a member of the warrior caste, a Kshatriya, like Mahavira), and caste in general. Buddhism, like the cults of the Hindu revival, is rooted in earlier beliefs, for example the mythology of light and dark (Buddha's was the dynasty of the Sun), and certain pre-Aryan beliefs about rebirth through death (fertility through sacrifice) and about detachment.

Buddhism became the dominant religion for a millennium among the ruling classes, and in a popularised form—which later supplied it with a mythology – was commonly practised by the masses. But Vedic deities or their derivatives continued to be worshipped, and fire and soma cults were widespread. The substratum of continuing belief in the old gods was the foundation on which the Hindu revival of the fifth century A.D. was built.

The new cults offered the more readily acceptable idea of incarnational deities and used ancient myths as the core of the religion. But they also incorporated in their teaching many of the philosophical ideas from the earlier *Upanishads*, which were the point of departure for Buddha. Hinduism thus became an all-embracing faith, able to claim even that Buddha, leader of its greatest rival, was merely a manifestation or avatar of its own supreme deity. Where the Brahmanic age postulated a father god or creator, and Upanishadic teaching suggested that beyond the creator god there was a universal spirit or supreme deity with which the spiritually gifted might become united by the path of meditation—with or without austerities, Hindu belief identified the gods of the supreme triad with the universal spirit, but suggested that they not only embraced within their natures the gods of the old pantheon but also, through the notion of avatars, that they might become incarnate in the form of heroes on earth.

Hinduism's essential difference from Buddhism lies in this concern with events on earth and in the way in which it developed the Brahmanic innovation of dharma. Dharma became righteousness and justice embodied in social, caste obligations. To follow dharma was now the path to salvation rather than the mere performance of sacrifices. 'Worldliness' had another consequence. More rigorous sages taught physical asceticism instead of the debased sacrificial cults to attain spiritual disengagement and thus fusion with the universal spirit. But just as in the popular mind the yogi was admired for his physical prowess rather than for his spiritual achievement, so the new cults of Vishnu and Shiva, originally conceived as a spiritual counter to Buddhist abstractions, came in many cases to foster grosser polytheism and a return to pre-Vedic beliefs. The reversion to these is clearly seen in the great epics. Though the *Mahabharata* received its final form about the fifth century A.D. and continues to be considered scriptural to the present day, it was a collection of the myths current during the whole of the previous millennium.

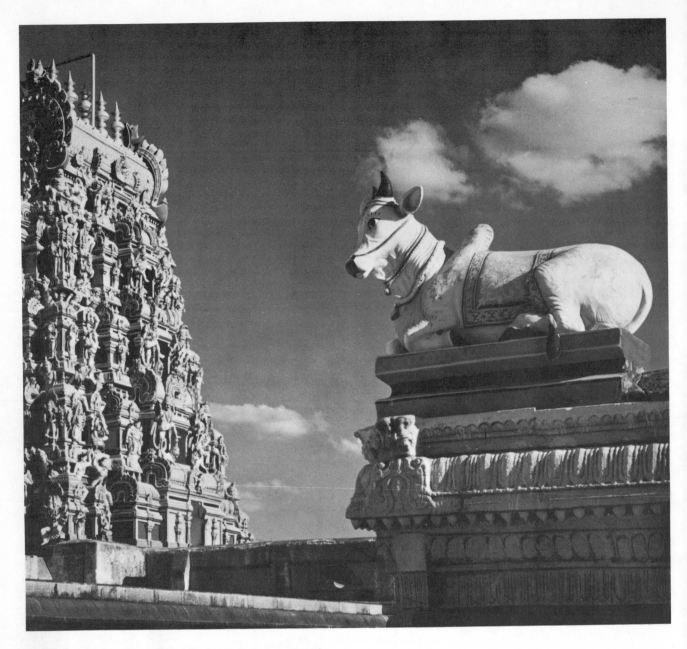

HINDU MYTHOLOGY
The Hindu triad

As we have seen, the idea of a triad of gods is rooted in the earliest Indian beliefs and seems to have its origin in solar cults, for the 'three-bodied' sun created with his fertilising warmth, preserved with his light, and destroyed with his burning rays. Though the triad remained, its members changed, so that the Adityas (Varuna, Mitra and Aryaman) gave way to Agni, Vayu and Surya, and Vayu in turn gave way to Indra. These deities were sometimes thought of simply as the three most important gods, sometimes as components of a single god embracing the world: Agni is the earth god, Vayu or Indra is the god of the atmosphere and Surya is the god of the sky. In the *Rig Veda*, Indra is closely united not only with Agni but also with Vishnu (in his early form). But in the Brahmanic and especially in the Upanishadic period Vishnu, not Indra, is the most important god left from the Vedic pantheon and is thus fitted to take his place in the triad. Similarly Rudra or Shiva is early identified with fire, from his role as god of red lightning, and can take the place of Agni. The first conjunction of the Hindu gods was in Harihara, where Vishnu and Shiva were treated as one deity. But this union ran counter to the tradition of the triad, and perhaps for form's sake Brahma, being officially the All-god, was added to make up a triad.

This triad was not, however, simply derivative from the fire triad: it introduced the new idea of conjunction and unity of creation, preservation and destruction, which fitted in with the new concept of a cycle of life, death and rebirth.

Left: Nandi, the bull mount of Shiva. Guardian of all quadrupeds, he is Shiva's chamberlain and provides the music for the Tandava, the dance of Shiva Nataraja. The approach to Shiva's temple at Perur.

To a great extent the triad as such was of mystic significance; but though the idea of a triune god embracing all three components was an old one, it became particularly important in the context of sectarian belief, where the followers of either Vishnu or Shiva sought to assert, and to prove by myths, that their particular god was not only the greatest but actually contained the triad within him. One such myth relates that Vishnu and Brahma fell into a dispute as to which of them was the more venerable. When they had been quarrelling for some time there appeared before them a fiery pillar, like a hundred universe-consuming fires.

Both gods were amazed at the sight and both decided that they must find the source of the column. So Vishnu took the form of a mighty boar and followed the column downwards for a thousand years, while Brahma took the form of a swift-moving swan and travelled upwards along the column for a thousand years. Neither reached the end and so returned. When they met again, wearily, where they had started, Shiva appeared before them; they now recognised that the column was Shiva's lingam, and acknowledged him as the greatest and most venerable of the gods.

Brahma

As Creator, Brahma is sometimes said to have been the first of the gods, the framer of the universe and the guardian of the world. At other times, however, he is said to be himself the creature of the supreme being, Pitamaya, the self-existing father of all mankind. In the Puranas Brahma is held to be the son of the supreme being and Maya, his energy; or he is thought to have hatched out from the golden cosmic egg, which floated on the cosmic waters; or to have been born from a lotus which sprang from Vishnu's navel.

Though he is sometimes thought to be self-created, Brahma's role, when he is considered as one of the triad of Hindu gods, is exclusively that of creator, his earlier position as All-god generally passing either to Vishnu or to Shiva. As the world is already created, much more interest is aroused by these other gods, the Preserver and Destroyer, who 'captured' the myths originally ascribed to Brahma, such as his ten forms, which we shall consider as Vishnu's avatars. Only traces of these myths survive, for example in Manu's creation myth, where Brahma appears as a fish. Brahma often figures in the main body of Hindu mythology as the inferior of Vishnu or Shiva, or as the victim of a sage or demon, who by practising austerities forces Brahma to make a concession which leads to a situation where Vishnu or Shiva must intervene to set matters right.

Formally, Brahma is revered as the equal of Vishnu and Shiva. He is the god of wisdom, and the four Vedas are said to have sprung from his heads. His heaven is said to contain in a superior degree all the splendours of the other heavens of the gods and of the earth.

Brahma rides a goose and is depicted with red skin and wearing white robes. He has four arms and carries the Vedas and his sceptre, or a spoon, or a string of beads, or a bow, or a water jug. His most salient features, however, are his four heads. Originally he possessed only one head, but he acquired four more, and then lost one. Having created a female partner out of his own substance, Brahma fell in love with her. This modest girl, who is variously called Satarupa, Savitri, Sarasvati, Vach, Gayatri and Brahmani, was embarrassed by his fervent look, and moved to avoid his gaze. But as she moved to the right, to the left and behind him, a new head sprang out in each of these directions. Finally, she rose into the sky, and a fifth head appeared there to look at her. Brahma joined with this girl, who was his daughter as well as his wife, to produce the human race.

It was Shiva who deprived Brahma of his fifth head, though the story of how this occurred varies. All versions, however, illustrate the tension existing between them. Though it is sometimes said that they were born simultaneously of the supreme being and immediately contested for superiority, some declare Shiva sprang from Brahma's forehead; others claim that Shiva created Brahma, who worshipped him and acted as his charioteer. As for Brahma's fifth head, according to one version Brahma claimed that he was superior to Shiva, who thereupon cut off the head with his nail. A second version states that Shiva cut off the head because Brahma told Vishnu a lie in an effort to establish his superiority over Vishnu. In a third version Shiva punishes Brahma for drunkenly committing incest with his daughter. A variant of this myth relates that the daughter was Sandhya, Shiva's wife, who tried to escape her father's advances by changing into a deer, but was pursued through the sky by Brahma in the shape of a stag. Shiva, who witnessed all this, shot an arrow which cut off the head of the stag, and Brahma then paid homage to Shiva. The fourth account says that Brahma wanted Shiva to be born as a son to him and that Shiva, though he had promised Brahma that he would grant him any boon, kept his promise but punished him for his insolence by pronouncing a curse which deprived him of one head. But Shiva thus committed Brahminicide, for Brahma was considered the chief of the Brahmins. He was paralysed for his crimes and thus open to attack by a demon created by Brahma. He fled and was forced to perform penances.

Apart from being the progenitor of the human race in general, Brahma was the father of Daksha, who was born from his thumb. Daksha became chief of the Prajapatis, sages associated with Brahma's creation. Though Daksha gave his daughter to Shiva as a wife, he insulted the god until, cowed by his violence, he was forced to acknowledge Shiva's superiority to him and to his father, Brahma.

Shiva

Rudra, Shiva's Vedic forerunner, was the red god of storms and lightning, the terrifying god living in the mountains and god of cattle and medicine who must be propitiated. As god of lightning, Rudra became associated with Agni, god of fire—and consumer and conveyor of sacrifice. With Rudra as his antecedent, Shiva could claim as his inheritance the position of priest of the gods and of candidate for divine supremacy.

By contrast with Brahma, a personalisation of a relatively late abstract principle, Shiva could combine with his Vedic antecedents features reaching even farther back than the Vedic age. He had characteristics of the Indus god of yoga, and his powers, especially in the epics, were said to derive from the practice of austerities, that is from yoga rather than from sacrifice. Such powers heightened his claims as priest of the gods. In the aspect of a yogi Shiva is depicted with a snow-white face, is dressed in a tiger skin and has matted hair.

Rudra's original character as god of cattle is extended by combining it with that of the pre-Aryan Lord of the Beasts. The bull is of course universally considered a symbol of fertility, and this aspect of the lord of cattle had attached to Rudra. But the pre-Aryan Lord of the Beasts exacted sacrifice, because of the ritual connection of sacrifice (death, murder and violence) with plant and animal fertility—a basic cult of agricultural peoples and the foundation of Indian mythology in pre- and post-Aryan periods. The fertility-giving aspect of Shiva is thus reinforced by identification with the yogic Lord of the Beasts, and at the same time the idea of violence present in Rudra is underlined. Shiva Bhairava, the Destroyer, is thus by extension Shiva

the bringer of fertility, the creator, the 'Auspicious'. In this sense his activity as destroyer is essential to that of Brahma as creator, and Brahma is thus sometimes said to be inferior to Shiva. For this reason Shiva is known as Mahadeva or Iswara, Supreme Lord. His supreme creative power is celebrated in the worship of the lingam or phallus.

Shiva repeatedly demonstrates his mastery of austerities as the source of power. Thus in the epic version of the slaying of Vritra by Indra, Vritra has obtained power to create illusions, endless energy, unconquerable might and power over the gods because Brahma cannot deny it to him after his practice of austerities. Shiva alone of the gods has sufficient strength gained by yoga to pit against that obtained by Vritra. It is Shiva who, by backing Indra and lending him his strength, enables him to overcome Vritra.

On another occasion Shiva acquired strength to make him superior to all the gods combined. At one time the asuras had obtained a boon from Brahma which consisted of the possession of three castles which could only be conquered by a deity and then only if he could destroy them with a single arrow. From these bastions the asuras made war on the gods, none of whom was strong enough to shoot the fatal shaft. Indra, king of the gods, asked Shiva for his advice; Shiva replied that he would transfer half his strength to the gods and that they would then be able to overcome their enemies. But the gods could not support even half of Shiva's strength, so instead they gave half of their own strength to Shiva, who proceeded to destroy the asuras. However, he did not return the gods' strength to them but kept it for himself, and ever after was the greatest of the gods.

He is often depicted as a demon-slayer, in which role he is called Natesa, and is seen dancing on the body of an asura. He sometimes wears an elephant skin belonging to an asura he killed.

His boons were also positive: he was worshipped as giver of long life and god of medicine, and his help was inestimable as strengthener of warriors. He was in a sense indiscriminate in this role, for he was ready to give help to anyone who would worship him. Thus in the *Mahabharata* Arjuna is said to have journeyed to the Himalayas to propitiate the gods before the outbreak of the great war, but got into a fight with a mountaineer who was Shiva in disguise. When he discovered who his adversary was he worshipped him and was not only forgiven but also given a powerful magic weapon. On the other hand Aswathaman, who was on the opposing side in the Bharata war, and who also fought tenaciously with Shiva until he realised who he was, threw himself on a sacrificial fire in the god's honour, this being the only offering he could make; as a reward for this Shiva entered into his body, so enabling him to slay all about him.

Among Shiva's beneficent roles is that of distributor of the seven holy rivers. The Ganges, which winds round Brahma's city on Mount Meru in the Himalayas, descends from the mountains in great torrents. Shiva, in order to break the fall, stands beneath the waters, which wind their way through his matted locks and divide into seven, the holy rivers of India. Shiva performed a vital service to the gods and thus to the world during the churning of the ocean of milk, the object of which was to produce amrita, or ambrosia, which was to strengthen the gods in their struggle against the demons. After some time the serpent Vasuki, whom the gods were using as a churning rope, vomited forth poison, and this was about to fall into the ocean of milk, contaminate the ambrosia and thus destroy the gods. But Shiva stepped forward, caught the poison in his mouth, and was saved from swallowing it himself only by the efforts of his wife Parvati, who by strangling him held the poison in his throat, which turned it blue.

Apart from his blue throat, Shiva is represented as a fair man, with five faces, four arms and three eyes. The third eye appeared in the centre of his forehead one day when Parvati playfully covered his eyes and thus plunged the world into darkness and put it in danger of destruction; it is a powerful weapon, for by fixing it upon his enemies Shiva can destroy them with fire. With this eye he kills all the gods and other creatures during the periodic destructions of the universe. His other weapons are a trident called Pinaka, which is a symbol of lightning and characterises Shiva as god of storms; a sword; a bow called Ajagava; and a club with a skull at the end, called Khatwanga. Further weapons are the three serpents which twine around him and may dart out at enemies: one coiled in his piled up, matted hair and raising its hood above his head; one on his shoulder or about his neck; and one which forms his sacred thread.

In addition to the weapons, most of Shiva's personal attributes emphasise the violent aspects of the deity, for which he is most generally known. These include his head-dress of snakes and necklace of skulls, which he wears when haunting cemeteries as Bhuteswara, lord of ghosts and goblins. In the character of Bhairava his violent nature is intensified, for he is then said to take pleasure in destruction for its own sake. When depicted in such roles Shiva is attended by troops of imps and demons. In his role as stern upholder of righteousness and judge, he carries a drum shaped like an hourglass and a rope with which to bind up sinners.

Apart from the lingam, personal attributes which characterise Shiva as god of fertility are the bull Nandi which accompanies him or whose symbol in the shape of a

Shiva Bhairava—Shiva in his fearsome aspect as the Destroyer. Bronze, ninth century.

crescent moon he wears on his brow, encircling his third eye, and the serpents which twine about him. Many of Shiva's violent aspects are symbolised in the characters of his consorts, who are particularly associated with his bloody rites. The yoni, which is their emblem as the lingam is his, is known as his shakti, or female energy.

Shiva likes to dance in joy and in sorrow, either alone or with his wife Devi, for he is the god of rhythm. Dancing symbolises both the glory of Shiva and the eternal movement of the universe, which it serves to perpetuate. But by the Tandava dance he accomplishes the annihilation of the world at the end of an age and its integration into the world spirit, so that it represents the destruction of the illusory world of maya. Maya no longer refers to Varuna's inscrutable laws governing the universe; it is that which governs life on earth, the illusion of material reality, and that from which by various means the faithful seek to free themselves. When dancing Shiva represents cosmic truth; he is surrounded by a halo and accompanied by troops of spirits. He is watched by anyone fortunate enough to be granted the vision. When the serpent Shesha saw the dance he forsook Vishnu for several years and gave himself up to austerities in the hope of seeing it again. The gods themselves assemble to behold the spectacle, which was treated as proof of Shiva's superiority over Vishnu by some hermits who till then had lauded only Vishnu. Even demons are affected by his dance when he performs it in cemeteries, thus bringing the unclean evil spirits into the orbit of his spiritual power.

But Shiva is generally depicted immobile, as an ascetic —naked, his body smeared with ashes and his hair matted. His meditation and austerities build up his spiritual strength, giving him unlimited powers to perform miracles—and also strengthening his powers as fertility god, for the two roles are not so antithetical as might at first appear from the myth in which he kills Kama, god of desire, by burning him up with the fire from his third eye. Though Shiva may have struck Kama dead for having interrupted his meditations, the effect of Kama's shaft was not thereby nullified. By still further delaying his union with Parvati, thereby causing Parvati herself to perform austerities in the hope of arousing his interest and causing all the gods to hope anxiously for the consummation of his desire, Shiva in effect heightened the desire and strengthened the force of his role as fertility god. The child produced from his union with Parvati was one of the strongest of the later pantheon: Karttikeya, god of war, who to some extent supplanted Agni.

It was the angry sage Bhrigu who caused Shiva to be worshipped in the form of the lingam. He was sent by the other sages to test the three gods of the triad to see which was the greatest. When he reached Shiva the god did not welcome him; he was engaged with his wife and would not be interrupted. For this lack of respect due to a sage, Bhrigu cursed Shiva to be worshipped as the lingam.

Brahma also failed to gain Bhrigu's approval, for he was too occupied with his own self-importance to receive the sage with due courtesy. Vishnu was sleeping when Bhrigu reached him and the sage rudely kicked him in the ribs. Instead of rising in wrath Vishnu, full of concern, asked him if he had hurt himself, gently rubbing the foot which had injured him. Bhrigu went away proclaiming that this was the god most worthy of adoration—such compassion and humility before a sage was the mark of greatness.

Shiva quarrelled with many of the gods, for though he claimed the right to judge their actions and to punish them, many of the other gods in turn considered him to be a Brahminicide because he struck off one of Brahma's heads, for which offence he was condemned to be a wanderer and to perform penances. The gods mocked at him as an ugly, homeless mendicant, unclean, ill-tempered and a haunter of cemeteries. Eventually, however, like Brahma and Vishnu, Shiva acquired a heaven of his own. This was situated on Mount Kailasa, in the Himalayas, and was the scene of his austerities and where the Ganges descended on his head.

Though Shiva quarrelled with many of the gods, his most open disputes were not with Vishnu, his real rival, but with Brahma. The quarrel was continued in a feud with Daksha, Brahma's son, who became Shiva's father-in-law. When Daksha called together the assembly at which his daughter Sati was to choose her husband, he issued invitations to all the gods except Shiva, whom he considered to be disqualified because of his impure habits and unkempt appearance. But as Sati had long been a devotee of Shiva and wished to marry no one else, she was disconsolate to discover Shiva's absence. After searching the assembly hall she prayed to him to appear and threw the garland into the air, where Shiva appeared and received it. Daksha was thus forced to allow the marriage.

Shiva had not, however, forgotten the initial insult, and later, when Daksha held an assembly to which all the gods were invited, he repaid it in kind. As Daksha entered all the gods rose to greet him, except his father, Brahma, and his son-in-law, Shiva. Brahma, of course, owed no such deference to his own son: but the disrespect from his son-in-law enraged Daksha, who declared to the assembled gods and sages his low opinion of Shiva, a disgrace to the reputation of the guardians of the world, who encouraged others to transgress and himself flouted divine ordinances and abolished ancient rites (sacrifice). Daksha protested against Shiva's habit of haunting cemeteries accompanied by ghosts and spirits, looking like a madman, with no clothes, smeared with ashes, with matted hair, and with skulls and human bones about his person; and he denounced his habit of calling himself 'Auspicious' (Shiva) when in fact he was dear only to the mad and to

Right: *Shiva and Parvati. It was such dalliance with his consort on the occasion of the sage Bhrigu's visit that led to Shiva being worshipped in the form of the lingam. Rajput painting, eighteenth century.*

the beings of darkness. Having delivered himself of his tirade, Daksha returned home to plan his next move against Shiva, which was to hold a great sacrifice without inviting his son-in-law to be present.

Daksha's revenge was, however, to miscarry. Sati, seeing all the gods trooping off to the sacrifice, enquired where they were going and was disconsolate when she heard that they were all going to her father's home. Accordingly she went herself to see her father and pleaded with him to invite Shiva. But Daksha merely repeated the strictures he made at the earlier assembly; upon which Sati, to vindicate her husband's honour, jumped into the sacrificial fire and was consumed by its flames. Shiva, hearing of this, stormed into Daksha's house and, producing from his hair some of the demons with whose company Daksha reproached him, destroyed the sacrifice. In the uproar which followed he scattered all the gods and cut off Daksha's head.

He then gave himself up to insane grief over Sati's death, retrieving her body from the embers and clasping her to him and calling on her to answer him. So violent was his emotion and the rhythm of the dance into which he threw himself, encompassing the world seven times, that the whole universe and its creatures suffered too. Finally Vishnu, to put an end to this frenzy of mourning, cut Sati's body, which was still in Shiva's arms, into fifty pieces, and thus restored him to his senses. Shiva repented of his murder of Daksha and brought him back to life; but the head could not be found, so a goat's head was used instead.

But this was not the end of the feud. When Sati was reborn as Parvati and again married to Shiva, Daksha held another sacrifice and once more failed to invite Shiva. Parvati spied the festivities from her seat on Mount Kailasa and informed Shiva who, furious, rushed to the scene. Accounts of what followed vary.

According to the famous version which is perpetuated in the *Mahabharata*, Shiva pierced the offering with an arrow and thereby inspired such fear in the gods and sages that the whole universe quaked. Shiva then attacked the gods, putting out Bhaga's eyes and kicking Pushan as he was eating the offering and knocking out his teeth; or alternatively causing Pushan to break his teeth on the arrow embedded in the offering – whereupon the gods acknowledged Shiva as their lord and refuge.

More interesting are the versions of the myth which introduce Shiva's true rival, making the issue less the feud with Brahma than a dispute with Vishnu for supremacy. According to one, Shiva hurled Pinaka, his blazing lightning trident, which destroyed the sacrifice that Daksha was holding in honour of Vishnu and then struck Narayana's (Vishnu's) breast. Narayana hurled it back with equal vigour at Shiva, and a battle flared up between the two gods which was halted only when Brahma intervened, persuading Shiva to propitiate Narayana.

Right: Ardhanarisvara, or Shiva and his shakti or female nature, combined in one image. He-she is seen riding the bull Nandi. The seductive one-breasted torso is surmounted by the high-domed head which represents the lingam. The essential nature of Shiva is seen in the reconciliation of opposites. From the Elephanta caves.

There is even more violence in the version of the myth told in the Puranas; here when Shiva heard from Parvati that he had been excluded from the sacrifice, he created a 'being like the fire of fate', called Virabhadra, whose looks and powers were terrifying, and sent him, together with hundreds of thousands of specially created demi-gods, to the place of sacrifice. These creatures broke up the sacrifice, causing the mountains to totter, earth to shake, winds to roar and the sea to be disturbed. The gods were routed: Indra was trampled underfoot, Yama's staff was broken, Sarasvati's nose was cut off, Mitra's eyes were put out, Pushan had his teeth knocked down his throat, Chandra was beaten, and Agni's hands were cut off. Then either Daksha admitted Shiva's supremacy, or the intervention of Vishnu, who seized Shiva by the throat, forced Shiva to desist and acknowledge Vishnu as his master.

Vishnu

In the Vedas Vishnu distinguishes himself only for the 'three steps' with which he measures out the extent of the earth and the heavens. The significance of this act is amplified to include other functions in the epics, where Vishnu is equated with Prajapati, the creator and supreme god. As Prajapati he encompasses Brahma, Vishnu himself as preserver, and Shiva as destroyer. As the preserver he is the embodiment of the quality of mercy and goodness, the self-existent, all-pervading power which preserves and maintains the universe and the cosmic order, dharma. Vishnu is the cosmic ocean, Nara, which spread everywhere before the creation of the universe, but is also called Narayana, 'moving in the waters'; in this character he is represented in a human form, sleeping on the coiled serpent Shesha, or Ananta, and floating on the waters. Brahma is sometimes said to have arisen from a lotus growing from his navel as he slept thus. After each destruction of the universe Vishnu resumes this posture.

According to Vishnu's adherents, he is unlike Brahma and Shiva in that he has no need to assert his own superiority. Indeed, his mildness combined with his power prove that he is the greatest of the gods. As the preserver, Vishnu is the object of devotion rather than of fear, and this affection is similarly extended to his wife Lakshmi, goddess of fortune.

When Vishnu is not represented reclining on the coils of the serpent Shesha, with Lakshmi seated at his feet, he is shown as a handsome young man with blue skin, dressed in royal robes. He has four hands; one holds a conch shell or Sankha, called Panchajanya, which was once inhabited by a demon killed by Krishna; the second hand holds a discus or quoit weapon called Sudarsana or Vajranabha, also an attribute of Krishna's, given to him by Agni as a reward for defeating Indra; the third hand holds a club or mace called Kaunodaki, presented to Krishna on the same occasion; the fourth hand holds a lotus, or Padma. He also has a bow called Sarnga, and a sword called Nandaka. He is usually either seated on a lotus with Lakshmi beside him, or riding on his vehicle, Garuda, who is half-man and half-bird.

Vishnu's heaven is called Vaikuntha, and is sometimes said to be on Mount Meru, though this is more often given as the location of Indra's heaven. With a circumference of 80,000 miles, Vaikuntha is made entirely of gold and precious jewels. The Ganges flows through it, and is sometimes said to have its source in Vishnu's foot. Vaikuntha contains five pools, in which grow blue, red and white lotuses; Vishnu and Lakshmi are ensconced amid the white lotuses, where they both radiate like the sun.

Though Vishnu existed as a god in Vedic times, his role as preserver is essentially a late development. It depends upon two assumptions. First, the theory of samsara, which teaches that every man is born many times over and that each life represents a punishment or a reward for his previous life, according to how well he has followed his dharma, or the path of duty laid down for him in that particular condition of life. If in each life he has faithfully performed his duty, he may hope to progress steadily upwards, until he becomes a saint, or even a god. On the other hand, if he does not perform his duty he progresses as steadily towards life as a demon. The second assumption is that gods and demons represent the two poles of existence, and that both are active in the world, a constant struggle being carried on between the two forces. In the normal course of events, good and evil are evenly matched in the world; at times, however, the balance is destroyed and evil gains the upper hand. Such a situation is deemed to be unfair to men and at such times it is Vishnu as preserver who intervenes by descending to earth in a human incarnation or avatar.

Such avatars are therefore not chance events, and during each one Vishnu has a specific task to perform. It is sometimes thought that Vishnu is called upon to descend to earth in this way once in each cycle of universal time. There are ten avatars in the present Mahayuga, the first four of which are said to have occurred during the Kritayuga, and the seventh, eighth and ninth of which are the best known. Late texts, however, say that there are twenty-two, or even that they are innumerable.

With the eighth incarnation, that of Krishna, which became very popular at a relatively late stage, a new and important idea is added to the older beliefs. Since Brahmanic times it had been believed that a man's progressive rise through countless lives to the level of god—'to enter Indra's heaven'—should not be the ultimate aspiration; it was far better to practise austerities (yoga) until the point where the soul became entirely unattached to the individual and was able to fuse with the universal spirit. The achievement of this release (moksha) became the ultimate aim, only to be attained by certain gifted spirits, and it absolved them from the weary round of existences to which they were otherwise doomed. Now the Krishna myth introduced an important variant to this belief, for in the course of the *Mahabharata* the god explains that there is another route to the release of the soul through bhakti, or devotion to a particular god (in this case Krishna speaks only of devotion to himself, who as Vishnu can in any case be equated with the universal spirit). Thus by concentrating his thoughts on the god a man can hope to merge his soul with him and earn release in a far more attractive way than the old discipline of austerities and yogic concentration. It is this which explains the enormous popularity of Krishna, who is the most widely worshipped avatar of Vishnu. It may be remarked in passing that this aspect of his cult has obvious similarities to Semitic beliefs in a saviour god and that the episodes of Krishna and the cowgirls resemble Dionysiac cults.

An interesting twist to the theory of bhakti is seen in the myth relating to Sisupala, King of Chedi, who hated Krishna so much that he thought of nothing else but him or Vishnu, even in his sleep and even as he lay dying. And the consequence of this was that Sisupala too gained release, simply from concentrating his thoughts so exclusively on the god. Besides the avatars, Vishnu has a thousand names, the repetition of which is a meritorious act.

Nevertheless, Vishnu's especial function as preserver remains linked to the older beliefs and is exercised through his avatars, when he descends to earth as a great hero and saves mankind and the universe. As a mortal hero, Vishnu guards the righteous, destroys evil-doers and establishes the reign of law, dharma.

Vishnu's avatars

Matsya

Vishnu's first incarnation, as a fish, is one borrowed from the mythology of Brahma, and already described in connection with Manu. In the Vishnu myth, the sage is called Vaivaswata, and is the seventh Manu and progenitor of the human race. The object of the incarnation was to save Vaivaswata. Vishnu took the form of a small golden fish with one horn, but grew until he was forty million miles long, when he predicted the deluge. He gave Vaivaswata further help by towing his ship with a rope attached to his horn and by advising him to allow the ship to descend slowly with the waters rather than allowing it to become high and dry on the peak of the Himalayas.

One version of this story gives a further purpose for the incarnation. During one of the periods of universal chaos, while Brahma was sleeping, the Veda, which had emerged from his mouth, was stolen by a demon called Hayagriva. As Matsya, his fish incarnation, Vishnu saved Manu but also instructed him in the true doctrine of Brahma's eternal soul, and when Brahma woke killed Hayagriva and restored the Veda.

Kurma

The second incarnation, as a tortoise, Kurma, is also borrowed from the Brahma myth—a relatively simple one where Brahma or Prajapati assumes the form of a tortoise in order to create offspring. In the Vishnu myth the means of creation and the objects created are more complex. During one of the periodic deluges which destroyed the world in the first age some things of value were lost, the most important of which was amrita, the cream of the milk ocean, whose absence threatened the continued existence of the universe. Accordingly Vishnu descended to earth as a tortoise to help recover these objects. Gods and demons together set about producing amrita by churning the ocean of milk, using Mount Mandara as a churning stick. Such was the weight of Mount Mandara that the operation would have been impossible unless Kurma had lent his curved back as a pivot on which to rest it. With Vishnu (Kurma) supporting the whole, with the help of the potent herbs which they had thrown into the ocean, and using the serpent Vasuki as a churning rope, gods and demons proceeded with the task, and in due course all the precious objects lost in the deluge rose up out of the milky ocean.

The ocean gave forth not only the water of life, amrita, but also Dhanwantari, bearer of the gods' cup of amrita and their physician; Lakshmi or Sri, goddess of fortune and beauty, Vishnu's wife; Sura, goddess of wine; Chandra, the moon, which Shiva took; Rambha, a nymph, who became the first of the lovely Apsaras; Uchchaisravas, a beautiful white horse, which was given to the demon Bali, but afterwards seized by Indra; Kaustubha, a jewel, which went to Vishnu; Parijata, the celestial wishing tree, which was later planted in Indra's heaven and belonged to his consort Indrani; Surabhi, the cow of plenty, which was given to the seven rishis; Airavata, a wonderful white elephant, which became Indra's mount after he stopped riding a horse; Sankha, a conch shell of victory; Dhanus, a mighty bow; and Visha, the poison vomited out by the serpent, which Shiva nearly swallowed.

Varaha

Two main versions exist of Vishnu's third incarnation, as a boar. The first of these versions again derives from an earlier Brahma myth, and claims that Brahma and Vishnu, who were one, took the form of a boar, a water-loving creature, in order to create the world out of the cosmic waters. The boar, Varaha, having observed a lotus leaf, thought that the stem must be resting on something, so

The preserver and protector, Vishnu holds first place in the hearts of many Hindus. This eighteenth-century painting from Jaipur shows him in the centre of his avatars – his incarnations on earth when his supreme power is put to the service of mankind. Nine have appeared but there is another still to come. Victoria and Albert Museum

he swam down to the depths of the ocean, found the earth below and brought a piece of it to the surface.

The second version of the myth relates that Brahma had been induced by the propitiation of a demon, Hiranyaksha, to grant him the boon of invulnerability. Under cover of this boon Hiranyaksha began to persecute men and gods and even stole the Vedas from Brahma and dragged the earth down to his dark abode under the waters. But Hiranyaksha, when reciting the names of all the gods, men and animals from whose attacks he wished to be immune, forgot to mention the boar. Accordingly Vishnu took the form of a boar forty miles wide and four thousand miles tall, dark in colour and with a voice like the roar of thunder. He was as big as a mountain, mighty as a lion, with sharp white tusks and fiery eyes flashing like lightning. With his whole being radiating like the sun, Vishnu descended into the watery depths, killed the demon with his tusks, recovered the Vedas and released the earth, so that it once more floated on the surface.

Narasinha

Vishnu's fourth incarnation was designed to free the world from the depredations of the demon king Hiranyakasipu who, like his brother Hiranyaksha, had obtained from Brahma the boon of immunity from attacks by man, beast and god; he had Brahma's assurance that he could be killed neither by day nor by night, neither inside nor outside his house. Protected by this immunity, Hiranyakasipu overreached himself. He forbade worship of all the gods

Vamana, Vishnu's dwarf avatar, who by his unsuspected ability to grow to gigantic size won back the celestial kingdom for the gods after they had been driven from it by the Daitya Bali. Stone sculpture, eleventh century.

Left: *The lion avatar. Vishnu as Narasinha destroys his enemy Hiranyakasipu. A ceiling panel from the Vimalashan temple at Mount Abu, eleventh century.*

and substituted worship of himself. He was therefore particularly incensed to discover that his own son Prahlada remained an ardent devotee of Vishnu. Hiranyakasipu tried persuasion and he tried torture, but still Prahlada refused to give up his worship of Vishnu, claiming that Vishnu was omnipresent and omnipotent. Hiranyakasipu, enraged at his son's obstinacy, finally ordered the serpents to fall upon him and bite him to death. But Prahlada was unaffected by this attack and remained obdurate; the serpents meanwhile fell into feverish disarray, their fangs broken and fear in their hearts. Vast elephants were sent against Prahlada; he was thrown over precipices; he was submerged under water. But all to no avail: Hiranyakasipu could not kill his son. Finally, one evening, the demon king, in exasperation at his son's repeated assertion of Vishnu's omnipresence, pointed out a pillar in the doorway of his palace and demanded to know if Vishnu was there inside it. Prahlada declared that he certainly was, whereupon Hiranyakasipu said that he would kill him, and he kicked the pillar. At this Vishnu stepped out of the pillar in the form of Narasinha, a creature who was half-man and half-lion, and tore Hiranyakasipu to pieces. The circumstances of Hiranyakasipu's death fell outside the conditions of Brahma's boon, for the time was evening—neither day nor night, the place was the doorway of the palace—not inside nor outside the demon's house, and the assailant was a man-lion—neither man, beast nor god.

Vamana

Vishnu's fifth incarnation took place in the second age, the Tretayuga. During this time the Daitya Bali, grandson of Prahlada, became king. Bali did all in his power to propitiate the gods by honouring them. He ruled well and was loved by his people, but as far as the gods were concerned his one defect was his great ambition. Having extended his kingdom as far as he could on earth, Bali could direct this ambition only in one direction—towards the kingdom of the gods. The celestials consulted together and Indra was advised by the sage Brihaspati that the power Bali had gained by his sacrifices could not be resisted—Indra would inevitably lose his kingdom to Bali. Brihaspati's prediction was accurate, and the gods were turned out.

The gods again consulted together and it was decided that Vishnu should become incarnate as the son of Aditi and Kasyapa, one of the seven rishis. This child grew up as the dwarf Vamana. Relying on Bali's reputation for generosity, Vamana approached the king and asked for the gift of three paces of land. The gift was no sooner granted than Vamana began to grow to enormous size. He then made two paces, which covered all the earth and the heavens and thus won back for the gods the whole of Bali's kingdom. But Bali's merits, acquired through sacrifice and austerities, had to be recognised; accordingly Vamana relinquished his right to a third pace and Bali was granted dominion over the remaining area of the universe, the nether regions, called Patala. Bali was also permitted to visit his lost kingdom once a year, and this visit is regularly celebrated in Malabar by his still devoted subjects.

Parasurama

The sixth incarnation, like the fifth, took place in the second age, the Tretayuga, at a time when the Kshatriya caste was exercising a tyranny over all men, including the Brahmins. In order to restore the power of the priestly caste, Vishnu came into the world as Parasurama, the youngest son of a strict Brahmin hermit, Jamadagni. One day Jamadagni's wife happened to see a young couple frolicking in a pool and was filled with impure thoughts. When she returned home Jamadagni divined her thoughts and was incensed, deciding that she did not deserve to live. As each of his sons returned from the forest Jamadagni bade him strike off his mother's head, but they refused and were cursed by their father to idiocy. Finally Parasurama came back from the forest, and he alone of the sons did as his father instructed and struck off his mother's head with the axe, Parasu, which was given to him by Shiva and for which he was named. Jamadagni was pleased by his son's obedience, and offered to grant him a boon. Parasurama immediately asked that his mother should be restored to life and that he himself should become invincible in single combat and enjoy long life. Both boons were granted, and life continued as before at the hermitage, with Parasurama's mother restored to purity.

One day, however, a powerful Kshatriya king called Kartavirya, who had a thousand arms, was hunting in the forest and called at the hermitage, where he was offered hospitality by Jamadagni's wife, who was alone at the time. While a guest of the house, Kartavirya caught sight of Jamadagni's wonderful cow Kamadhenu, which could grant all desires. Kartavirya decided that such a miraculous animal should be the possession of a king rather than of a hermit, so he departed, driving the cow before him, despite the helpless protests of his hostess. When Parasurama arrived home shortly thereafter and heard what had happened, he set off immediately, overtook Kartavirya, killed him in single combat and returned with the cow. When Kartavirya's sons heard of his death they came marching with all their troops on the hermitage. There they found the aged Jamadagni alone and killed him. When Parasurama returned to find his father dead, he vowed vengeance on the whole Kshatriya caste. His vow was accomplished in the course of twenty-one campaigns against them, in which all their menfolk were exterminated, their blood filling five large lakes.

Having killed all the rulers, Parasurama gave the earth into the care of the Brahmin sage Kasyapa, father of Vishnu's former avatar Vamana, father of the Adityas and of the world. Parasurama himself retired to the mountains, his main purpose achieved. Though he was an avatar of Vishnu, he was indebted to Shiva, who had among other things given him the axe Parasu.

While he was still living, another avatar of Vishnu

Ravana rallies his demons against the army of Rama, whose wife he holds captive in the fortress of Lanka. Moghul painting from a Persian translation of the Ramayana, *sixteenth century.*

Left: *The Rajarani temple, one of a number at Bhubaneswar, a ruined city in Orissa sacred to the worship of Shiva. Tenth century.*

appeared on earth and Parasurama became jealous of him. The seventh was Ramachandra, generally called Rama. Both avatars figure in the two epics, the *Ramayana*—which celebrates Ramachandra, and the *Mahabharata*. In the course of the *Ramayana*, Parasurama is annoyed with Ramachandra for having broken the bow of Shiva, and challenges him to a trial of strength. In this Parasurama is defeated and consequently excluded from a seat in the celestial world. The rivalry appears also in the *Mahabharata*, where Parasurama, armed with Shiva's bow, is knocked senseless by Ramachandra, armed with Vishnu's. It is Parasurama who instructs Arjuna in military skills durng Arjuna's twelve-year period of exile, imposed for an involuntary breach of marital propriety. Parasurama fights with Bhishma, the son of the goddess Ganga, whose allegiance is to Arjuna's enemies, the Kauravas; but neither of them can defeat the other, for both are protected by magic boons.

Ramachandra (*Rama*)

Vishnu's seventh incarnation, accomplished even while the sixth was still on earth, had as its purpose to quell the most dangerous and powerful demon king who had ever appeared. This was Ravana, ten-headed rakshasa king of Lanka (Ceylon), whose strength was overcome only after the epic struggles related in the *Ramayana*.

Like Hiranyaksha and Hiranyakasipu, Ravana had practised austerities in order to propitiate Brahma, who had granted him immunity from being killed by gods, Gandharvas or demons. Under cover of this immunity and the benevolence of Shiva, whom he carefully propitiated, Ravana persecuted gods and men. The gods consulted on how they could be rid of Ravana, and decided that the only way was for a god to take human form, for Ravana had been too proud to ask for immunity from men. Vishnu agreed to be that god, and all the others said that they would lend their powers to men and animals. Vishnu was accordingly born on earth to a certain king, Dasaratha, who after many years without an heir had performed the horse sacrifice. Four sons were born to him as a result. The oldest, called Ramachandra (Rama), was born to Kausalya; the second son, Bharata, to another wife, Kaikeyi; and two more sons, Lakshmana and Satrughna, to a third wife, Sumitra. Rama, whose mother had been the principal queen taking part in the sacrifice, partook of half Vishnu's nature; Bharata of a quarter, and Sumitra's sons of an eighth each. Thus the incarnation was divided among four mortals for this great task.

Rama and Lakshmana were particularly close and even as boys killed many rakshasas who were persecuting poor

Left: Parasurama—Rama with the Axe—was the sixth avatar, and was still living when the seventh, Ramachandra, appeared. His coming delivered the world from the tyranny of the warrior Kshatriyas, whom he destroyed in twenty-one campaigns. Kangra painting, eighteenth century. Victoria and Albert Museum

hermits. One day they heard that King Janaka's beautiful daughter Sita was to be married. Sita was actually an incarnation of Lakshmi, Vishnu's wife, and had received her name, meaning 'furrow', because she had been born of her own will in a field opened up by a plough. A contest was to be held and the man who could bend a bow given to Janaka by Shiva was to receive Sita's hand. Rama was the winner of this contest, actually breaking the bow.

Shortly after Rama's marriage to Sita, Dasaratha decided to abdicate in his favour and the coronation day was

Ramachandra, the gentle Rama, seventh avatar of Vishnu. Copper statue from south India, twelfth century.

proclaimed. But meanwhile a malicious servant of Queen Kaikeyi stirred up her resentment at the preferment of Rama over her own son Bharata, and during Bharata's absence from the court incited her to ask the King for a boon. Without asking what it was Dasaratha consented. He was appalled when he discovered that the boon was Bharata's succession to the throne, but he had given his word and was forced to grant it, and furthermore to send Rama into exile in the forest for fourteen years. Despite Rama's protests, Sita insisted on accompanying him, and together they set off into exile to the sounds of lamentation from the people and from Dasaratha, who died of grief within a week. Lakshmana, devoted to his brother, went with Rama and Sita.

Bharata, who during all this had been away, was furious with his mother on his return, blaming her for his father's death. He spared her only out of filial duty, and went to the forest and tried to persuade Rama to return; but Rama declared that he was in honour bound to remain in exile. Bharata returned to the capital, Ayodhya, and proceeded to reign as viceroy, preserving a pair of Rama's sandals on the throne as a symbol of the rightful king.

In the forest, meanwhile, Rama and Lakshmana incurred the wrath of Ravana's sister, the rakshasi giantess Surpanakha. She first fell in love with Rama, who resisted her advances, saying that he was married, but that Lakshmana might wish to have a wife. But Lakshmana also spurned her. Suspecting that Lakshmana too was in love with Sita, Surpanakha attacked her and tried to swallow her. But Lakshmana in turn attacked the giantess, cutting off her nose, ears and breasts.

Surpanakha sent her younger brother Khara to avenge her. He gathered an army of fourteen thousand rakshasas and sent an advance party to attack. Rama killed these first and then destroyed Khara and his entire army. Surpanakha now sought vengeance through her older brother Ravana, but could arouse his interest only by pointing out that Sita was very beautiful and would be a fitting wife for him. Ravana accordingly set out to capture Sita by a ruse (for he knew the true identity and power of Rama). He sent an enchanted deer to the clearing where Sita liked to pass the time. The creature was so beautiful that she wanted to possess it and asked Rama and Lakshmana to capture it for her. When the brothers had gone Ravana approached in the disguise of an ascetic and seized her. He made off with her to Lanka in his aerial chariot.

Overleaf left: Radha and Krishna in the grove. The love of Krishna for the beautiful cowgirl is beloved of Hindus and celebrated in hundreds of songs, stories, and pictures. Nurpur painting of the eighteenth century. Victoria and Albert Museum

Overleaf right: Krishna subduing the serpent demon Kaliya, which inhabited the River Jumna and had been terrorising the people living along its banks. Though only a boy, Krishna overcame Kaliya by dancing on his heads. Chola bronze of the sixteenth century. Victoria and Albert Museum

On the way Jatayu, an incarnation of Garuda, Vishnu's mount, and king of vultures, fought Ravana but was fatally wounded, living only long enough to return and tell Rama what had happened. Sita also implored the forest and the River Godavari over which she was flying to inform Rama of her fate. When they reached Lanka, Ravana tried to woo her, but she rejected all his advances. He then tried to threaten her into marriage, declaring that he would kill and eat her, but Sita was saved by the intervention of one of Ravana's wives. Ravana dared not force her because, as an inveterate wife-seducer, he was at this time doomed to die if he ever again ravished the wife of another.

Meanwhile, after a lengthy search for Sita, Rama and Lakshmana discovered Jatayu who, as he lay dying, told them the story of her disappearance. Rama piously cremated Jatayu's body, and then set about making plans to recover his wife. He made an alliance with the monkey king Sugriva, son of Indra, who had been exiled from his own kingdom by his half-brother Bali (to be distin-

guished from the Daitya king who figured in the fifth avatar). In return for their help in regaining his kingdom, Sugriva promised to support Rama and Lakshmana against Ravana. Bali was soon killed and Sugriva restored to his throne. After some delay Sugriva raised an army of monkeys and bears, led by his general the celestial Hanuman, son of Vayu, the wind, and marched south towards Lanka.

Meanwhile, Hanuman, who could fly, went ahead and crossed the sea to Lanka, where he found Sita alone in a garden in Ravana's palace. He told her of the plans being made for her deliverance and gave her Rama's signet ring as a token. Pleased with his success, Hanuman then frolicked in the enemy's garden, pulling up the plants; but he was caught by the rakshasas and brought before Ravana. Still ebullient, Hanuman raised himself on the coiled mound of his long tail so that he was seated higher than the king. Ravana was about to kill him, but the monkey-general managed to stay his hand by claiming diplomatic immunity—messengers from the opposing side could not be killed. Ravana nevertheless ordered the rakshasas to set fire to Hanuman's tail, by wrapping it in oily rags and lighting them. But at this moment the monkey made his escape and, trailing his burning tail and jumping from building to building, he succeeded in setting fire to the whole of Lanka.

Hanuman flew back to the mainland and rejoined Rama, giving him valuable information about Ravana's defences. Lanka was indeed a mighty fortress, for it had originally been built by Visvakarma for the god of wealth, Kubera. The vast city, which was built mostly of gold, was surrounded by seven broad moats and seven great walls of stone and metal. It had originally formed the summit of Mount Meru which, as we shall see, was broken off by Vayu and hurled into the sea.

Shortly after Hanuman's return a bridge across the strait to Lanka was completed, despite the efforts of creatures from the dark depths of the ocean to prevent it being built. Its chief architect was a monkey leader called Nala, who was a son of Visvakarma and had the power to make stones float on water. The bridge is therefore sometimes called Nalasetu (Nala's Bridge), though its usual title is Rama's Bridge.

A mighty battle was now fought before the gates of the city. Ravana's forces included his son Indrajit, who acquired his name and the boon of immortality from Brahma in return for the freedom of Indra, whom he had captured during Ravana's attack on Swarga, Indra's heaven, and whom he had taken prisoner to Lanka. Indrajit succeeded twice in injuring Rama and Lakshmana, but on each occasion they were cured by a magic herb which Hanuman flew all the way to the Himalayas to obtain. Meanwhile

Rama and Bharata taking leave of each other in the forest where Rama had taken exile. Bharata agreed to return with his army to Ayodhya to rule his father's kingdom only on condition that he should be regarded as Rama's viceroy. Delhi miniature, seventeenth century.

Kumbhakarna, Ravana's brother, a giant whose appetite was insatiable, was devouring hundreds of monkeys. But the monkeys were inflicting heavy losses upon the rakshasas. Finally all the rakshasa generals were killed and the battle resolved into single combat between Rama and Ravana.

As the whole company of gods looked on, these two fought a deadly battle and the earth trembled during the encounter. With arrows, Rama struck off Ravana's heads one after the other; but as each one fell another grew in its place. Finally Rama drew forth a magic weapon given to him by Agastya, a renowned sage and noted enemy of the rakshasas. This weapon was infused with the energy of many gods: known as the Brahma weapon, the wind was in its wings, sun and fire reposed in its heads, and in its mass lay the weight of Mounts Meru and Mandara. Rama dedicated the weapon and let it loose; it flew straight to its objective in the breast of Ravana, killed him, and returned to Rama's quiver. This was the moment for great rejoicing among the gods, who showered Rama with celestial garlands and resurrected the monkeys fallen in the great battle which saw evil defeated.

Now Rama and Sita could be reunited; but to the amazement of all Rama, when he saw his wife again, spoke coldly to her; he found it hard to believe that she had been able to preserve her virtue as Ravana's captive.

Right: The rakshasi Surpanakha, her advances rejected by both Rama and Lakshmana, attacked Sita in a jealous rage. Lakshmana cut off her nose and ears and she called on Ravana to avenge her. Gupta-style relief, fifth century.

Below: Rama and Lakshmana defeat Sabahu and Marica, the rakshasas who try to interfere with the sacrifice of the sage Visvamitra. Marica is the rakshasa who turns himself into a beautiful deer at the request of Ravana, to inveigle Rama away from his home, thus allowing the capture of Sita. Relief from Prambanam, Java, eighth century.

Sita protested her unfailing love for Rama and declared her innocence, and determined to prove it by fire-ordeal. She ordered Lakshmana to prepare a burning pyre and threw herself on it; as she did so the sky proclaimed her innocence and the fire-god, Agni, led her before Rama, who now accepted her, saying that he himself had never doubted her but had only wished for public proof.

This seemed to be a happy ending, and the monkey army returned with Rama, Lakshmana and Sita to Ayodhya, where Rama was crowned. But though Rama's reign was one of unprecedented peace and prosperity, Ravana's mischief had not yet run its course. The people of the kingdom began to murmur, doubting Sita's innocence, and though she was pregnant at the time Rama felt obliged to send her away into exile. She took refuge at Valmiki's hermitage in the forest, where she gave birth to twin sons, Kusa and Lava.

These boys, who bore the marks of their high paternity, wandered into Ayodhya when they were about fifteen years old and were recognised by their father, who thereupon sent for Sita. In order that she should publicly declare her innocence, Rama called a great assembly together. In front of it Sita called upon Earth (her mother, for she was born of a furrow) to attest to the truth of her words. Earth made a sign, but it took the form of opening up beneath Sita and swallowing her up.

Rama, now heartbroken, for Sita was his only wife, wished to follow her. The gods had mercy on him in his despair and sent him Time, in the guise of an ascetic, with the message that he must either stay on earth or ascend to heaven and rule over the gods. Then the sage Durvasas also came to see Rama, and demanded immediate admission to his presence, threatening dreadful curses on him if he were refused. Lakshmana, who had received Durvasas, hesitated; he knew that the interruption of a conference with Time carried the penalty of death. But preferring his own death to the curses of Durvasas on his brother he went to fetch Rama. Then he calmly went to sit by the riverside to await death. Here the gods showered him with garlands before they conveyed him bodily to Indra's heaven. Rama's end was more deliberate; with great dignity and ceremony he walked into the River Sarayu, where Brahma's voice welcomed him from heaven and he entered into the 'glory of Vishnu'.

Above left: Jatayu, incarnation of Garuda and king of the vultures, swooping down on Ravana as he abducts Sita in his magic chariot Pushpaka. Jatayu was fatally wounded, but lived long enough to tell Rama what had happened. From a copy of a Moghul painting, seventeenth century.

Left: Hanuman receiving instructions from Rama, while Lakshmana looks on. The bonds that unite the monkey general to Rama are those of selfless loyalty, for which he was rewarded with the boon of immortality. Trichinopoly painting, 1820. Victoria and Albert Museum

Right: Rama's forces, led by the monkeys and bears, approach the walls of Lanka where Ravana's demons wait to engage with them. Kangra painting, eighteenth century.

Krishna

Vishnu's eighth incarnation attracted to it an even greater body of mythology than the seventh, though its purpose was relatively simple: to kill Kansa, son of a demon and tyrannical king of Mathura. Of the many myths surrounding Krishna the most popular, which concern the aspects of the god in which he receives the greatest worship, have nothing to do with the reasons for his incarnation as an avatar of Vishnu. Indeed the Dionysiac myths concerning the young Krishna, with their strong Greek influence, have little to do with the ideas current during the great mythologising period of the epics. Sometimes, Krishna is considered as a great deity in his own right and then his brother Balarama is said to be Vishnu's eighth incarnation. Krishna's life falls into four main parts: childhood, when he performed great feats of strength; youth, when he dallied with the cowgirls; manhood, when he performed the task for which he had been born; and middle age, when he became the great ruler of Dwarka and took part in the Bharata war, acting as Arjuna's charioteer and pronouncing his great teaching on the subjects of dharma and bhakti.

Krishna's birth and childhood. During the second age of the world the Yadavas of northern India, whose capital was Mathura, were ruled over by King Ugrasena. They were a peace-loving, agricultural people, who could have lived quietly had a misfortune not befallen their queen, Pavanarekha. One day as she was walking in the forest she was waylaid and raped by the demon Drumalika, who took the shape of her husband Ugrasena. Drumalika resumed his demon form and revealed that the son to be born, Kansa, would conquer the nine divisions of the earth, be supreme ruler, and struggle with one whose name would be Krishna. Ten months later Kansa was born and as Pavanarekha remained silent about his true paternity Ugrasena assumed the son was his own. As he grew up his evil nature showed itself. He was disrespectful to his father. He murdered children, and forced the defeated King Jarasandha of Magadha to yield up two of his daughters whom he took as wives. Next he deposed his father, ascended the throne and banned the worship of Vishnu. He extended his kingdom by conquest and committed many crimes.

The gods, at the entreaty of Earth, decided it was time to intervene; Vishnu should restore the balance of good and evil. Vishnu made use of two Yadavas loyal to him.

Sita proving her innocence by fire-ordeal as Rama, Lakshmana, Hanuman, Sugriva and Jambavan look on. By rescuing her from the flames, Agni publicly vindicated Sita's honour and they all returned to Ayodhya. Moghul painting, seventeenth century.

They were Devaka, an uncle of Kansa, and Vasudeva, to whom Devaka's six elder daughters were married. Vishnu ordained that the seventh daughter, Devaki, should also be married to Vasudeva. He plucked a black hair from his own body and a white one from the serpent Ananta, or Shesha, on whose coiled body he reclines, declaring that the white hair would become Devaki's seventh son, called Balarama; the black hair would become her eighth son, called Krishna.

At Devaki's wedding, however, a voice warned Kansa of these preparations for his downfall; but he agreed to spare Devaki on condition that each of her sons should be killed at birth. Accordingly, her first six sons were slaughtered as soon as they drew breath. She then became pregnant with a seventh son, and Kansa received a second warning, for he heard that gods and goddesses were being born in the shape of. cowherds. He therefore ordered the systematic killing of all the cowherds that could be found and this endangered the life of Nanda, Vasudeva's closest friend. Nevertheless it was Nanda who was chosen to help preserve Devaki's seventh and eighth sons. Vasudeva sent another of his wives, Rohini, to stay with Nanda,

and Vishnu had the child in Devaki's womb transferred to that of Rohini. In due course Balarama was thus born to Rohini and Kansa was given to understand that Devaki had miscarried.

But the time came for Devaki to conceive again. Kansa took the precaution of imprisoning both mother and father. He had them manacled together and set men, elephants, lions and dogs to guard the prison. But the eighth child was Krishna and he reassured his parents from the womb. Indeed when he was born all Kansa's precautions were seen to have been in vain; the manacles fell away and the baby Krishna, assuming the form of Vishnu, ordered his father to take him to the house of Nanda—where Nanda's wife Yasoda had just been delivered of a child— and to substitute the two babies. Krishna then resumed his infant form and Vasudeva put him in a basket, placed it on his head and left the prison freely, for the doors had swung open and the guards had fallen asleep.

On his way Vasudeva came to the River Jumna and attempted to ford it; but the waters rose steadily until they nearly submerged him. At this point Krishna stretched out his foot from the basket and placed it on the waters, which thereupon subsided, allowing Vasudeva to pass. At Nanda's house he found that Yasoda's baby was a girl but he took her back to the prison, whose doors reclosed and where the guards, waking up, suspected nothing. They announced the birth of a girl to Kansa, who himself attempted to smash the infant's body on a rock. But the baby was transformed into the goddess Devi who, having told Kansa that his future enemy had escaped him and that he was powerless, herself vanished into heaven.

Nanda, who did not suspect that Krishna was not his own son, arranged a great celebration of the birth, to which he invited all the cowherds and their wives. During the festivities the Brahmins foretold that Krishna would be a slayer of demons, would bring prosperity to the land of the Yadavas and would be called Lord of the Cowgirls.

His childhood revealed his dual character. At times he seemed just an exceptionally lovable boy; in other episodes he began to show his strength and was recognised as a god.

During his first year Krishna was three times attacked by a demon. The first one was Putana, a child-killing ogress who, taking the form of a beautiful girl, was allowed to suckle Krishna. But the poison she had put on her breast could not harm Krishna who, on the contrary, sucked so hard that he drew all the life out of Putana, who resumed her monstrous form as she died. The second enemy was Saktasura, a monstrous flying demon who lighted on a cart loaded with pitchers beneath which Krishna was lying. But though the cart collapsed as Saktasura planned, it crushed him rather than Krishna, who had turned the tables with a well directed kick. The third attack took the form of the Trinavarta, a whirlwind demon who snatched Krishna out of Yasoda's lap. A great storm arose as Trinavarta flew away with Krishna, but Krishna twisted the demon round and smashed him against a rock, at which the storm subsided.

As Krishna began to grow up he amused himself and, despite themselves, his mother and all the womenfolk, with various pranks involving stealing the cowgirls' curds and butter, upsetting their pails of milk and blaming their children for his own mischief.

But this idyllic childhood was interrupted by the efforts of Kansa who, still searching for any child who might be the one destined to kill him, had sent demons to attack all children of Krishna's age. He overcame in turn a cow demon called Vatsasura; a crane demon called Bakasura, who swallowed Krishna but was forced to release him when Krishna became too hot; and a snake demon, Ugrasura, who swallowed Krishna but whom Krishna burst open from within by expanding his own body. Again and again Krishna was attacked by Kansa's demons, but on each occasion he extricated himself, killing the ass demon Dhenuka, subduing the snake demon Kaliya

Above: *At dead of night, while Kansa and all his guards are asleep, Vasudeva takes the newborn Krishna, escapes from the prison and, right, at Nanda's house, exchanges the infant Krishna for Yasoda's newborn daughter. Prahari painting, eighteenth century.*

Right: *Yasoda with the infant Krishna and his fair-skinned brother Balarama. Kangra painting, eighteenth century.*

Krishna suckled by the rakshasi Putana, who intended to murder the child by poisoning her breasts. Udaipur painting, 1740.

Left: *The Brahmins' wives, irresistibly attracted to Krishna, give to him and his companions the food meant for their husbands. Kangra painting, eighteenth century.*

by dancing on his heads, and swallowing up a fire sent to consume Krishna and his companions in a forest. Balarama, who was Krishna's constant companion, also killed some demons, such as Pralamba, a demon in human form.

Krishna's youth. During his childhood, Krishna showed his defiance of the world of demons. During his youth he demonstrated his attitude to the Brahmins and to Indra and the Vedic gods. One day when Krishna and his companions were hungry they smelled food and found that it was being cooked by some Brahmins in preparation for a sacrifice. They asked for some to eat, but were angrily rebuffed. The Brahmins' wives, however, were eager to oblige; Krishna had a reputation as a stealer of hearts and they disobeyed their husbands and brought him food, recognising him as God and feasting their eyes on him. When they returned, gratified, to their husbands they found them not only forgiving but angry with themselves for having missed this unexpected opportunity of serving the young god.

Right: *Krishna as a cowherd, surrounded by shepherds and their flocks. The ambiguity of Krishna's nature stands out in the contrast between this milking scene, which marks Krishna's promotion to the rank of cowherd, and the episode on Govardhana, where his companions just as easily accepted his divinity. Relief from the 'Five Pandava Cave' at Mahabalipuram, early seventeenth century.*

Krishna then persuaded Nanda and the other cowherds that their sacrifices to Indra were useless, for Indra was an inferior deity and subject to defeat by demons. Krishna convinced them that their salvation lay either in following their duty of being ruled by their fate, or in worshipping their early nature divinities, which in their case were contained in the spirit of the mountain, Govardhana, on which they grazed their flocks and which sheltered them and their beasts. The cowherds accordingly performed a great ceremony in honour of the mountain, and were rewarded for their devotions by the manifestation of Krishna himself as the spirit of Govardhana. Indra was enraged and, forgetting who Krishna really was, sent a terrible storm with torrents of rain to punish the cowherds. Krishna protected them from the flooding that this seven-day storm would normally have produced by raising the mountain on one finger, giving the cowherds shelter underneath. Indra admitted his defeat. He descended to earth accompanied by his white elephant Airavata and the cow of plenty, Surabhi, and worshipped Krishna.

The story of the Brahmins' wives hints at an aspect of the Krishna myth which receives more attention than any other: his amorous adventures with women, in particular the married cowgirls (*gopis*). All these stories are noted for the beauty of their sensuous descriptions, but though a symbolic, spiritual meaning is ascribed to them all, it must be remarked that in later life Krishna repudiated his cowgirl loves and became the model husband and

Krishna, in royal robes and standing on a dais of lotus petals, playing the flute to the delight of animals and cowgirls. His playing was the prelude to the gopis' abandonment with him. Rajput painting, seventeenth century.

Right: *The Rasalia, Krishna's dance with the cowgirls. His divine figure is seen partnering each of the gopis in the outer circle as well as the preferred one, Radha, in the centre. The cowgirls' swinging robes betray their agitation. Painting on cotton.*

Below: *Krishna seizing and breaking the neck of the bull demon who came at dusk to attack him and sent the cattle, cowherds and cowgirls into panic flight. Pahari painting, nineteenth century.*

embodiment of married bliss. However, as is often said in Indian scriptures, the gods are not to be judged by human moral standards—and many of the cowherds and cowgirls were, moreover, divine incarnations on earth.

Krishna's amorous adventures began when he was young, and developed naturally from his childhood teasing of the cowgirls. One day when a group of them, already smitten with love for him, went bathing in the River

Jumna in an attempt to make their wishes come true, Krishna came across them as they were calling out his name. He stole their clothes and hid with them in a tree. Despite their earlier pleas the cowgirls were mortified at the situation and tried to hide their nakedness beneath the water; but Krishna told them that Varuna inhabited the water so they were no better off in it. He insisted that each of the cowgirls come forward to the tree to receive back her clothes. Sending them away after all this teasing, Krishna mollified them by promising that he would dance with them in the following autumn.

When autumn came, Krishna went one moonlit night into the forest and played upon his flute to call the cowgirls, who all slipped away from their husbands and went to join him. After some teasing on his part the dance began, sending the lovesick girls into ecstasies of delight, each one dancing with Krishna as if he were her lover. But Krishna slipped away with one of them and when the other girls realised they were alone they set out with lamentations to look for him. First they found his footprints, accompanied by those of a girl. But the girl, too sure of herself and proud at being singled out, had asked Krishna to carry her; annoyed, he abandoned her on the spot. The others found her, and after their endless search and entreaties that he should return, Krishna relented.

They took up the dance again. The girls became frantic with desire and, using his powers of delusion, Krishna made each believe that he was dancing with, embracing and loving her. The dance and its erotic delights continued for six months and ended with the whole company bathing in the River Jumna. The girls returned to their homes, and found that no one knew they had even been away.

The story of the girl who was singled out is elaborated in Indian poetry (rather than in myth), where she is called Radha. The plight of the lovelorn girl is described as she waits for Krishna while he dallies with others, and the emotions of each of them at the various stages of their story, their misunderstandings and the fulfilment of their love, became the classical images of Indian love poetry.

In the myth, though Krishna returned once or twice to the cowgirls, this great dance of love marks the climax of his idyll and the end of his youth.

The slaying of Kansa. Meanwhile, the attacks of Kansa's demons continued. One of them took place at night, when Krishna and Balarama were with the cowgirls. Sankhasura, a yaksha demon, came among them and attacked some of the girls; hearing their screams, Krishna pursued Sankhasura and cut off his head. On another night, a bull demon careered among the herd, but Krishna caught it and broke its neck.

About this time Kansa was informed by a sage of the identity of his future killer and the rest of the story. He immediately cast Vasudeva and Devaki into prison and laid plans to capture Krishna. He decided that the best way would be to lure Krishna to Mathura but he made some more attempts to kill him in the forest by sending Kesin, the same asura who had once fought and nearly overcome Indra, in the form of a horse. But again Krishna was equal to his opponent; he thrust his hand down the throat of the horse, causing it to swell within. The horse burst apart. Then Kansa sent the wolf demon to waylay Krishna. He disguised himself as a beggar; but once more Krishna was prepared, and when the demon resumed his true form and attacked him, he seized him by the throat and strangled him.

Kansa now abandoned such tactics and sent the head of his court, Akrura, to invite Krishna to attend a great sacrifice to be held at Mathura in honour of Shiva. But Akrura was a secret devotee of Krishna and warned him that Kansa had arranged for him to be killed in a match with a wrestler called Chanura, and that he had also stationed at the gates a savage elephant which was to trample Krishna to death should the other plan fail.

Despite the protests of the cowgirls, Krishna, Balarama and a party of the cowherds set off for Mathura, where news of their arrival had gone before them. In Mathura the women leant from their windows and rooftops to greet Krishna; Kansa's tailor himself made them new clothes; another of his servants, the hunchback Kubja, anointed Krishna with perfume, in return for which he straightened her back.

At the gate of the city Krishna picked up the great bow of Shiva and broke it into pieces (just as Rama had broken it) and killed all the guards. As he entered Mathura the great elephant attacked him, but after a mighty struggle was overcome. Balarama and Krishna took the tusks and paraded around with them. Then Chanura and the other wrestlers attempted to worst the brothers, but one after the other were routed. Kansa, now desperate, ordered his demons to bring forth Krishna's parents and his own father Ugrasena; they were to be put to death together with Krishna and Balarama when the brothers were overcome. When news of this reached Krishna he slew the remaining demons without mercy, and then Kansa himself and his eight brothers.

The main object of his life, the killing of Kansa, was now achieved but Krishna was not yet satisfied. Kansa's allies were still at large and powerful enough to disturb the balance of good and evil just as Kansa had done. Having restored Ugrasena to his rightful throne and been reunited with his real parents, Vasudeva and Devaki, Krishna himself abandoned the pastoral life and became a sort of feudal prince, thus entering the last phase of this life.

Krishna the prince. Krishna was shortly justified in his decision to continue the fight against the demons, for another, a former rival of Kansa named Jarasandha, soon summoned up great armies of demons at the insistence of his two daughters, Kansa's widows. Among his many allies was another demon, Kalayavana. Seventeen times Jarasandha and his armies attacked Mathura and were defeated by Krishna and Balarama single-handed, and each time the troops were slaughtered but Jarasandha was released so that he might return, bringing more demon troops to be slaughtered.

Finally Krishna wearied of these battles and decided to build a new capital which would be easier to defend. He assigned to Visvakarma, the divine architect, the task of building in one night the fortress city of Dwarka. When it was completed all the Yadavas were transported to the new capital; on the way the demons were allowed to believe that they had encircled them on a hill and destroyed them by fire.

Right: Rukmini, on the eve of her marriage to Sisupala, sends a letter to Krishna imploring him to intervene. In order to accompany Vishnu in his various avatars, Lakshmi was incarnated as Sita, Radha, Rukmini. Garhwal painting, eighteenth century.

Krishna was now ready to settle down and sought wives for himself and his brother. Balarama married a princess called Revati and Krishna heard of a beautiful princess called Rukmini, who was meanwhile told of Krishna by Shiva and Brahma disguised as beggars. Both fell in love at the mere description of the other, and the stage was set for a great romantic passion which was to supersede all those of Krishna's youth. There were, however, obstacles to be overcome before the pair could be brought together and married.

Rukmini was betrothed (on the advice of her evil brother Rukma) to Sisupala, a cousin of Krishna but an avatar of the demon whose other avatars were Hiranyakasipu and Ravana. Just before the wedding was due to take place Rukmini sent a letter to Krishna beseeching his intervention. He answered it by arriving on the wedding morning while Rukmini was praying to Devi and snatching her away in his chariot. Rukma, Sisupala and Jarasandha—who was present with his demon army for the wedding—decided to avenge this, but Balarama routed the demons and all but Rukma fled. He tried to kill Krishna, but was taken captive. Rukmini begged for his life and Balarama released him (just as Jarasandha was always released).

Krishna now married Rukmini and celebrated the defeat of yet more demons at the time of his nuptials. In the same way he married seven further wives; each marriage was opposed in some way by demons and so brought about the destruction of yet more evil. Thus Krishna married Jambavati, daughter of the king of the bears, Jambavan, and Satyabhama, daughter of Satrajit, and Kalindi, daughter of the sun, and four other girls, in each case after struggles with demons.

He now seemed to have achieved the aims for which he was born, and Earth appealed to Brahma, Vishnu and Shiva for a reward for her part in securing the presence of Krishna in the world. She requested a son who would never die and who would never be equalled. The three gods granted her a boon but not quite in the form that she expected, for they also warned her that the son, Naraka, would be attacked by Krishna and killed by him at Earth's own request.

Naraka became the powerful king of Pragjyotisha and conquered all the kings of the earth; he became an implacable enemy of the gods in the sky and routed them; carried off the earrings of the mother of the gods, Aditi, and wore them in his impregnable castle at Pragjyotisha; he took Indra's canopy and placed it over his own head; took into captivity sixteen thousand one hundred girls, earthly and divine; and finally, taking the form of an elephant, he raped the daughter of Visvakarma, the divine architect.

The gods' prophecies were duly fulfilled. Krishna attacked and defeated Naraka, though he was assisted in his defence of Pragjyotisha by the five-headed arch-demon Muru and his seven sons. When the vast demon armies had been defeated the palace was opened to reveal the countless jewels Naraka had amassed besides the earrings of Aditi, the canopy of Indra, and the sixteen thousand one hundred virgins. Krishna took all these girls back to Dwarka and married them, for on seeing him all had fallen in love with him.

Krishna now settled down with his sixteen thousand one hundred and eight wives and was able to delight them all simultaneously. In due course each of them bore him ten sons and one daughter, and despite the great number of his wives, he was sensitive to their least whim and ready to pander to their every desire. One day he gave Rukmini a flower from the Parijata or Kalpa tree, the heavenly wishing tree which grew in Indra's heaven and belonged to Indrani. A sight of this tree rejuvenated the old, and when Krishna's third wife, Satyabhama, saw the present he had made to Rukmini, she asked him to bring her the whole tree. So Krishna set off for Indra's heaven, taking with him Indra's canopy and Aditi's earrings, and asked for the tree. But Indra had not forgotten his humiliation over the Govardhana episode and refused, whereupon Krishna seized the tree and made off with it. Indra raised forces and pursued him but was defeated; however,

Krishna returned the tree of his own free will a year later.

The demons meanwhile were not forgotten; many of their leaders whom Krishna and Balarama had earlier defeated were plotting revenge. Jarasandha had by now imprisoned twenty thousand rajas, so Krishna set out with two of his Pandava cousins, Bhima and Arjuna, to release them.

On the way Krishna offered good counsel. He informed Bhima that the way to overcome Jarasandha was to split him in two, and after single combat against the demon lasting twenty-seven days Bhima succeeded in tearing him in half. The next to be dealt with was Sisupala, who had never forgiven Krishna for depriving him of his bride Rukmini and never ceased attacking him. But Krishna repeatedly spared his life because he had promised Sisupala's mother that he would forgive him a hundred wrongs. At a great sacrifice held by Yudhisthira, Sisupala stepped forward to contest the decision to treat Krishna as the most honoured guest, saying that Krishna was of low caste, associated with cowherds, a thief, a philanderer and an enemy of Indra. But this was his hundred and first attack. Krishna let him speak, but then stood up, cast his magic quoit weapon, Sudarsana, and killed him instantaneously. Some time later, Sisupala's two brothers were also killed.

Sisupala with his retinue. Krishna's cousin Sisupala became his implacable enemy after the beautiful Rukmini, his intended wife, was abducted by Krishna with her own connivance. He was eventually killed by Krishna, who decapitated him with his discus. Garhwal painting, eighteenth century.

Right: *The battle between Bhima and Jarasandha, worshipper of Shiva and father-in-law of the demon Kansa, who attacked Krishna at Mathura seventeen times and on each occasion, though defeated, was released. He refused to set free the twenty thousand rajas he had captured and met his end in combat with Bhima. Carving from Garhwal, fifth century.*

The climax of Krishna's long battle with the forces of evil came, as we shall see, in the struggle between the Pandavas and the Kauravas. Throughout his career Krishna had been related by family ties to both gods and demons. So in the *Mahabharata* he was related to both the good Pandavas and the evil Kauravas. He took no active part in the battles, only giving advice and letting the mortal warriors fight out the epic struggle. The most important advice he gave is contained in the *Bhagavad Gita*, where he explained to Arjuna that all is illusion, including battle and death in arms, and that it is not the prerogative of man to question his duty: he must merely follow it, and leave the higher perspective to the gods. Nevertheless, through his intervention Krishna finally secured that for which he came to earth—even though to the human protagonists the struggle must have seemed futile.

Krishna now decided that he could return to heaven. But his own mortal end seems tragic; the weapons which were to destroy the Yadava race and bring about his own death were created as the result of a curse by some Brahmins who had been mocked by Yadava boys, one of whom, Samba, was Krishna's son by Jambavati. The Brahmins declared that Samba, who had dressed up as a pregnant woman, would give birth to an iron club that would cause the downfall of the Yadavas. In due course

the club was 'born', and though it was smashed by order of King Ugrasena and thrown into the sea, splinters from it escaped destruction; one was swallowed by a fish, later found and made into an arrow head; the others grew into some rushes hard as iron.

Portents now began to appear in Dwarka of impending destruction, and the Yadavas, frightened by the storms and lightning, misshapen births and other horrors appearing all about them, asked Krishna how they might avert catastrophe. On his advice the men set out on a pilgrimage to Prabhasa. But after performing the various rituals, the Yadavas fell to drinking by the river and were assailed by a destructive flame of dissension. In the fight which ensued Krishna's intervention only made their fury greater, and by the end they had all been killed either by each other or by Krishna, who became angry with them. The weapons they used were the rushes growing by the river bank—which were the very ones which grew from the splintered club.

Both Krishna and Balarama were now free to leave the earth. Balarama performed austerities by the sea-shore, and dying, was rejoined to the Absolute. Shesha or Ananta, the divine serpent from whose white hair Balarama was born, flowed out from his mouth. The ocean came to meet him, carrying other serpents in its waters.

Krishna too assumed a yogic posture of abstraction. He sat beneath a fig tree with his left heel pointing outwards. A passing hunter, his arrow tipped with the one remaining splinter of the iron club, mistook Krishna's foot for a deer and shot at it, thus piercing Krishna's one vulnerable spot and mortally wounding him. The hunter, coming closer and recognising Krishna, immediately asked his pardon. He was forgiven and granted liberation.

Finally, before he died, Krishna sent word to Dwarka that the city would shortly be engulfed by the ocean and warned the remaining Yadavas to leave. But first a great funeral was held for Krishna and Balarama. Vasudeva, Devaki and Rohini, who died of grief at the news of Krishna's death, were placed on the funeral pyre with his body and that of Balarama; they were joined by Krishna's eight principal wives, Balarama's wives, and King Ugrasena, who threw themselves on the flames.

Buddha

Vishnu's ninth incarnation, appearing at the start of the Kaliyuga (the present age), clearly represents an attempt to subordinate Buddhism to the Hindu system, and in it the means employed to preserve the world differ radically from those in all the other avatars. Vishnu in his Buddha incarnation was not the straightforward heroic upholder of virtue, but rather the devious devil's advocate, who propagated ideas which would lead to wickedness and weaken the opponents of the gods, causing them ultimately either to be destroyed or to turn back for their salvation to their old faith in the traditional gods.

The doctrines supposedly put forward by Buddha bear only a distorted relation to Buddha's teaching as understood by his followers. He is said to have taught that the world has no creator and therefore no universal spirit of whom Brahma, Vishnu and Shiva are manifestations. The three supreme gods of the Hindus were therefore just ordinary mortal beings on a par with men. The doctrine of samsara and the associated idea that men should follow their duty, dharma, as prescribed for them according to their caste had no validity; for death was no more than peaceful sleep and annihilation; heaven and hell existed only on earth, the one being pleasure and the other bodily suffering. Sacrifices were of no value, for the only true blessing was the individual's release from ignorance.

The pursuit of pleasure was to be narrowly interpreted; to propagate this doctrine Lakshmi was incarnated as a woman who taught her disciples that since the body after death simply crumbled, heaven on earth was to be sought exclusively through sexual pleasures.

Ironically, as we shall see, the Buddhists did in some sense turn to Hindu belief, though this movement was far from stemming from Buddha's hedonistic teaching —rather the reverse. The mythology and cosmology that became attached to Buddhism as it became a popular mass religion, rather than a philosophers' creed, were rooted in Hindu belief, and the Hindu gods even inhabited some of the lower heavens of the Buddhist cosmos.

Kalki

The tenth and last incarnation of Vishnu has yet to come. It will usher in the end of our present age. Social and spiritual life will have degenerated to their lowest point. Sovereigns will set the tone for the final decline; they will be mean-minded and of limited power but during their short reigns they will attempt to profit to the maximum from their power. They will kill their subjects and their neighbours will follow their example, and nothing will count but outward show. Even the Brahmins will have nothing to distinguish them but their sacred thread, while the apparent wealth of the materialists will be an empty display, for real worth will have departed from everything. Truth and love will disappear from the earth, falsehood will be the common currency of social existence and sensuality the sole bond between man and wife. India will lose its sacred associations, and the earth will be worshipped for its mineral treasures alone. The sacred rites will disappear: mere washing will pass for purification; mutual assent will replace the marriage ceremony; bluff will replace learning; and the robes of office will confer the right to govern. Finally even the appearance of civilisation will vanish: the people will revert to an animal existence, wearing nothing but the bark of trees, feeding upon the wild fruits of the forest, and exposed to the elements. No man will live for longer than twenty-three years.

At this point of degeneration Vishnu will appear in person on earth, riding a white horse, Kalki, which is his tenth incarnation. Vishnu will ride through the world, his arm aloft and bearing a drawn sword blazing like a comet. He will accomplish the final destruction of the wicked and prepare for the renewal of creation and the resurgence of virtue in the next Mahayuga.

The white horse of Vishnu's tenth avatar being led towards him so that he may mount it and with his blazing sword destroy a universe at the lowest point in its moral decline. Pahari painting, eighteenth century.

Right: Indra as a Hindu god. Though he still bears weapons, he no longer gives the impression of being a warrior god, seated in dignified luxury on his white elephant, Airavata. Trichinopoly painting. 1820. Victoria and Albert Museum. (Indra's heaven, Swarga, is shown in the endpapers to this book.)

The Vedic gods in Hinduism

As we have seen, many Vedic mythological episodes and the functions of the great Vedic gods were transferred in Hinduism to Brahma, Vishnu and Shiva. Nevertheless, the greatest of them remained as objects of veneration, especially Indra, Yama, Varuna, Agni, Surya, Vayu and Soma. These, together with an eighth, Kubera, the new god of riches, were known as the 'world-guardians'. With the shift of power to the new triad the functions of the old gods changed in their significance; in their lesser roles they were rivalled in importance by new figures: gods such as Karttikeya and Dharma, the goddesses who became the consorts of the great gods and appeared in as many forms, the animal deities, deities associated with physical phenomena—especially rivers, sages or rishis, and the forefathers—Manes or Pitris.

Indra

Indra is still king of the celestials, though of course he has no power or influence over the Triad. His functions remain much the same as in the Vedic period, though many aspects of his character are more emphasised, particularly the less worthy ones such as his love of soma, his crime of Brahminicide, his flirtations, and his impotence before the curses of sages, which sometimes cause him to be worsted by demons.

As god of storms, Indra remains a fearful figure, hurling lightning and thunderbolts and using the rainbow as his bow. But he is no longer altogether the warrior god: he exercises his power in more dignified fashion as regent of the atmosphere and guardian of the eastern quarter of the compass. Instead of riding a chariot or his wonderful horse Uchchaisravas, he mounts the massive white elephant Airavata. His power rests on right rather than force. It is even sometimes said that Indra is a title rather than an individual god, and that it is awarded every three thousand six hundred years to the god or mortal of greatest merit. The 'merit', however, may consist only in having performed one hundred sacrifices and according to this the present Indra owes his position to trickery: he is said to have snatched away the offerings of some mortals who were performing the requisite sacrifices, and to have sent voluptuous nymphs to distract others who were trying to acquire merit by the performance of austerities.

Indra resides in great splendour in his heaven, Swarga, which is situated on Mount Meru and whose capital is called Amaravati. Swarga is still a magnificent abode, though Indra and his wife, Indrani, now preside only over minor deities and the souls of those virtuous men who have merited a respite from the round of rebirths on earth.

The king of the celestials still wages constant war against the demons, but not always successfully – partly because according to the new beliefs power is to be obtained not through drinking of soma, from which the demons were always excluded, but from the performance of sacrifices or austerities to propitiate the supreme triad, at which the demons are adept; and partly because Indra is hampered by his old crime of Brahminicide (which the slaying of Vritra is now considered to be), which pursues him in the personified form of Chandala. To escape his guilt Indra had to go into hiding, and was eventually freed

Left: *Surya, attended by Ushas and Pratushyas who drive away the darkness. God of the sun, Surya's brilliant countenance overwhelmed his wife Sanjna, so her father Visvakarma shaved away an eighth of his brightness. Thirteenth-century carving, Hoysala style. Victoria and Albert Museum*

Above: *Durga was born fully grown, a beautiful woman with ten arms. She destroyed the demon Mahisha who threatened to dispossess the gods, carrying in each of her arms one of the gods' weapons. Chamba painting, eighteenth century. Victoria and Albert Museum* from it only by the diligent performance of sacrifices. All through this time he was at the mercy of all and sundry. A certain King Nahusha gained supremacy over the three worlds and decided to abduct Indrani; he was foiled and Indra's honour saved only because Agastya, one of the thousand rishis who bore the king's chariot up to Swarga, was annoyed because Nahusha accidentally touched his foot and pronounced a curse on him, so that he fell down to earth again as a serpent.

Another king who gained control of the three worlds by propitiation of the gods was Bali, who defeated Indra and expelled him from his heaven, and who could not be removed from heaven and earth without the intervention of Vishnu in his Dwarf avatar.

Ravana, the demon king of Lanka, whose great power also derived from his Brahmin ancestry and his religious exercises, was another who humbled Indra. When Ravana's forces marched against Indra's the king of the gods found himself utterly incapable of defending Swarga. He himself was captured by Ravana's son, Meghanada, who had been granted the boon of invisibility by Shiva. Meghanada bound up the god and took him to Lanka, where he held him hostage. Indra had to serve him as a menial along with the other gods who had been captured. Agni was forced to cook for Ravana, Varuna to carry water for him, Kubera to supply his money and Vayu to sweep his palace. All the other gods, headed by Brahma, had to go to Lanka to sue for their release, and Brahma offered Meghanada the title Indrajit, 'conqueror of Indra'. The demon accepted the title, by which he was thereafter known, but demanded a still higher ransom: he demanded immortality. Such was Indra's abject condition that Brahma finally had to agree to pay this high price.

On another occasion Indra gave to a pet elephant a garland presented to him by the sage Durvasas, who was an emanation of Shiva and the same sage who caused the death of Lakshmana. By this slight Indra incurred the curse that his sovereignty over the three worlds should be subverted, fulfilled when Indra and the other gods became so weak that they were overcome by the Daityas, who were led by their ally, Raji. Indra, ousted from his heaven, was reduced to a pitiable condition and this god, who once could command the offerings of a hundred sacrifices, had to go the rounds of the other gods begging a little sacrificial butter. Through their own fault, however, the Daityas enjoyed only a short-lived triumph. In their pride they neglected to observe their duties; the world went into a decline and there was no longer any amrita. On Vishnu's advice therefore Indra suggested to the Daityas that gods and demons together should make a concerted effort to remedy this. They agreed and this led to the famous churning of the milk ocean, during which the demons were cheated out of their agreed share of the amrita and so deprived of the power to resist the newly

strengthened gods. Thus Indra was reinstated in his heaven only by ruse.

According to a variant of the same story, Raji was granted by Brahma the ability to command a victorious army in the unceasing war between gods and demons. The demons were the first to seek his aid, but they were refused it when they would not promise to make him their king. The gods were less loyal to their leader and agreed to accept Raji if he could lead them to victory. Accordingly after the defeat of the demons Indra was made to step down from the throne. Raji did not, however, remain in Swarga, and left Indra as his regent there. Indra regained his dominion by another piece of trickery; after the death of Raji he refused to recognise the rights of succession of Raji's five hundred sons. The sons attempted to seize their patrimony but were foiled by Brihaspati, who confused them and led them to ruin.

Indra's sensuality is much dwelt upon in later times. His love of soma—acknowledged as a source of strength in the Vedic period—leads him into weakness and moral laxity, for intoxicants are now frowned upon and forbidden to ordinary mortals. The example of Indra's sexual prowess is often cited in justification of others' lapses. He is said to have chosen his wife, Indrani, for her sensuous appeal, and furthermore to have won her by committing a double crime. She was the daughter of Puloman the demon who, discovering that Indra had ravished his daughter, was about to pronounce a curse on him; Indra, however, forestalled this by slaying him. Though Indrani remained his principal queen, Indra early embarked on an endless series of love affairs, usually with married women.

One of the most famous of these concerned Ahalya, wife of his teacher, the sage Gautama. Ahalya was the first woman made by Brahma and she surpassed all others in beauty. One day when Gautama was away from his hermitage Indra entered and began protesting his passionate love for her. Ahalya, flattered by his attentions, was about to succumb when her husband returned home and found the pair together. He immediately cursed Indra to be branded with his lechery and to bear upon his body a thousand marks of the yoni (female sexual organ). Later, however, recognising that Indra's crime was one of intention rather than of commission, he relented and the 'thousand marks of disgrace' were transformed into a thousand eyes. Indra, however, was not to be deterred in his overpowering desire for Ahalya. With the connivance of the moon, who took the form of a cock and crowed at midnight, Indra managed to lure Gautama out of his house in order to perform his morning devotions. He then assumed the form of the sage and took his place beside Ahalya. This time Gautama returned too late, and cursed both his wife and Indra. Ahalya was turned into a stone and had to wait to resume her old form until she was kicked by Vishnu, during his incarnation as Rama. Indra was cursed to become a eunuch, but was rescued from this dismal state by the intervention of the gods and was forgiven after performing a sacrifice. Punishment was nevertheless meted out, and it took the form of Indra's humiliation at the hands of Ravana and Indrajit.

Yama

In Hindu belief Yama is no longer the benevolent figure who welcomes the dead to heaven. He presides not over the delightful abode of the Manes or Pitris but over hell, a place of punishment. His gloomy palace, Kalichi, is situated in the lower regions in the southern quarter of the compass, of which he is the regent. All souls must pass before his throne of judgment in Kalichi, where his recorder, Chandragupta, reads out from a great book the sum of the dead man's virtues and sins. According to this register a judgment is passed by Yama, who may consign the soul to one of his hells, to the abode of the Pitris, or to another life on earth.

Yama also keeps another register—the great Book of Destiny in which is recorded each man's allotted span of life. When the Book of Destiny shows that a man must die, Yama sends his messengers forth to fetch him. He occasionally sets forth himself, his green skin dark against his blood-red robes, coppery eyes staring out of his grisly face. He rides a buffalo and carries a heavy mace and a noose, which he puts round the necks of his victims in order to drag them back to his abode.

Many ways were found to elude Yama, the most effective being propitiation of one of the Triad. As propitiation could take the form of mere repetition of the god's name, many sinners tricked him in this way. For example, a wicked man called Ajamila had spent his whole life flouting his obligations and neglecting all respect due to the gods. He had a son called Narayana (one of the names of Vishnu), and he called for him as he lay on his deathbed. Vishnu, hearing his name, was bound to send his servants in answer to the call and they found the emissaries of Yama already on the scene. Yama was persuaded to recall them and Ajamila did not die. But he repented of his sinful life and, becoming a hermit, practised austerities to such good effect that he obtained liberation.

In the same way another wicked man was delivered by Shiva. He was a robber who inadvertently pronounced one of Shiva's names, Hara, when engaged in his crimes, for he constantly shouted out *Ahara* ('bring the booty') and *Prahara* ('strike'). Though he had pronounced the

Above: Yama, fearsome ruler of hell. As he rides forth on a buffalo, inexorably summoning men to the kingdom of the dead, his coppery eyes stare out from his green skin. He wears crimson robes and bears a trident, a mace and a noose with which to bind up his victims. Trichinopoly painting, 1820. Victoria and Albert Museum

Savitri begs Yama, the god of death, to restore her dead husband. This much-loved story has echoes in the myths of other cultures, and in India was one of the many painted at great speed by the bazaar artists in the early nineteenth century for sale to the pilgrims to the Kalighat temple in Calcutta. Victoria and Albert Museum god's name unwittingly he was nevertheless acquitted and granted rebirth as a king.

Another episode concerned a real worshipper of Shiva. This man, Markandeya, was an ardent devotee of the lingam and worshipped it night and day. But his span of life set out in the Book of Destiny was only sixteen years. When this period expired Yama sent his messengers to fetch Markandeya. But they, finding their victim clinging to the lingam, dared not touch him. Yama, inexorable, came in person and tried to detach Markandeya from the lingam. Having failed to do so, he put his noose round the two together and started to drag them towards hell. Shiva immediately appeared in person and, furious at this outrage to himself, kicked Yama to death – whereupon all beings became immortal. But this was soon found to be a great disaster for the world, which was plunged into misery. At the request of all the gods, Yama was therefore brought back to life.

That he was not always unmoved by the sufferings of his victims is illustrated in the story of Savitri and Satyavan. The daughter and only child of King Aswapati was named after the goddess Savitri, or Sarasvati, who had granted the king this only child after eighteen years of supplication. The goddess promised Aswapati that his child would be greater than any son.

As Savitri grew up she became supremely beautiful and of celestial bearing; so beautiful was she that none dared to ask for her hand in marriage. Aswapati therefore sent her forth to search for a husband in all the neighbouring courts. But Savitri found no young man whom she wanted for a husband. At last, almost despairing, she wandered into a hermitage in the forest, where she found the blind king Dyumatsena who had been exiled from his kingdom, and his son Satyavan. Though they were living the rough life of hermits, their noble bearing immediately attracted her and she fell in love with Satyavan.

Savitri then returned to her father's court and told him of her choice. Aswapati enquired of the sage Narada whether he approved of Satyavan. The sage informed him that the young man possessed all the princely qualities that could be desired, for he was brave, virtuous and handsome. But, Narada added, Satyavan's name was written in Yama's Book of Destiny, and he had only one more year to live. The king advised Savitri to choose another husband, but she declared that she had given her troth and could never love another man. Narada, consulted once more, bowed before such constancy and advised the king to consent, assuring him all would be for the best.

Savitri and Satyavan were accordingly married and settled down to live at the hermitage with the aged Dyumatsena. Savitri was sweet-natured and virtuous, and she appeared to be happy despite the growing heaviness of her heart as the year progressed. Her cheerful nature endeared her to her father-in-law and to the other hermits, and when on the last day of the year she asked for permission to accompany Satyavan when he went to the forest to cut wood, her request was granted.

The two set out, Savitri following and keeping careful watch on her husband, who seemed to be in low spirits. Finally, deep in the forest, Satyavan selected a tree and began to cut it down. As he was working he suddenly felt a great pain in his head, called out to Savitri, and fell to the ground. Savitri, weeping, cushioned her husband's head in her lap. Then the terrifying crowned figure of Yama appeared and, without uttering a word, plucked Satyavan's soul out of his body and fastened his noose around his neck. Dragging the body behind him, he then set off towards the south.

When Yama had gone some way he chanced to look behind him and saw Savitri, faithfully following the body of her husband. She declared that, as it was written in the scriptures, death had no power to separate husband and wife and that her duty still lay in following her husband. Yama, touched by this devotion, spoke gently to her, telling her that she must not follow any further, but that as reward for her devotion he would grant her any boon other than the life of her husband. Savitri asked that the sight of her father-in-law Dyumatsena should be restored, and this boon was granted.

Yama turned again southwards, but had not gone far before he found Savitri still following. Once more he felt sorry for the lonely figure, and asked her to name another boon, attaching to it the same condition. This time she asked that Dyumatsena should be restored to his throne. Yama granted this boon also but he ordered Savitri to turn back and resumed his journey, travelling far into the realm of twilight. As he approached the portals of his own abode, Yama turned once more and was amazed to see Savitri still following. He deemed that such courage and devotion merited yet another boon, and asked her to name it. She now asked one for herself: that she should bear one hundred sons. Yama assented, but had scarcely finished speaking when Savitri pointed out that without a husband the boon could never be fulfilled. Yama was forced to concede her point, and release Satyavan, sending the two back to the realm of the living with his blessing.

When Satyavan opened his eyes, he found his head resting in Savitri's lap and the forest dark about them. He reproached Savitri for allowing him to sleep so long, but she soon explained what had happened. The two returned to the hermitage, where they found Dyumatsena with his sight restored and having just received a message to say that the usurper of his throne was dead.

Varuna

Varuna had already fallen from his position as supreme god in Vedic times. In Hindu belief his position has declined still further and of his former character of celestial deity he retains only the title of regent of the western quarter of the compass. The mythological explanation of this fall is that a great conflict occurred between gods and demons and that when it was over each of the gods was assigned a clearly defined sphere of influence so that no such conflicts should arise again.

From this time on Indra remained the atmospheric god of battle, while Varuna was ousted from guardianship of the sea of heaven, whence he had sent rain, and given instead overlordship of the terrestrial oceans, where he kept watch over the various demons of the ocean darkness.

In order to subdue these creatures Varuna still carries his noose; but as his palace is now situated on a mountain called Pushpagiri, which lies beneath the waters, he also has to carry a covering made from a cobra's hood in order to keep dry. Varuna travels about his realm on a monster fish called Makara, who has the head of a deer and the legs of an antelope. His retinue includes rivers, snakes and demons, and he is often surrounded by a troop of a thousand white horses.

Although his realm is the ocean, Varuna enters into the common fray during the wars between the gods and the demons—a departure from his earlier character, when his power was exercised by force of will alone. Varuna now also descends to a lower moral plane. He and Mitra (or sometimes Surya) were so aroused by the beauty of the nymph Urvasi that their seed fell on the ground. This was collected into a jar of water, and from it was born Agastya, whose first shape was that of a lustrous fish and who was to become a sage of great ascetic virtues. Apart from his important role in the *Ramayana*, where he subdued all the rakshasas of southern India, Agastya was known for having swallowed up the waters of his father's realm, which had offended him by hiding in their depths demons trying to escape just retribution by the gods.

Agni

In Hindu times Agni has taken over Varuna's role as king of the Pitris, or fathers. He assumes this function by virtue of parentage not ascribed to him earlier, according to which he is son of Angiras, one of the seven rishis as well as being one of the ten Prajapatis, or progenitors of mankind. As a Prajapati Angiras became naturally king of the Pitris, and Agni in due course inherited the title. Agni equally passed his earlier attributes to his father, who became known as priest of the gods and lord of sacrifices.

Agni is now worshipped less as fire than as the purifier of sacrificial offerings and as such he is honoured at all solemn ceremonies, such as those of marriage and death. His seven tongues are ceaselessly employed in licking up the butter used in sacrificial ritual; just as Indra has an insatiable appetite for soma, so Agni devours quantities of oblations and like Indra he is weakened by his greed. On one occasion, according to the *Mahabharata*, he ate so many sacrificial offerings that he became exhausted. Thinking to recover his strength by consuming a forest, he set about his destructive work, but was prevented by

Agni, the great fire god of Vedic times, later assumed a different role. He became the purifier of sacrificial offerings and on solemn occasions was paid great reverence. Stone sculpture, eleventh century.

Indra; later, however, he accomplished his design with the help of Krishna and Arjuna, Indra's son. In his role as fire Agni is still generally represented as a red man with three flaming heads, riding on or accompanied by a ram.

As king of the Pitris, Agni merely extended the old role of smoothing the path of sacrifice and of conveying to his abode the pure aspects of the mortal soul.

Confusion over the nature of Agni first arose from his association with Indra, who robbed him of some of his power but lent him aspects of an atmospheric god; and then with Shiva, who because of his association with Rudra robbed him of other attributes, such as that of slayer of the demons of disease. As well as being king of the Pitris and consumer of sacrifice, Agni is sometimes considered to be a sage; sometimes identified with a star; and frequently said to be a Marut. In this last capacity he is represented as a man with four arms, clothed in black, with smoke forming his standard and his headdress. He carries a flaming javelin and rides in a chariot whose wheels are the seven winds and which is drawn by red horses. At other times he is identified with the old Rudra, and his forty-nine sons are held to be the Maruts.

Surya

In Hindu times the god of the sun has absorbed the characteristics of all three Vedic sun gods: Surya himself, Savitri and Vivasvat. The Hindu Surya is no longer said to be one of the sons of Dyaus, but rather, like Savitri and Vivasvat, he is thought to be the son of Aditi and the sage Kasyapa, grandson of Brahma and progenitor of the human race. At other times Surya is said to be the son of Brahma himself.

Surya retains many of the characteristics of his Vedic forerunners, though he is no longer pictured as a handsome golden youth but rather as a dark red man, with three eyes and four arms. Like the Vedic Surya, he rides in a golden chariot drawn by seven horses, each one representing one day of the week; but he no longer directs the chariot himself, for he has acquired a legless charioteer called Arun, a brother of Garuda who symbolises the dawn. At other times again his charioteer is said to be Vivasvat and the god himself is pictured as copper-coloured, dwarfish and with red eyes.

Surya is considered to be a benefactor of man. His symbol, the swastika, is a sign of munificence. He is celebrated as a slayer of demons; on one occasion terrifying rakshasas tried to devour him, but he destroyed them with his light.

His illegitimate children were many and included Karna, son of Kunti and one of the Kaurava leaders in the *Mahabharata*, and Sugriva, the monkey king who became the ally of Rama in the *Ramayana*. One of his sons became the ancestor of the solar race. His most famous progeny, however, were the children of his wife Sanjna. The story of Sanjna and Surya repeats with variations the myth of Vivasvat and Saranyu. Sanjna was the daughter of Visvakarma (Tvashtri in the Vedas). In the early years of their marriage she bore Surya three children. These were the Manu Vaivaswata and the twins Yama and Yami, who became the first man and woman and, later, deities—Yama, king of the dead, and Yami, goddess of the River Yamuna. But as time passed Sanjna found the brilliance of her husband's presence insupportable and she fled, leaving her handmaiden, Chhaya ('Shade') in her place. In her retirement Sanjna lived in the forest disguised as a mare and devoted herself to religious exercises. After some time Surya spied her out as she was grazing in a field; he took the form of a horse and approached her. From this union were born the twin horsemen, the Aswins, and another, less important son called Revanta. The character of the Aswins differs little from the Vedic conception, though perhaps their role as luminary deities is stressed less than that as physicians of the gods.

For some time Surya and Sanjna lived together as horses, but they finally tired of life as animals and changed back into human form. Surya now brought his wife home with him and agreed, in order to prevent a recurrence of her flight, that his father-in-law Visvakarma should place him on his lathe and shave away an eighth of his brightness, from every part of his body except his feet. Thereafter the couple lived happily together. Even the fragments which had been removed from Surya had strength and

beneficent qualities, and from them Visvakarma made Vishnu's discus, Shiva's trident, Karttikeya's lance, and the weapons of Kubera and all the other gods.

Vayu

The god of wind in Hindu belief has fallen far from his eminence as one of the Vedic triad. He is a destructive god of intemperate character and violent desires. He roams everywhere over the earth and in the heavens, though his abode is in the north-west quarter, of which he is regent. He is also said to be the king of the Gandharvas, who live in the foothills of Mount Meru. This fact, however, did not lessen the violence of Vayu's attack on the heavenly summit of that mountain. He was incited to break off the summit by the sage Narada (who is also sometimes credited with being chief of the Gandharvas). For a full year Vayu expended his full force against the mountain, but it was nobly defended by Garuda, who spread his wings to protect it from the buffeting winds. At the end of a year, however, during a short absence of Garuda, Vayu, informed of his opportunity by Narada, attacked once more and was successful. He hurled the detached summit down into the sea, where it became the island of Lanka (Ceylon).

Vayu's lusts seem to have been equally indiscriminate. Though married to a daughter of Visvakarma, he is credited with a number of illegitimate children, among them Hanuman, the monkey general, who owed his ability to fly to his paternity. Another son was Bhima, one of the Pandava heroes in the *Mahabharata*, a man of violent temper and voracious appetite and a great demon-slayer. Bhima came to be Vayu's son more respectably than did Hanuman, for he was conceived by his mother Kunti as a result of a prayer to Vayu. Vayu tried to seduce en masse the hundred daughters of King Kusanabha, and when they resisted gave them all crooked backs.

One of the wheels of the sun-temple at Konarak, in Orissa, which was built in the shape of a giant solar chariot. Each of the wheels, almost ten feet in diameter, symbolises the eternal cycle. A.D. 1240-1280.

Certain sects give Vayu a less violent character, regarding him as a sort of holy spirit and attendant of Vishnu and Lakshmi. He is sometimes called the 'bearer of perfumes'.

Soma

Soma, also known as Chandra, is entirely identified with Hindu belief in the moon—though one of the explanations of his origin still equates him with amrita, for it claims that he was produced from the churning of the milk ocean. More common accounts of his lineage say that he was the son of Dharma; or that he was the son of Varuna, lord of the ocean, from which the moon arises. Yet another account links Soma with Surya, though it is not clear whether Surya is the father of Soma; or, taking Surya as female, Soma is said to be married to Surya. More certain is the belief that Surya nourishes the moon with water from the ocean when Soma is exhausted by the many beings who feed upon his substance. For during half the month thirty-six thousand three hundred divinities feed upon Soma and thus assure their immortality, while during the remaining half of the month the Pitris feed upon Soma; Soma also nourishes men, animals and insects, for the moon not only gives them pleasure, but the watery nectar of its light also sustains the vegetable life on which mortal creatures feed. This account neatly combines the two aspects of Soma; as the amrita or nectar from which the gods derive their strength; and as the moon, whose substance waxes and wanes according to the calendar.

Soma was married to the twenty-seven daughters of the sage Daksha, who are personifications of the lunar asterisms. But Daksha had as much trouble with this son-in-law as he had with his other, Shiva. Soma showed such a preference for one of his wives, Rohini (Hyades), that the others became wildly jealous, and went to their father to complain. Daksha's remonstrances were of no avail, so the sage pronounced a curse on Soma which afflicted him with consumption and childlessness. Despite their earlier anger, however, Daksha's daughters soon grew sorry for their husband and went back to their father for advice. Daksha was unable to retract the curse completely but he succeeded in modifying it, so that Soma should suffer from consumption only periodically, for fifteen days at a time.

He soon proved himself to be free of the curse of childlessness. He performed the great horse sacrifice, which both demonstrated and procured universal dominion and fertility. Protected by the influence of the sacrifice, Soma became arrogant and daring, and one day abducted Tara, wife of Brihaspati, sage and preceptor of the gods and often associated with the planet Jupiter. Despite Brihaspati's great occult power he was unable to do anything. None of his entreaties or the sermons of the other sages in any way affected Soma, who with his assurance of universal dominion felt himself quite secure. Brihaspati appealed to

Brahma but not even he could persuade Soma to return Tara. Brihaspati then turned to Indra, who decided that the only way would be to take Tara by force. But Soma heard of these plans and promptly made an alliance with the asuras. He was also supported by the sage Usanas, who had an ancient feud with Brihaspati. Brihaspati commanded the support of most of the other gods, under the leadership of Indra. Though the war produced many fierce clashes, during one of which Soma was cut in two by Shiva's trident, it was inconclusive.

Brahma then made another appeal to reason, and again asked for the return of Tara. By this time Soma had become bored with her and to everyone's surprise agreed to send her back to Brihaspati. He restored her to her husband, but it was then seen that she was pregnant. Brihaspati refused to accept her back until the child was born, so Brahma, in order to have done with the affair commanded this to happen at once. When the gods beheld the infant they were dazzled by its great beauty, and both Soma and Brihaspati at once claimed parentage. Only Tara could say who was the true father but she was reluctant to speak out. Finally, after a great deal of coaxing, she admitted that the child was Soma's. He was named Budha, and was to become the ancestor of the lunar race.

Brihaspati, naturally, was enraged with his wife and cursed her to be reduced to ashes but Brahma felt the punishment to be too severe and revived Tara, had her purified, and persuaded Brihaspati to take her back. Soma was punished for his infidelity; his father, Varuna, disinherited him. But Lakshmi, who since she also was born out of the milk ocean was Soma's sister, decided to campaign on his behalf. She approached Parvati, and asked her to enlist Shiva's aid. Shiva agreed, and to honour Soma he wore the crescent moon on his forehead. But when Brihaspati caught sight of Shiva thus arrayed at the next assembly of the gods, he declared that Shiva was dishonouring the company by his presence. A great dispute arose between them which had to be referred to Brahma for settlement. Brahma declared in favour of Brihaspati and Soma was thereafter relegated to the outer atmosphere and forbidden entry into heaven. (This can be interpreted as yet another myth explaining how intoxicants came to be banned.)

As he travels about in the atmosphere, Soma is represented as a copper-coloured man, trailing a red pennant behind his three-wheeled chariot, which is drawn either by a pied antelope or by ten white horses.

Overleaf left: *The Vimla Vashi temple at Dilwara, dedicated to the goddess Sarasvati, is built of white marble. The interior of the dome is elaborately carved with gods, worshippers and animals in eleven concentric circles. Eleventh century.*

Overleaf right: *Sarasvati, goddess of learning, making music as patroness of the arts. Her gentle grace belies her independent character. When Sarasvati became identified as consort of Brahma her earlier role of river goddess was forgotten. White marble relief from the Vimla Vashi temple at Dilwara, eleventh century.*

Kubera, the bejewelled but hideous god of wealth and guardian of the north. Enthroned on the Himalayas, where he guards the treasures of the earth, Kubera bears a sack over his shoulder and a casket in his right hand. Gupta style sandstone, sixth century.

this deformed creature some form of locomotion, so he had Visvakarma build him a magic chariot, Pushpaka. Pushpaka is an aerial chariot which can move of its own accord and is so large that it contains a whole city. As it moves over the earth it rains jewels. Pushpaka was stolen by Ravana, Kubera's half-brother, who took it to Lanka and made great use of it in his attacks on the gods, as well as to abduct Sita. When Rama defeated Ravana he used Pushpaka to transport himself and Sita, together with Lakshmana and the entire army of monkeys and bears back to Ayodhya.

Ravana also stole Kubera's original palace of Lanka, which had been built for the rakshasas by Visvakarma. Though the city by rights belonged to the rakshasas they had all deserted it, expecting an attack by Vishnu, which they feared even though Lanka was the richest and best fortified city then in existence. So Kubera took possession of a ghost city. But the rakshasas soon determined to reoccupy it, and sent the daughter of one of their leaders to try and woo Kubera's father. She succeeded, and from their union was born Ravana and three other sons. Ravana, by performance of austerities, obtained from Shiva the boon of invincibility and so was able to defeat Kubera and to seize and retain Lanka and Pushpaka.

As Lanka could not be restored to him Visvakarma built Kubera a palace on Mount Kailasa, in the Himalayas. He has another city called Alaka, which is also in the Himalayas and the richest city in the universe, and a garden of great beauty called Chaitraratha, on Mount Mandara.

Kubera's domains are all in the high Himalayas, partly because he is guardian of the north, but also because the mountains are the repository of mineral wealth. Aided by his attendants, the Kinnaras, Kubera watches over the earth's storehouse of gold and silver, jewels and pearls and its other treasures, as well as the nine Nidhis, special treasures whose significance is not clear.

Karttikeya

Karttikeya, or Skanda, is the chief battle god of the Hindu pantheon. In this role he replaces Indra and Agni, his father (to the extent that Agni, by his association with Indra, was considered as a warrior). In his role as defender of the gods, Karttikeya is more single-minded than either of his predecessors and seems to be interested in little else than military exploits. He is not even interested in women, in fact according to most he dislikes them and will not suffer them to enter his temples; as a bachelor, he is also called Kumara. But other accounts say that he has a wife

New gods

Kubera

In the Vedic period Kubera was the chief of the evil beings living in the abodes of shadow and darkness. It was not until Hindu times that he was elevated to the ranks of the gods and became one of the eight guardians of the world (though he remained king of the yaksha demons). There are two versions of how this hideous dwarf obtained the boon of immortality. One relates that he performed austerities for thousands of years and was elevated to the rank of the gods as a result.

The other claims that in a former life Kubera was a thief. One night he was robbing the temple of Shiva (himself known as lord of robbers) when his lighted taper was blown out. His ten successive attempts to light his taper in Shiva's temple earned for him such merit that in his next life he was born as the god of wealth.

Though in this elevated capacity he has his person covered in jewels and other ornaments, he retains his ugliness and deformity. His white body is dwarfish; he has three legs and only eight teeth. Brahma had to grant

Right: Karttikeya or Skanda, six-headed and twelve-armed god of war, born in order to rid the world of the demon Taraka. His mount is the peacock Paravani. Image from the interior of the temple at Perur.

The marriage of Shiva and Parvati was brought about by Kama at the urging of the other gods, who foresaw that the fruit of the union would be the warrior god Karttikeya. The marriage is attended by Vishnu, Brahma, and Indra. Trichinopoly painting, 1820. Victoria and Albert Museum

called Kaumari or Devasena and at one time wooed Siddhi and Buddhi. He is represented riding on Paravani, a peacock, and carrying a bow and arrow. He has six heads springing from one body and six pairs of arms and legs. He is called Subrahmanya in southern India.

Accounts of his origin, of how he came to supplant the earlier warrior gods, and of his strange appearance are generally of great complexity. The simplest relates that he was born of Agni's seed thrown into a sacrificial fire;

Kama, god of love, bearing his sugar-cane bow strung with humming-bees and his flower-tipped shaft of desire and accompanied by his wife Rati, seen shaking a cymbal. Kama is riding a peacock, symbol of impatient desire, rather than his usual parrot. South Indian wood carving.

he was afterwards received by the Ganges and later still fostered by the Pleiades (Krittikas), in honour of whom he developed six heads and acquired the name Karttikeya.

According to another version Karttikeya was born in order to rescue the gods from extreme humiliation at the hands of the asuras. Because Shiva had relinquished his position as military commander of the gods and taken to the life of a hermit, the asuras had been able to defeat the gods and to drive them out of their kingdom. They were in despair, particularly Indra, who was reduced to the life of a forest wanderer, meditating unceasingly on how he could regain his kingdom.

One day as he was thus occupied in the forest he heard cries for help from a nearby glade and, running to the spot, found the demon Kesin trying to ravish a young girl of great beauty. Indra drove the demon away. The girl turned to Indra afterwards and asked him to help her to find a husband. She told him that her name was Devasena, which means 'army of the gods'. Agreeing to help, Indra decided that a military husband would be suitable for this girl and that, strengthened by a wife with this auspicious name, he would be able to lead the celestial hosts to victory. He went to Brahma to enjoin his help, and Brahma decided that the most suitable parents for this future hero would be Agni and Ganga, goddess of the sacred Ganges.

Accordingly Brahma arranged that at a sacrifice held shortly after by the seven great rishis, Agni should emerge from the sacrificial fire and instantly fall in love with the wives of the sages. But these were virtuous ladies, so Agni said nothing and went into the forest to try and forget them. But his efforts to quell his desires met with no success. While he struggled with himself in the forest he was seen by Swaha, daughter of Daksha, and she fell in love with him. But Agni, occupied with thoughts of the other women, rejected her advances. Swaha was endowed with some of her father's divine power and knew the reason for Agni's coldness, so she disguised herself as one of the rishis' wives and approached him again. This time Agni's scruples were overcome; and Swaha returned five times more disguised each time as a different rishi's wife. By these six unions with Agni, Swaha acquired six seeds from him, and these were carefully preserved and nurtured in a golden reservoir of Ganges water. By virtue of extended devotional chanting by the rishis over the sacred waters there was eventually born from the six seeds a boy with six heads, twelve eyes, twelve arms and twelve legs. This was Karttikeya, who when he grew up married Devasena and drove the asuras out of the kingdom of the gods.

According to other versions, Karttikeya was the son of Shiva. Again he was born to combat asura power. An asura named Taraka had so propitiated Brahma by the performance of austerities that Brahma was forced to grant him the boon that he desired: invulnerability to all but a son of Shiva. At this time Shiva had no sons and had just lost his wife Sati, who had thrown herself on to her father Daksha's sacrificial fire. The god was in no mood to marry again and was engaged most ferociously in the practice of austerities, so Taraka considered that he had nothing to fear. Protected by his boon, he set about extending his domains, and managed to subdue not only the creatures of earth but also to inflict humiliation on the gods. Indra was forced to give him his wonderful white horse, Uchchaisravas, one of the 'fourteen precious things' yielded up by the churning of the milk ocean; the rishis had to hand over the cow that granted all desires, Kamadhenu, which had been in the care of Jamadagni during Vishnu's incarnation as Parasurama; Kubera had to yield him his thousand sea-horses; and Vayu was forced to obey Taraka's command. In their terror, the sun gave no heat and the moon remained full at all times.

The gods consulted together on how they could put down the tyrant and persuade Shiva to marry again. They decided that Sati should be reborn as the beautiful Parvati, daughter of the Himalayas. When Parvati came of age to marry she began to perform austerities in the hope of rendering herself worthy in the eyes of the great god. But Shiva took no notice of her, absorbed as he was in his own meditations. After several years of this Indra, despairing of Parvati's success without outside assistance, ordered Kama, the god of love, to approach the great ascetic and arouse desire in his heart. Accordingly Kama went to Mount Kailasa, where he found Shiva sunk in yogic meditation, impervious to all around him, having silenced the very birds and stilled the leaves of the trees about him with the majesty of his presence. Kama hardly dared to accomplish his mission and stood looking on for some time. Just then, however, Parvati came into sight, gathering flowers and looking so charming and beautiful that Kama dared to hope that Shiva would be gratified to see her. He loosed his arrow. As the shaft of love struck Shiva, desire woke in his heart and he perceived Parvati. But at the same time he saw Kama and, filled with anger at his audacity, instantaneously burned him to ashes by fixing on him his third eye.

Though desire had been woken in Shiva's heart, the lord of asceticism did not give way to his passion, and was not even moved by several years more of austerities on the part of Parvati. Finally, however, he consented to marry her, to the delight of the other gods. But their pleasure was premature, for many years passed by and no children were born. Once more they consulted together and decided this time to send Agni as their ambassador to Shiva and to urge him to beget a son. Agni chanced to reach Mount Kailasa just as Shiva had left his wife and, taking the form of a dove, managed to pick up a seed of the great god. He immediately hastened back with it to Indra. The seed of Shiva, however, could not be supported by one of the lesser gods and as Agni travelled his burden seemed to grow heavier and heavier until finally, as he was passing over the Ganges, he was forced to drop it. There on the banks of the river arose a child as beautiful as the moon and as brilliant as the sun. This was Karttikeya. As he appeared on the bank of the Ganges the six Pleiades, daughters of six rajas, came to that spot to bathe. Each of them claimed the beautiful boy, and each wished to give him the breast; so Karttikeya acquired six mouths and was suckled by all of his foster-mothers.

When the child grew up he duly became commander of the celestial hosts and slew the demon Taraka.

Visvakarma

The name Visvakarma, which means 'omnificent', was at first the title of any strong god, such as Indra or Surya; but it gradually came to refer to the divine artificer, honoured not only for the creation of the universe but also for having initiated sacrifice and then given the example by sacrificing himself. In Hindu times Visvakarma assimilates the function and mythology of the Vedic Tvashtri, and in this new place in the hierarchy his role is restricted to that of architect of the gods.

In this capacity Visvakarma built the heavens of all the gods and their palaces, such as Indra's Vaijayanta, Kubera's and then Ravana's Lanka, and the Pandavas' palace at Indraprastha. Like Tvashtri, he created many of the chariots, including Kubera's Pushpaka; he also produced animals, such as Indra's fabulous horses. Perhaps his most famous artefacts were the gods' weapons, including Indra's thunderbolt or discus weapon, Karttikeya's lance and Shiva's trident, all of which, according to the Hindu version of the myth, were fashioned from the fragments of Surya's substance which fell blazing to earth when Visvakarma put the sun god on his lathe to reduce his effulgence. In addition he made weapons for the epic heroes.

Besides his daughter Sanjna or Saranyu, who became the husband of Surya, Visvakarma's progeny includes Nala, fathered on a monkey queen. Nala possesses some of his father's skills, and by making stones float built a bridge to Lanka for Rama and his troops. Visvakarma also taught the art of architecture to men.

Dharma

Dharma appeared as a new god in Hindu times, when the path of duty became the road to salvation. Just as Soma and Agni had in Vedic times become personified gods because of their importance in sacrificial rites, so now the god Dharma personified justice, virtue and righteousness. Dharma was an ancient title of Yama, who is still known as Dharmaraja when considered as judge of the dead.

Dharma is said to be the son of the sun, and often seems to stand mid-way in importance between the supreme triad of gods and Indra and the other deities. He married Sraddha, the goddess of faith, and became father of Kama, the god of love. Apart from this, however, Dharma has attracted little mythology, unlike Soma and Agni.

Kama

Kama's name, too, was known in the Vedas, when he was identified as the creative spirit which welled up in Purusha or Prajapati, when that god found himself alone in the cosmic waters at the beginning of time. Some of the Vedas exalt Kama's role still further, saying that he was self-existent, sprung from the cosmic waters, and himself the supreme god and creator whose first emanation was desire, and whose second was the power to achieve that desire. In this role Kama is equated with the creative aspect of Agni. When Brahma became identified as the creator god, Kama was said to have sprung from his heart. Alternatively, when viewed as a creative moral force, Kama is considered, as we have seen, to be the son of Dharma.

In later times Kama became a more frivolous god, still concerned with creation but identified more with sexual desire. In this role he is thought to be the son of Vishnu and Lakshmi, goddess of beauty.

Kama is the most handsome of the gods, an ever-youthful man riding a parrot. He carries a bow made of sugar-cane and strung with a line of humming-bees, and with it shoots the five shafts of desire, which are tipped with flowers. He is accompanied by his wife, Rati (passion), and his friend, Vasanta (spring), who strings his bow and selects for him the shaft tipped with the flower considered suitable for the current victim. He is surrounded by troops of beautiful nymphs, the Apsaras, of whom he is lord; one of them carries his red banner, which bears the emblem of the monster fish Makara, the vehicle of Varuna.

Kama loves to roam about and amuse himself by inspiring passion in those he sees about him, and he is quite frivolous in the use he makes of his powers. According to one account, which makes him the son of Brahma, he had no sooner been born than he shot one of his arrows at his father, thus causing him to commit incest with his daughter—and incidentally to lose one of his heads at the hand of Shiva. Gods as well as mortals have been victims of Kama. He loves to wander about, especially in springtime, loosing his shafts indiscriminately, but with a preference for innocent girls, married women and ascetic sages.

Kama himself suffered most on the one occasion when he hesitated to use his power. Shiva was quick to burn him to ashes as a punishment for interrupting deep meditation but, despite Shiva's protests, the shaft had done its work and Shiva was unable to obtain peace until he married Parvati. During all this time Kama lay dead and love disappeared from the earth, which became an arid desert. At length the gods approached Shiva, who agreed to allow Kama to be reborn as Pradyumna, son of Krishna and Rukmini, and he was ultimately reunited with Rati. The god of desire thus fittingly became the son of the other deity in the pantheon associated with erotic love. After his death in a drunken brawl in the form of Pradyumna, he returned to his own form and function as Kama.

Goddesses

Sarasvati

In the Vedas Sarasvati was a water deity, goddess of a river of the same name which flowed west from the Himalayas, through the home of the early Aryans. In early times the river and its goddess were celebrated for purifying, fertilising and enriching powers, and for flowing clear into the sea. At present, however, the river peters out in the desert, and according to the *Mahabharata*, this is the result of a curse pronounced by the sage Utathya when Varuna stole his wife. By depriving Varuna of water for his ocean, he hoped to force the god to return her.

The next stage in Sarasvati's mythological history was her identification with the holy rituals performed on her banks; this led to the belief that she influenced the composition of the hymns and thus to her identification with Vach, the goddess of speech. She is said to have invented Sanskrit, and one account says that it was she who discovered soma or amrita in the Himalayas and brought it to the other gods. Vach was at one time attributed with very wide powers, accompanying and supporting all the celestial gods. She originated in the ocean and pervaded heaven and earth; she was the power behind all phenomena and mistress of all.

Later myths diminish her power. She was said to be identical with Viraj, the female half or being created out of the substance of Purusha or Prajapati, and thus the instrument of creation. Most generally, however, and up to the present day, she is considered to be the creature and consort of Brahma, and is called mother of the Vedas which sprang from his heads. As Brahma's wife she provides the power to execute what Brahma has conceived with his creative intelligence. She is goddess of all the creative arts and in particular of poetry and music, learning and science. She is represented as a graceful woman with white skin, wearing a crescent moon on her brow; she rides a swan or peacock, or is seated on a lotus flower.

Sarasvati has a haughty nature and is disputatious. One myth tells that she was originally the wife of Vishnu, along with Lakshmi and Ganga. But Vishnu could not endure their quarrelling, so he gave Sarasvati to Brahma and Ganga to Shiva. On another occasion she was too idle to arrive on time for a sacrifice to be performed by Brahma in which his wife had to take part. Brahma sent a messenger to fetch her, but she sent back the message that she was still at her toilet and that he should wait. Brahma was incensed at this reply and asked the assembled gods to provide him with another wife. Gayatri, the daughter of a sage, was offered to him, and he married her

Sarasvati as goddess of poetry and music, standing on a lotus and accompanied by a swan, her vehicle. As Brahma's wife and the medium through which he executes his creative will, she is patroness of all the creative arts. Ivory statuette.

Lakshmi, or Sri, embraced by her consort Vishnu. She is feminine beauty personified and goddess of fortune (usually of good fortune). Daughter of the sage Bhrigu, she was reborn during the churning of the milk ocean, as one of the 'fourteen precious things'. From the temple at Khajuraho, c. A.D. 1000.

Right: Devi, the Great Goddess, 'shakti' or female energy of Shiva, accorded worship both as the consort of Shiva and as a power in her own right; both as an auspicious and as a terrifying deity. Chola bronze, eleventh century.

immediately and completed the sacrifice. When Sarasvati eventually arrived on the scene, she in turn displayed her fury and cursed Brahma to be worshipped no more than once a year. Henceforth she nevertheless had to accept the presence of Gayatri, but was mollified by the latter's promise to remain always in second place.

Lakshmi

Lakshmi, also known as Sri, attained importance as the consort of Vishnu. Her previous existences, described in the Vedas, make her the wife of Varuna or of the sun. Alternatively, like Sarasvati, she is said to have issued from Prajapati. In these early times she is associated with both good and bad fortune.

Lakshmi is now generally thought to have existed first as the daughter of the sage Bhrigu and to have taken refuge in the ocean of milk during a period when the gods were exiled from their kingdom as a result of a rishi's curse. She was reborn during the churning of the milk ocean as Lakshmi, one of the fourteen precious things. She emerged from the ocean froth fully grown and radiant, bearing a lotus in her hand. As soon as the gods saw her each of them wanted her as his wife. Shiva was the first to claim her, but as he had already seized the moon Lakshmi's hand was accorded to Vishnu, whom Lakshmi herself preferred. It is sometimes said that it was Shiva's despair at this judgment that led him to catch in his mouth the poison vomited by the serpent.

Thereafter Lakshmi was reborn as Vishnu's consort in each of his incarnations. For his incarnation as the dwarf, Vamana, Lakshmi was born from the waters, floating on the flower of a lotus. For this reason she was called Padma (lotus) or Kamala. When Vishnu was born as Parasurama, Lakshmi was Dharani, the earth. When he became Rama she was the faithful Sita, born from a furrow in a ploughed field. When he was incarnated as Krishna, she entered both phases of his life: as the cowgirl Radha and as his wife, Rukmini. As Rukmini, she was the mother of Pradyumna, Kama's reincarnation.

Lakshmi thus has a clear share in Vishnu's activities as preserver, and this reinforces her earlier character as goddess of fortune and giver of wealth. Despite her complete fidelity, most strikingly shown in her incarnation as Sita, she is also described as the 'fickle goddess', for the wheel of fortune is ever-changing.

Lakshmi is generally represented as a beautiful golden woman, usually sitting or standing on a lotus, her symbol. Though she really has four arms, as the ideal of feminine beauty she is often represented with only two. She is usually worshipped in conjunction with her husband, when she is portrayed as exhibiting her devotion to him by massaging his feet as he lies on the coils of the serpent Shesha; or seated beside him on a lotus; or riding with him on Garuda. When she is worshipped alone she is considered to be the female energy of the supreme being, 'mother of the world'.

Devi

Devi, or Mahadevi (Great Goddess), is the most complex and the most powerful of the goddesses. She owes both characteristics to the combination of her ancestry in the great mother goddess of pre-Aryan times and to her high place as Shiva's consort, when she is known as his 'shakti' or female energy, and mirrors in her nature her husband's variety of roles. For each of these roles she has a different name (Sati, Parvati, Durga, Kali), and they may roughly be divided into mild characters and fierce. As we have seen, this duality may also be traced back to the pre-Aryan goddess, who was both bringer of fertility and exacter of living sacrifice.

Of the mild forms of Devi, the first was Sati who, as we have related, was the daughter of the sage Daksha and married to Shiva at her own insistence and against her father's wishes. She later burnt herself to death on her father's sacrificial fire in order to defend her husband's honour. When Shiva, dancing to express his grief at her death, held her body locked in his embrace, it was cut out of this arms by Vishnu. Each of the places where the fifty pieces of her body fell became sacred; this is the origin of the worship of the yoni, the female organ. Sati is considered to be the ideal Hindu wife, and the example of her self-immolation let to the practice of suttee.

When the gods had need of a military commander Shiva had Sati restored to him. She was reborn as Parvati ('from the mountains') the daughter of Himavan, god of the Himalayas, and Mena—whence she is also called Haimavati. In this incarnation she is the sister of Ganga, goddess of the Ganges, which also comes from the Himalayas. Shiva's grief at the death of Sati was such that Parvati saw no difficulty in fulfilling the purpose of her new incarnation; she had only to wait for Shiva to come and woo her again. So she passed her days happily, singing and dancing and making herself beautiful. But she waited in vain, for Shiva had embarked on his career of asceticism and showed no interest in her. So Parvati sought to please him by herself practising austerities and was so assiduous in her devotions that she changed the colour of her skin from its original black to golden; in this form she is also known as Uma, Light or Beauty. But still Shiva was unmoved, so the gods sent Kama to enflame Shiva's heart with one of his arrows.

Kama succeeded in rousing Shiva's passion, with what results to himself we have seen, but the great god retained his willpower and would not give way to his emotions. As a last resort, Parvati took up the practice of severe penances—eating nothing, lying in icy water and torturing her body. As she was thus engaged a Brahmin came to her and asked why she was destroying her lovely body. He laughed when Parvati said that she wanted to marry Shiva, describing him as a dirty, foul-tempered old beggar who had no home and haunted cemeteries. Parvati agreed with this description but said that she loved and venerated Shiva all the same. The Brahmin then painted Shiva in even blacker colours, until finally Parvati refused to listen any more, put her hands over her ears and shouted at the Brahmin. At this the Brahmin revealed himself as Shiva, told Parvati to cease her penances, and sent her back to her father. In due course Shiva came to her home in the Himalayas and married her.

As we have seen, their marital relations were not ideal, and it required the intervention of Agni and the help of Ganga before they produced the desired son, Karttikeya. Though they were often happy—Parvati did her best to entertain her husband and be an amiable wife—they frequently quarrelled. Often these disputes were caused by Shiva wishing to curse someone whom Parvati wished to bless.

Their most serious quarrel also occurred over a devotional matter. One day Shiva was reading aloud texts from the scriptures and explaining obscure points to Parvati, when

Parvati. The wife of Shiva in her beautiful womanly form. Chola bronze, eleventh century.

Uma, the golden goddess, the form of Devi personifying light and beauty. South Indian copper figure, c. twelfth century.

he looked up and saw that she had fallen asleep. He reproached her for her lack of interest in these important matters but she claimed that she had not been asleep, she had merely closed her eyes in order to concentrate better. Shiva therefore asked her what he had been talking about, and she could not answer. As a punishment for her inattention and for her lie, Shiva cursed her to fall from Mount Kailasa to earth, and there to become a fisherwoman.

Left alone to practise his meditation, Shiva soon found that thoughts of Parvati prevented him from concentrating. He had to wait some time, however, before regaining her. His first move was to send his servant Nandi (the bull) down to earth in the form of a shark, which persecuted the fisherfolk among whom Parvati was living by breaking their nets. Nandi became the greatest scourge along the coast and the fishermen decided to offer the hand of Parvati, the most beautiful maiden of the village, to the man who could rid them of the shark. When he

heard of this offer Shiva immediately took the form of a fisherman and caught the shark. After his marriage to Parvati they returned to Mount Kailasa.

Light and beauty in the person of Uma is one form of the golden goddess; another is that of fertility goddess or harvest bride, when she is known as Gauri or Jagadgauri. Another manifestation is as Amvika, Shiva's (or Rudra's) sister. When Shiva is considered as the first man and creator, Purusha, Devi is held to be his female half. She is sometimes called Jaganmata, mother of the world.

The name most commonly given to the fierce form of Devi is Durga. She is a beautiful yellow woman with ten arms who rides on a tiger; but despite her grace she has a menacing expression, for she was born to kill. She was created out of the flames which issued from the mouths of Brahma, Vishnu and Shiva and the other gods, specifically to kill demons, in particular the buffalo demon Mahisha, who by practice of austerities had gained the strength to drive the gods out of the celestial kingdom. Durga was born fully grown and beautiful; she was immediately armed by the gods and sent forth against Mahisha. In each of her ten hands she held one of the gods' special weapons, symbols of their divine power. Among these were Vishnu's discus; Shiva's trident; Varuna's conch shell; Agni's flaming dart; Vayu's bow; Surya's quiver and arrow; Yama's iron rod; Indra's thunderbolt; Kubera's club; a garland of snakes from Shesha; and as a charger a tiger from the Himalayas. As Durga approached Mahisha's domain in the Vindhya mountains, she was seen by the demon, who tried to capture her. But Mahisha had no power against Durga, though he attacked her in many quickly changing forms, and she finally killed him with a spear.

Devi's next campaign was against a demon called Durga, from whom she was to acquire her name. The demon Durga had overcome the three worlds and driven Indra and the lesser gods from their heaven and into the forests to live. He abolished all religious ceremonies and the reading of the Vedas, and the gods and their wives were forced to worship him. Rivers changed their courses, fire lost its strength and the stars disappeared. Durga pervaded all the natural world, producing rain when he wished and forcing the earth to bear heavy crops even out of season. The gods asked Shiva to help and he suggested that they address themselves to his wife. Devi agreed to help and first sent them Kalaratri (dark night), a creature which she specially created. Kalaratri, however, was unsuccessful in his battle against the demons.

Devi therefore decided to enter the conflict herself and set forth from Mount Kailasa. Arrayed against her was a demon army of 100,000,000 chariots, 120,000,000,000 elephants, 10,000,000 horses and innumerable soldiers. She faced this with various beings which she called to her assistance. A mighty battle now began, in which Devi was attacked by a rainstorm of arrows and a shower of trees and rocks which had been torn up by the demons. But Devi, who had grown a thousand arms, hurled at Durga a weapon which destroyed much of his army. Durga retaliated with two flaming darts, but Devi turned both aside with a hundred arrows. Another arrow, a club and a spike were turned aside by the goddess, who managed to seize the demon and plant her foot on him. He struggled free and renewed the battle. Devi now produced nine million beings from her own body and these destroyed the entire army of the demon; she also brought forth the weapon Sashonu, which protected her from the hailstorm produced by Durga. Then the demon hurled a mountain at her; she cut it into seven pieces and rendered them harmless by shooting arrows at them. Now Durga took the form of an elephant as large as a mountain, but was cut to shreds by Devi's scimitar-like nails. He next became a huge buffalo, which tore trees up with its breath and cast them, together with stones and mountains, at the goddess. But Devi pierced him with her trident and forced him to

resume his normal shape—a demon with a thousand arms and a weapon in each hand. With her thousand hands the goddess now seized his arms and threw him down; she then transfixed his breast with an arrow and he died, the blood pouring out of his mouth. After this victory Devi assumed the name of her newly vanquished enemy, Durga.

On another occasion the goddess was sought out by the gods, who were being persecuted by two demon brothers, Sumbha and Nisumbha, who by virtue of eleven thousand years of austerities had obtained from Shiva immunity from harm by any god. As the only goddess capable of defeating the demons, Durga was approached by the gods and agreed to help them. Taking the form of a very beautiful woman she went to the Himalayas, where she was seen by demon spies, Chunda and Munda. They went back to their masters saying that there was in the forest a woman who would please them. Sumbha sent a messenger to Durga with a proposal of marriage; but she replied that she had vowed to marry only a man who could defeat her in single combat. Sumbha's counter to this challenge was to send his general, Dhumralochana, with an army to seize her. When she saw the army approaching, Durga began to roar, and thereby destroyed the general and most of the great army. When news of this defeat reached Sumbha and Nisumbha, they sent a fresh army commanded by Chunda and Munda. But the goddess devoured them all, thirty to a hundred demons at a mouthful, and cut off the heads of Chunda and Munda.

Sumbha and Nisumbha now set forth themselves, leading another army. This time Durga produced several other goddesses from her hair, and a mighty battle was fought between the goddesses and the demons. Eventually all the demon army was destroyed, and Durga engaged first Sumbha and then Nisumbha in single combat, killing them both. The goddesses celebrated their victory by devouring the bodies of the slain demons.

Even more terrifying than Durga is Kali, the black earthmother, whose rites involve sacrificial killings—at one time of humans—and who is associated with dark, obscene rites and devil-worship. She has black skin and a hideous tusked face, smeared with blood, the brow bearing a third eye, like Shiva's. She has four arms, and holds in one a weapon, in another the head of a giant, dripping blood; the other two are raised to bless worshippers; the hands end in claws. Her body is naked except for her 'ornaments', which include earrings made of little children, a necklace of snakes, another of skulls, another of the heads of her sons, and a belt from which hang demons' hands.

Kali developed her thirst for blood after killing the demon Raktavira whom Brahma had granted a boon whereby every drop of blood which fell from his body was able to produce thousands more like him. The only way in which Kali could kill him therefore was to hold him up, pierce him with a spear and drink all his blood as it

Durga dispatching a demon enemy. Her trident is perhaps Shiva's, for the gods often lent her their weapons and invested her with their strength when they found themselves powerless against their enemies. Despite her murderous power Durga wears a serene expression. Post-Gupta style sculpture, eighth century.

Two Dakinis carved from human bone, originally ornaments worn on the apron of an exorcist. Tibetan, eighteenth century.

gushed out. She is often portrayed with her tongue hanging out and her mouth dripping blood.

Once she gave free rein to her blind lust for destruction nothing could stop her. On one occasion Shiva himself had to mingle among the demons whom she was slaughtering and allow himself to be trampled underfoot in her dance of victory, as this was the only way to bring her to her senses and save the world from collapse. She was in this sense said to have subdued her own husband, and to this she owes her name, Kali, 'conqueror of time'. Devi, goddess of fertility, had conquered Shiva, who as the inexorable destroyer was equated with Time.

Aspects of Kali are Chandi, the fierce, and Bhairavi, the terrible, in which she is the counterpart to Shiva's aspect of Bhairava, when he takes pleasure in destruction.

The triad of goddesses

The consorts of the Hindu triad are grouped together in a corresponding female triad. They are said to have been originally one goddess. The story is that one day Brahma called upon Vishnu to discuss with him what they should do about a demon called Andhaka, who was a son of Kasyapa and Diti and who had a thousand arms and heads and two thousand eyes and feet. He owed his name (darkness) to the fact that though he was not really blind, he pretended that he was. One of his many crimes was to attempt to seize the Parijata tree from Swarga. Brahma and Vishnu decided that Shiva should be present at their discussion and summoned him to Vaikuntha. The three gods sat for some time deliberating and then looked at one another. As their glances met they produced a combined energy that summoned up a feminine form so brilliant that it illuminated all the heavens, and which was coloured red, white and black. As each of the three great gods wished to possess this deity she divided herself into three forms, which represented Past, Present and Future. These were the white goddess, Sarasvati; the red goddess, Lakshmi; and the black goddess, Parvati.

Aditi

In Hindu belief Aditi is still referred to as mother of the gods, but this now means all the gods, not simply the Vedic Adityas. She is now definitely considered to be the mother of Vishnu, not his wife, and in different incarnations she bore him twice. She was the wife of the sage Kasyapa and mother of Vamana, Vishnu in his dwarf avatar; and she was Devaki, mother of Krishna. For this reason Vishnu is sometimes called Aditya.

Indra also acknowledged Aditi as his mother (again when she was the wife of Kasyapa), and made her a present of the famous earrings produced at the churning of the milk ocean. We have already seen how these earrings were stolen by the demon king Naraka until recovered by Krishna and eventually brought back and handed over to Indra again.

Saranyu

Saranyu is a goddess whose mythology became more complex as her role became less important. In the Vedas she is identified with Ushas, though said to be the daughter of Tvashtri, and is married to Indra. In later times she loses her celestial character—indeed, she cannot bear and helps to diminish the brilliance of Surya, her husband—and becomes an artificer, like her father.

The story of her marriage is in its essentials the same as that of her earlier form, when married to the Vedic Vivasvat, and that of Sanjna, married to Surya. According to the final version Saranyu was the daughter of Visvakarma and twin sister of Trisiras and was married to Surya. She bore him twin children, Yama and Yami; but shortly thereafter, finding her husband's brilliance oppressive, she created an exact replica of herself and departed, leaving the replica behind her to look after the twins. Surya was unaware of what she had done, and fathered another child on the substitute; this was Manu, a royal rishi, who was the equal of his father in glory.

The secret of Saranyu's departure was kept for some years. Surya was unaware of her absence until one day the false consort became angry with the boy Yama, who had kicked her, and uttered against him a curse which caused his leg to be affected with sores and worms. The curse took immediate effect and this revealed the deception to Surya, for a mother's curse cannot harm her own son. He drove away the impostor and gave to his son a cock which picked off the worms and cured the sores, though Yama was left with a shrivelled foot. Then Surya went in search of his real wife whom, as in other myths, he eventually discovered in the form of a mare, and with whom he united to produce another set of twins, the Aswins.

On their return Surya, as related before, was shaved down by Visvakarma. Saranyu then helped her father to create the gods' powerful weapons from the superfluous brilliance of her husband's being.

Prithivi

While in the Vedas Prithivi has a creative role as wife of Dyaus and mother of Indra and Agni, in Hindu belief her role is rather that of nourisher or sustainer and she is associated with Vishnu, often as the deity who called the attention of the other gods to the depredations and the oppression of the demons and to the need for Vishnu's intervention. But just as she neglected to look after Indra when he was born, so in this later role she was not always generous to those who looked to her for nourishment.

At one time the world was governed by a wicked king called Vena, who prohibited worship and sacrifice; for this reason the sages who had installed him as king beat him to death with sacred grass. But they soon regretted their action for without a ruler the world fell into anarchy; the people were at the mercy of evil-doers and dying for want of

A Dakini, a female fiend attendant upon Kali, who like her takes pleasure in drinking blood and eating human flesh. The vessel on her head would no doubt be used for bloody oblations. North Indian brass image, tenth century.

Kali, the terrible aspect of Shiva's wife. Copper statue, sixteenth century.

food. So the sages took the body of Vena and rubbed his thigh; out sprang a dwarfish, flat-faced demon with black skin, and with his emergence the king was purged of his wickedness. Then the sages rubbed the king's right arm, and from it sprang the resplendent Prithu, a manifestation of Agni (or, some say, of Vishnu). Immediately on his birth Prithu, who was to become a celebrated sage, released his father's soul from hell and granted it liberation in heaven. All the creatures of earth rejoiced, thinking that this new king, who was at once invested with universal dominion, would rescue them from famine and oppression. But the fruits of the earth did not materialise and Prithu in anger took his bow and shot an arrow into the earth. Earth took the form of a cow and ran away; but Prithu pursued and caught her, and she promised to provide the customary fruits of the land if she were given a calf, so that she could produce milk. Prithu agreed and created the calf Manu Vaivaswata. Then he milked the earth-cow and passed her milk on to the people of earth, who consumed it in the form of grain and vegetables. The earth acquired the name Prithivi because Prithu was considered to be her father.

A variant of this myth relates that Prithu married the earth as soon as he was born, but that she refused to give up the treasures she had been concealing. Prithu therefore decided to kill the earth and thus end the famine. He chased her, but she took the form of a cow and sought asylum with Brahma. Brahma, however, refused to protect her and ordered her to return to her husband and obey him. Prithivi did as she was told, but on her return was severely beaten by her husband. Thus in the same way farmers constantly wound the earth with their ploughs and spades, but the earth, patient cow that she is, gives back nothing but good in the form of precious wealth and nourishment. The goddess can thus be seen as a symbol of patience.

Rati

Rati is the daughter of the sage Daksha. She is the goddess of sexual passions and wife of Kama, god of love, whom she usually accompanies when he wanders forth shooting his arrows of desire. Like her husband, she is usually a frivolous deity, also known as Mayavati, the deceiver. Her faithfulness to Kama was, however, exemplary and it was largely through her efforts and the enlistment of Parvati's aid that Shiva was persuaded to agree that Kama should be reborn after his destruction by Shiva's third eye.

Kama returned as Pradyumna, the son of Krishna and Rukmini; but as soon as he was born the sage Narada went to a demon called Shambhara and told him that the child was destined to kill him. Shambhara therefore transported himself magically to the room in Rukmini's palace where the baby lay, snatched it away and threw it into the sea, where a fish swallowed it. But the fish was subsequently caught by a fisherman and sold to Shambhara; when it

was opened in his kitchens Pradyumna, still alive, was revealed. Now the cook who had opened the fish's belly was none other than Rati who, following Narada's advice, had taken shape as a mortal woman and had become Shambhara's wife. In this guise she is often called Mayavati. As she beheld the baby Narada appeared and told her that this was her husband reincarnated. He furthermore gave her power to make the child invisible. She therefore rescued Pradyumna and was able to tend him and bring him up without her husband's knowledge.

When Pradyumna was grown up Rati one day spoke to him of love; he was at first horrified at these advances from her, for she was married to Shambhara and he had always thought her to be his mother, but she explained to him his true identity and her own, and they then lived as man and wife. In due course Rati became pregnant and Shambhara, learning of this, began to beat her; but Pradyumna then threw off his cloak of invisibility and killed Shambhara in single combat. This freed the couple from their need for disguise and allowed them to return to Dwarka and Pradyumna's parents. After Pradyumna's death, both resumed their original forms as Kama and Rati.

Diti

Diti was another daughter of the sage Daksha and was married to Kasyapa, by whom she was the mother of the Daityas. These demons and titans were enemies of sacrifice and were ultimately confined by Indra to the ocean depths, where they were ruled by Varuna. The loss of her children was the cause of Diti's great bitterness against Indra. She asked her husband Kasyapa to grant her the boon of a son who should be invulnerable and should kill Indra. Kasyapa agreed, but he made certain conditions: the first was that her pregnancy should last for a hundred years; and the second was that she should unfailingly maintain absolute piety and purity of her person throughout it.

Diti, with meticulous zeal, observed all the prescribed rituals and for nearly a century devoted all her attention to fulfilling the conditions. But Indra knew of her plan and watched her closely. His opportunity came in the last year of the century, when Diti went to bed without washing her feet. The boon was now powerless, but Indra made sure by plunging his thunderbolt into Diti's womb and dividing the unborn child into seven. The seven portions then began to weep so piteously that Indra repented his action and tried to comfort them, saying 'Ma rodih' ('Weep not'). But still they cried, and Indra grew angry again and divided each of them into seven. The forty-nine beings thus created were called the Maruts from Indra's words of comfort. Other myths explain why the Maruts are also called the Rudras. They relate that the forty-nine lumps of flesh were made into boys by Shiva at the request of Parvati, who became their adoptive mother. In this sense they were therefore the sons of Rudra (Shiva).

Shitala, the goddess of smallpox, whose protection is invoked against the disease. She is a popular deity with mothers, who seek her help for their children. Chola bronze from Tanjore, thirteenth century.

Manasa

Manasa is said to be the daughter of Kasyapa and Kadru and sister of the serpent-king Shesha; alternatively she is said to be the daughter of Shiva and a mortal woman (though sometimes she is identified with Shiva's consort in her Jagadgauri aspect). Unlike her brother, Manasa enjoys a widespread cult as a deity, mostly in Bengal, where she is invoked for protection against snake bites. She is certainly not of Aryan origin and the best-known myth about her concerns the way in which she forced recognition for herself.

Manasa grew angry with a rich merchant named Chand who addressed all his devotions to Shiva and as a result had been granted magic powers by him. She demanded his worship, and when he refused it destroyed his prized garden. He used his magic powers to reinstate it but she then appeared as a beautiful girl, who said she would marry him only if he would transfer his powers to her. As soon as he had done this she resumed her true shape and again demanded his worship. He refused, and she again destroyed his garden, this time irrevocably. Still

Chand refused to give in, and so Manasa persecuted him. Her first act was to bite his six sons to death. She then capsized his ships containing all his wealth and left him far from home, a castaway. On his slow journey back she inflicted many other hardships and reduced him to starvation, but still he refused to yield.

Eventually he reached home and settled down to rebuild his life. A new son was born to him, called Lakshmindra. But when Lakshmindra was betrothed to marry Behula the persecution began anew. It was predicted that Lakshmindra would die of a snake bite on his wedding night. Chand therefore had a house built entirely of solid metal by a famous architect and arranged for his son to live in it. But Manasa intimidated the architect and forced him to leave a small gap in the defences. So on the wedding night Chand's precautions in locking the metal door were of no avail. Behula, who lay awake for some time, saw one snake after another slip into the room, but she offered each one milk to drink and was thus able to capture it and tie it by the neck to a post. At length, however, she grew weary and fell asleep and another snake entered the room and bit her husband to death.

Next morning the dead body was laid on a raft and set to float down the river in the hope that a physician would see it and bring it back to life—for life is said to remain in the body for some time after death by snake-bite. Behula remained on the raft with the decomposing body for six months, until one day she saw a washerwoman, angry with her little son, kill him and then, by sprinkling him with water some time later, bring him back to life. Behula asked the washerwoman to perform the same miracle on her husband; but the washerwoman merely led her to Manasa, who explained that she would bring Lakshmindra back to life, but only if Behula would promise to convert Chand. Behula agreed and husband and wife then set off home.

When they reached Chand's house they sent in word that they would enter only if Chand would worship Manasa. The unhappy man's resolution broke at last, and on the eleventh day of the waning moon he honoured her. Ever since then Manasa has been recognised as a goddess, Manasa-devi.

Shasti and Shitala

Shasti is a feline goddess, who is depicted riding a cat. Like Manasa, she is of Bengali origin and little worshipped in other parts of India. She is invoked as the tutelary divinity of childbirth and the protectress of children.

Shitala is another goddess invoked for protection against the evil she causes. She is the goddess of smallpox, who roams the countryside, riding an ass, and searches for victims. She can be identified with Devi in her role as goddess of disease and resembles her in the fury of her attack. She is depicted wearing red robes and carrying reeds with which to chastise her victims.

Kama, god of love, riding a symbolic elephant composed of womankind, who seek his favour. In popular imagination the religious significance of Kama's role is often forgotten beneath that of the wilful master of sexual desire. Trichinopoly painting. Victoria and Albert Museum

Right: *Garuda, king of the birds, charger of Vishnu and Lakshmi and pursuer and devourer of the evil. This painting of the eighteenth century (when Radha was regarded as Krishna's permanent consort, and divine) shows his riders as Vishnu's and Lakshmi's avatars, Krishna and Radha.*

Animal deities

Ganesa

Ganesa is one of the most popular Hindu deities. As the remover of obstacles, he is propitiated at the beginning of every undertaking, whether it be a journey, the building of a house, the writing of a book—or even of a letter. He is also the god of wisdom and prudence, a good scribe and learned in the scriptures. It was he who, at the dictation of the sage Vyasa, wrote the *Mahabharata*. It is said that the reason why the epic is such a harmonious work is that before agreeing to write it down Ganesa stipulated that the dictation should never falter and that he should at all times be able to understand its meaning. Ganesa is also leader of Shiva's hosts, the Ganadevatas.

He is represented as a short, pot-bellied man with yellow skin and four arms and with an elephant's head bearing a single tusk. In his hands he holds a shell, a discus, a club or goad and a water-lily. He rides on or is accompanied by a rat. His pot-belly no doubt stems from his great partiality for offerings of food, especially fruit. Explanations of his parentage and the origin of his elephant's head vary. One version relates that Shiva was in the habit of surprising Parvati in her bath. As she disliked this habit she one day

scraped the scurf from her body, mixed it with oils and ointments, formed it into a man's figure, and gave it life by sprinkling it with water from the Ganges. She then set this figure, Ganesa, outside the bathhouse door to guard it. When Shiva tried to enter and found his way barred, he cut off Ganesa's head. Parvati was so overcome with grief when she emerged to find her son dead that Shiva sent out messengers to seek another head for him. The first creature they found was an elephant, so they brought his head back and this was planted on Ganesa's shoulders.

Another version is that Parvati had long prayed to Vishnu for a son and that when one was granted to her she was so proud of him that she called together all the gods to admire him. All the gods duly gazed at the beautiful child except Sani (Saturn), who looked down at the ground, for he was under the influence of his wife's curse, which caused any being that he fixed his eyes upon to be burnt to ashes. Parvati, however, thought that her son was immune to such dangers and insisted that Sani look at him and admire. So Sani looked, and Ganesa's head was burned to ashes. Parvati now turned on Sani and cursed

Left: Ganesa, the elephant-headed god, being waited upon by maidservants, one of whom fans him while the other offers him his favourite fruit. Apart from his usual features, Ganesa is here seen wearing two of Shiva's attributes: the crescent moon and the serpent coiled about his shoulders. In the foreground is the rat, his vehicle. Rajput painting, early eighteenth century.

him for having killed her son, so that he became lame. But Brahma comforted Parvati and told her that if the first available head were put on her son's trunk he would be able to restore his life. So Vishnu set forth on Garuda and the first creature he saw was an elephant sleeping beside a river. He cut off its head and brought it back to Parvati.

Yet another version that makes Parvati creator of Ganesa says that during one of the twilight periods between the ages a number of unworthy people had obtained access to heaven by visiting the shrine of Somnath, with the result that heaven was full to bursting while the hells were empty. With Indra as their spokesman, the gods asked Shiva for his help in rectifying this situation. On his advice they approached Parvati, who by rubbing her body produced a being with four arms and an elephant's head who would induce in men a desire for riches so strong they would never think of spending their time in pilgrimage.

Sometimes Shiva is said to have created Ganesa, and again there are several versions of this. One relates that Shiva was approached by the other gods and sages, who had been reflecting on the fact that there was no obstacle to the performance of good or bad deeds; they wished Shiva to create for them a being who would oppose the commission of sins. Shiva pondered for some time on how he could help in this matter and then turned his face to Parvati. As he looked a radiant youth of great beauty and endowed with the qualities of Shiva sprang forth from his dazzling countenance. All the heavenly hosts were amazed and captivated by his beauty. But Parvati was angered and jealous of her husband's son. She cursed him to be ugly, to have a pot-belly and to have an elephant's head. But Shiva countered this curse by declaring that the being whom he had thus created should be called Ganesa, son of Shiva and leader of Shiva's hosts; that success and failure should derive from him; that he should be great among the gods and in all spiritual and worldly affairs; and that he should be invoked first on all occasions, those that did not do so being doomed to failure. Another version of this myth ascribes Ganesa's deformity not to Parvati's curse, but to Shiva's previous crime of killing the sun; though he had restored the sun to life, Kasyapa had pronounced a curse whereby Shiva's son should lose his head. When Ganesa lost his head that of Indra's elephant was used to replace it.

Another myth explains why Ganesa has only one tusk. One day as Shiva was sleeping in his palace of Mount Kailasa, Parasurama (the avatar of Vishnu) came to visit him. Ganesa met him at the gate and told him that his father was asleep. Parasurama said he had little time and urged Ganesa to wake Shiva; but Ganesa thought, and

said aloud, that Parasurama was not a sufficiently important visitor for him to waken his father. The two then began to fight and Ganesa grasped Parasurama in his trunk and threw him with great violence into a spin. When Parasurama recovered his balance he drew forth his axe and hurled it at Ganesa. But Ganesa recognised the axe as his father's, for Shiva had given it to Vishnu when he became incarnated as Parasurama. Out of reverence for his father Ganesa therefore took the axe's blow on one of his tusks, thereby breaking it off. Parvati then appeared and was going to curse Parasurama for this act, when the gods intervened; Brahma promised her that to make up for the lost tusk Ganesa should be worshipped by the other gods.

He has two wives, Siddhi and Buddhi. His brother Karttikeya and he were rivals for their hands and agreed to decide which should marry them by a race in which the first to complete the circuit of the world should be the winner. Karttikeya set off and after long and weary travels returned home. There he found that Ganesa was already married to the two girls, having, as he said, made the whole tour of the world in the course of his deep studies of the scriptures—he was so gifted for learning and logic he had completed his tour of the world long before his less astute brother returned.

Garuda

Garuda is king of the birds; he mocks the wind with the speed of his flight and as the charger of Vishnu receives great veneration. He is the son of Kasyapa and Vinata, one of Daksha's daughters, and hatched from an egg which Vinata laid. He has the head, wings, talons and beak of an eagle and the body and limbs of a man. His face is white, his wings red and his body golden. When he was born he was so dazzlingly brilliant that he was mistaken for Agni and worshipped.

Garuda was born with a great hatred of evil and roams about the world devouring bad men—though his parents forbade him to eat Brahmins. Garuda is also famous for his relentless hatred of snakes, which he inherited from his mother, who was at odds with Kasyapa's principal wife, Kadru, the mother of serpents. The two wives had an argument over the colour of the horse Uchchaisravas, produced during the churning of the milk ocean. Each laid a wager on her own theory, and promised that whoever was wrong should become the slave of the other. Kadru was proved to be right and she imprisoned Vinata in the nether regions, where she was guarded by serpents. Garuda sought to release his mother, but the serpents demanded as a ransom a cup of the gods' ambrosia. So Garuda set off for the celestial mountain where the amrita was kept, surrounded by terrible flames which were fanned by violent winds that caused them to leap up to the sky. Garuda, however, his golden body bright as the sun, drank up many rivers and extinguished the fire. The next barrier was a fast revolving wheel with bright, sharp spokes but

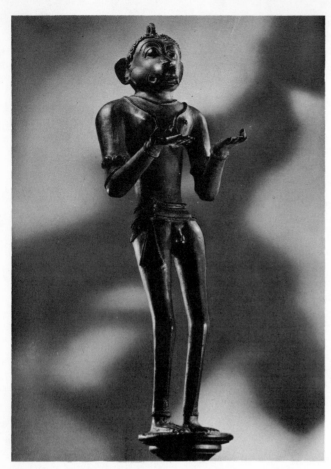

Hanuman, the monkey general of the Ramayana. *Divine in origin and with magical powers, he is nevertheless all monkey. This bronze statuette from Ceylon originally held a lamp, and probably stood before a statue of Rama. Fourteenth century.*

miles high. The tree, however, could not bear their weight, and was in danger of snapping and crushing some Brahmins. Mindful of his parents' prohibition on the killing of Brahmins, Garuda flew with the elephant and the tortoise to a mountain, where he consumed them both. He then resumed his journey and eventually reached the moon. Tucking it under his wing, he set off towards the nether regions. The gods, however, were determined not to lose the moon, and though their attacks could not defeat Garuda they forced a compromise on him. According to this Garuda was to return the moon and was to become the charger of Vishnu, and in return he was to become immortal and to have a higher seat than Vishnu's. Thus Vishnu rides Garuda, while Garuda's emblem appears on the flag flying at the top of Vishnu's chariot.

Hanuman

Hanuman is a monkey deity renowned for his learning, for his agility and speed, and for his faithful service to Rama. He was born of a monkey queen, Anjana, as one of the creatures fathered by the gods so that they could be of assistance to Vishnu in his incarnation as Rama, and has the ability to fly because his father was the wind god, Vayu. It is sometimes related that Vayu ravished Anjana in the forest; but the common account of Hanuman's parentage is more complex. It is said that as part of the ceremony that Dasaratha, Rama's father, performed so that he should be granted sons, he gave to each of his three wives a cake. Kaikeyi, who was the youngest of the three, received her cake last; she resented this and turned up her nose at it. At this a kite swooped down and snatched the cake (Kaikeyi later repented and became the mother of Bharata). The kite bore the cake into the forest where he found Anjana, an Apsara who had been transformed by a curse into a monkey; she was praying for a son, so when the kite dropped the cake Vayu came forward and directed it into Anjana's hand. Shiva then appeared before Anjana and told her to eat the cake; by swallowing it she conceived Hanuman.

As soon as Hanuman was born he felt hungry, and his mother could not satisfy him. Then he caught sight of the sun, and thinking it was a fruit he leapt after it. The sun took flight, but Hanuman chased him as far as Indra's heaven. Here, however, Indra intervened, and injured Hanuman's jaw with his thunderbolt. The monkey then fell back to earth; but his father was quick to avenge him by entering the bodies of all the gods and giving them colic. Indra then apologised to Vayu and agreed that Hanuman should become immortal.

Hanuman's immortality is more often considered to have been granted him as a reward for his loyal support of Rama.

Garuda made his body small and slipped through them. He then had to overcome two fire-spitting snakes, so he blinded them with dust and cut them to pieces. He then turned back to the wheel, broke it and, taking up the cup of amrita, flew with it to the nether regions. The gods, however, pursued him and Indra struck him with his thunderbolt. The two fought, and Indra was worsted and his thunderbolt smashed; Garuda felt no pain and continued until he reached the domain of the serpents. On his arrival his mother was released; but just as the serpents were about to drink the amrita Indra snatched the cup away from them. The serpents greedily licked up the few drops which had spilt on to the grass, and this was enough to make them immortal; but with its strength it also divided their tongues. That is why serpents have forked tongues.

A variant of the myth treats the amrita or soma demanded by the serpents as the moon, and so Garuda's quest for it takes a different form. Garuda set off for the moon, but on his long journey he felt hungry just as he was passing the pole star, the abode of his father Kasyapa. He asked his father where he could find something to eat, and Kasyapa sent him to a lake where a tortoise and an elephant were fighting. The tortoise was eighty miles long and the elephant twice that length, but Garuda seized them, one in each claw, and put them on top of a tree eight hundred

Right: *The Horse Court at Srirangam. Temples to the great gods became more elaborate with each succeeding century. The temple of Vishnu at Srirangam dates from the fourteenth century and contains five courtyards. The outer wall is nearly a thousand yards in length.*

His physical strength and agility made him an invaluable ally. He could not only fly at the speed of wind, but he also had the strength to uproot trees and mountains, and could alter his size at will and make himself invisible. In battle he was a terrifying figure, as vast as a mountain and as tall as a tower, with a yellow skin gleaming like molten gold; his face was as red as a ruby and his tail was of enormous length. As he faced his enemies he shattered them with his fierce roar.

We have already seen how Hanuman went to Lanka in advance of Rama and the army of monkeys and bears in order to deliver Rama's message to Sita and to spy out the land. On the way he had many adventures. Hanuman was informed by Sampati, brother of the vulture Jatayu, that the strait dividing Lanka from the mainland was a hundred leagues across. Angada, another of the monkeys, thought that he could leap across but was sure he would not have the strength to return. Hanuman also doubted that he could perform such a feat. But an old monkey advised Hanuman that if he would only have confidence in his strength and his divine origin he would be able to accomplish the task. So Hanuman went up to the summit of Mount Mahendra and meditated on his mission. As he sat there his body began to shake and grow until it was itself the size of a mountain. He knew that if he could do this, he would be equal to the task, so, roaring and with flashing eyes, Hanuman coursed through the sky. In mid-air he was intercepted by a female rakshasa called Saurasa, who opened her mouth so wide as to engulf him. He at

once shrank to the size of a thumb, but when he was inside her swelled again to his former size, escaping by bursting open and killing her.

When Hanuman reached Lanka he again reduced his size, to that of a cat, and wandered freely about, taking note of the city's defences and even wandering into Ravana's bedroom. As we have seen, he eventually found Sita, destroyed Ravana's pleasure gardens, was captured, and in his escape set fire to Lanka.

During the battle Hanuman proved himself to be a valiant warrior. But his greatest service was to fly to the Himalayas to bring herbs with which to cure Rama and Lakshmana of their mortal wounds. The rakshasas naturally set obstacles to his flight, and many other difficulties arose, all to be overcome. The first of these was a giant called Kalanemi, to whom Ravana had offered half his kingdom if he would kill the monkey god. Kalanemi therefore flew ahead of Hanuman, and when the latter reached the Himalayas, invited him to dinner. But Hanuman had been warned of his host's identity by an Apsara whom he had released from a curse. So he seized Kalanemi by the leg and hurled him all the way to Lanka, where he fell dead before Ravana's throne, and resumed his search for the herb. But he could not find it; Indra, who bore him ill-will, deliberately confused him in his search. Exasperated, Hanuman finally plucked up the whole mountain and flew off with it towards Lanka. He travelled at such speed that his passage created a whirlwind and Bharata, thinking that such turmoil could only be caused by an evil spirit, shot an arrow at him as he passed over Ayodhya. Hanuman fell to earth and Bharata, discovering his mistake, offered to shoot him on to Lanka on another arrow. But Hanuman refused this help and continued alone, only reaching Lanka late in the day. As he drew near he saw the moon was about to rise. He knew that this would stop the herb from working so he swallowed the moon and safely delivered the magic medicine to his master.

Hanuman found complete fulfilment in selflessness and service to his master. When the battle of Lanka was over and the hosts had returned to Ayodhya, Rama offered him any boon that he cared to name. Hanuman asked to be allowed to live for as long as men spoke of the deeds of Rama; he thus only incidentally acquired immortality, for the memory of Rama will never die.

Other mythological animals

Jambavan

Jambavan was king of the bears and leader of the army of bears which aided Rama in his battle against Ravana. Like Hanuman, he had been specially created for this purpose and his father was Vishnu. Jambavan was a wise counsellor, and as a reward for his services Rama conferred on him the boon that he should be vulnerable only to his own father. He was to be killed not by Vishnu himself but by his incarnation in the next age, Krishna.

During Krishna's reign as prince at Dwarka, one of the Yadavas, Satrajit, practised such rigorous austerities in honour of Surya that the sun god gave him a magic jewel, Syamantaka, which every day produced eight loads of gold, and protected its wearer against evil portents, wild animals, fire, robbers and famine. But it would only protect a virtuous wearer; it would bring disaster to the wicked. Krishna asked Satrajit to give him this jewel, and showed his anger when Satrajit refused. When the gem disappeared some time later it was generally thought that Krishna had stolen it. In fact its fate was quite different. Satrajit's wicked brother Prasena wore the jewel one day when he went hunting in the forest; because he was immoral he was exposed to the attack of a lion, who killed him and carried off Syamantaka. But Jambavan, who lived in a cave in the same forest, saw the jewel and, having killed the lion, took possession of it.

Meanwhile the general accusations against Krishna as thief and murderer of Prasena caused him to search for the real thief to vindicate himself. He eventually traced the jewel to Jambavan's cave. Leaving his followers outside, Krishna entered and challenged the bear king to relinquish the jewel. Jambavan resisted and the two engaged in single

Left: Sugriva, son of Indra, in combat with his half-brother Bali, who had usurped his throne. To the left, Rama and Lakshmana look on; to the right, Rama kills Bali with an arrow. Once Sugriva was restored to his throne he was able to help Rama against Ravana. Relief from Prambanam, Java, eighth century.

Seven-headed Naga, of the serpent race descended from Kadru and the sage Kasyapa. The Nagas' heads, based on those of cobras, are surmounted by hoods in which gleam the most precious jewels of the three worlds and which light up the darkness of Patala. Sandstone balustrade carving from Angkor Thom, twelfth century.

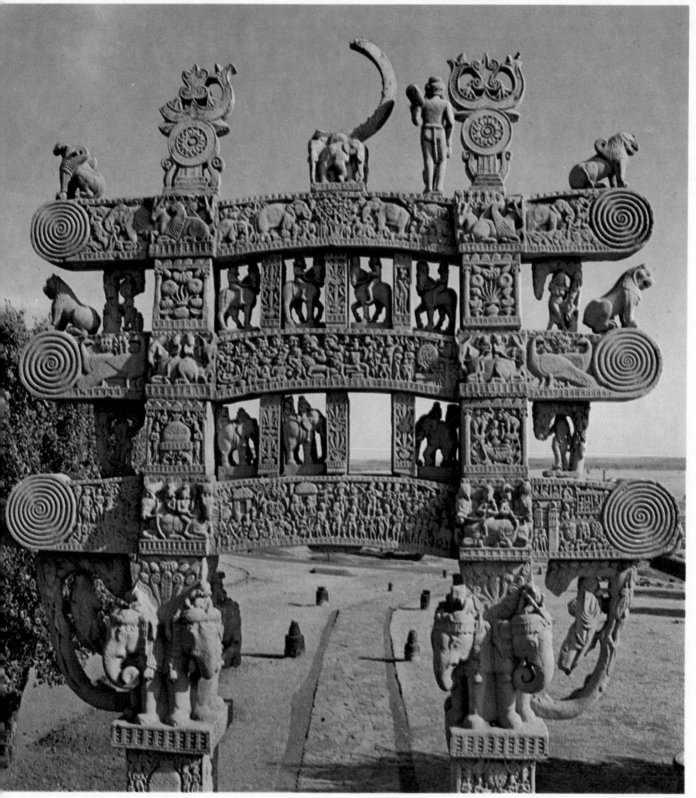

Left: *Arjuna propitiates the gods and gains the support of their divine weapons in the coming war with the Kauravas. He can be seen in the upper left-hand corner, standing on one leg. Shiva's appearance in response to the force of the hero's austerities signified that Arjuna's hopes would be fulfilled. Rock sculpture at Mahabalipuram, seventh century.*

Above: *The north gate of the Buddhist stupa at Sanchi. The sculptures, which date from the first century, B.C., are of subjects from the Jatakas —the myths which relate to Buddha's previous lives on earth. The great hemispherical domes called stupas were raised to honour the resting places of Buddha's relics. First century B.C.*

combat. After seven days Krishna's followers assumed that he had been killed and returned with the news of his death to Dwarka.

But in fact the struggle was to continue for another fourteen days, when Krishna finally managed to inflict a mortal wound on Jambavan. Knowing he was about to die, Jambavan realised that his opponent could be none other than Vishnu, his father and beloved master in the previous age. At this he begged forgiveness, gave Krishna the jewel and offered him the hand of Jambavati, his daughter, who became one of Krishna's principal wives. Jambavan died glorifying the name of Vishnu.

The jewel was given back to Satrajit, who in recognition of Krishna's honourable behaviour gave him his daughter Satyabhama as a wife; but Satrajit was subsequently murdered and the jewel stolen. Balarama and Krishna together set out in pursuit of the thief; but he had meanwhile given it to Krishna's uncle Akrura, so when Krishna killed the thief he found no jewel. Balarama accused Krishna of having stolen the gem himself, and this led to a serious quarrel. Eventually, however, Akrura produced the jewel, and though Krishna, Balarama and Satyabhama laid claim to it, Akrura was finally allowed to keep it.

Sugriva

Sugriva was a monkey king, the son of Surya, whose alliance Rama sought in his struggle against Ravana. He had been dethroned by his clever half-brother Bali, so Rama first helped Sugriva to regain his throne by killing the usurper. When he was re-established in his kingdom, Sugriva gave himself up to year-long celebrations; but as soon as Rama reminded him of his promise he devoted himself zealously to Rama's cause.

In the battle of Lanka Sugriva knocked Ravana's crown off his head, but he was then nearly killed by Kumbhakarna, who crushed him with a mountain and then made to eat him. But Sugriva surprised Kumbhakarna by biting him on the thigh and made his escape. He then killed many of Ravana's generals. Sugriva joined in the general rejoicing and victory celebrations at Ayodhya, but unlike Hanuman was granted no special boon, being sufficiently rewarded by the recovery of his kingdom.

Bali

Bali was born of the same monkey queen as Sugriva, but his father was Indra and he had greater powers than his half-brother. A great practiser of austerities, Bali had acquired a boon whereby he could assume half the strength of anyone he looked at. But he had once conquered Ravana without the benefit of this boon. Ravana's head had been turned by the sage Narada who, when he had one day visited Lanka, was offered a chair by Ravana, which his host merely kicked in his direction. As a punishment for this rudeness Narada decided to deliver him into Bali's power. He first flattered Ravana, telling him that he was more powerful than all the gods and that therefore he, Narada, wished only to worship in Lanka. But having given the demon an exaggerated idea of his own power, Narada mentioned that Bali had boasted he could overcome Ravana with one hand. As Narada had hoped, Ravana immediately set out to fight Bali. He found him looking as large as a mountain and performing his ablutions by the shore of the ocean, and came up behind him and grasped his tail. But Bali, without looking round and without interrupting his ablutions, used his tail to tie Ravana's hands together. Ravana pulled harder on the tail, trying to lever himself free by pressing against Bali's back; but Bali merely wound his tail round Ravana's ten heads and round his legs and set off on a tour of the western, eastern and northern oceans, keeping Ravana prisoner in his tail for twelve years. Ravana owed his eventual liberation only to Bali's generosity.

Rama killed Bali by a stratagem. He had Sugriva engage his half-brother in single combat while he hid behind a tree. As Bali's attention was focused on Sugriva, Rama was able to retain his full strength and kill him with an arrow. Bali protested against this unfair ruse, but Rama explained that he was fated to die thus. Bali, accepting this, died praising Vishnu, and recommending his son, Angada, to fight on Rama's side against Ravana.

The Nagas

The Nagas are the race of serpents who were sons of Kadru, the principal wife of the sage Kasyapa. The Nagas are the guardians of the nether regions, Patala, where they kept Vinata prisoner. Though most of them are considered to be demons, some of them succeeded in obtaining immortality from licking up the few drops of amrita which fell to the ground when Garuda came to rescue his mother, Vinata. These serpents are powerful rulers in Patala. Some of them have five hoods and others have seven, and the jewels which they wear on them light up the darkness of the nether regions. The Nagas possess the best gems in the three worlds.

Though most of the Nagas are considered to personify evil, some of them are worshipped, for they have acquired virtue through their connection with the gods. Thus Shesha, king of the Nagas, is the constant companion of Vishnu and forms the raft on which he lies when floating on the cosmic waters at the dawn of creation. Shesha, also known as Ananta, is the symbol of eternity, especially when he holds his own tail in his mouth, and he is said to support the heavens. Vasuki, who was used as the rope at the churning of the milk ocean, vomited forth the poison within him and became pure. He is worn by Shiva as a girdle and helps him to kill demons.

Ganga, goddess of the river Ganges, whose waters are represented about her. She was originally the river surrounding Brahma's city on Mount Meru. As daughter of the Himalayas, the beautiful Ganga was consort to all the gods of the celestial kingdom. Stone sculpture, twelfth century.

Mountains, rivers and pools as deities

Mountains

Mountains occupy an important place in Hindu mythology, a symbol of strength when certain gods in their fury grow to resemble mountains, and of oppressive weight when they are torn up and used as missiles by gods or demons. Some of them themselves count as deities. The most important of these are of course the Himalayas, which contain on their summits all the heavens. The greatest individual mountain within the Himalaya range is Meru, which bears on its summit Brahma's heaven and which acts as a pivot for the three worlds, and around which all the heavenly bodies revolve. At one time Vindhya, the deity of the mountains which form the northern border of the Deccan, became jealous of the powers of the Himalayas as personified in Himavan. Vindhya demanded of the sun that he should revolve around him just as he did around Mount Meru. But Surya refused, so Vindhya began to grow, hoping to tower above Himavan and hide him from the sun. The gods therefore called upon the sage Agastya, who was Vindhya's preceptor, and asked him to use his influence. Agastya called upon Vindhya to bow down so that he could more easily make a journey to the south and back. Vindhya did as he was asked out of respect for his teacher, and Agastya crossed over his lowered back; but Agastya never returned, so Vindhya is still bowed low.

Himavan took the form of a man when the gods wished Sati to be reborn, and became the father first of Ganga and then of Parvati. His wife was called Mena. Mount Mandara is a revered mountain in the Himalaya range and was thought to be the only one mighty enough to serve as the pole in the churning of the milk ocean. Mandara became the home of Durga. Mount Kailasa, the home of Shiva, became involved in a dispute between Indra and Karttikeya over their relative powers. To settle the matter they ran a race around Kailasa, but then disagreed again as to who was the winner, although in fact Karttikeya had won. They appealed for a verdict to Kailasa, who thought to propitiate Indra by declaring in his favour. For this injustice Karttikeya hurled his lance at the mountain and split it open, thus creating the Krauncha pass. On another occasion Indra punished the mountains for their stubborn independence by cutting off their wings.

Rivers

Ganga, the elder daughter of Himavan and Mena, was a holy river which wound three times round the city of Brahma on the summit of Mount Meru. She was married to the gods and remained in heaven until she was brought down to earth through the efforts of Bhagiratha, grandson of Sagara, king of Ayodhya.

Sagara was a scion of the solar race but his power gave him no satisfaction for he had no sons. He therefore propitiated the sage Aurva, who promised him that one of his wives would have one son while the other would have sixty thousand sons. Kesini, the daughter of Vidharba, chose to have one son, who was called Asamanjas; while Sumati, the daughter of Kasyapa, had the sixty thousand, which burst out of a gourd to which she gave birth. Asamanjas grew up to be an immoral youth and his father abandoned him; the other sons were no better and the gods complained to Vishnu and the sage Kapila about their behaviour. Vishnu therefore arranged to humble Sagara and his sons.

Sagara decided to perform the horse sacrifice as a sign of his universal dominion, and planned to dethrone Indra. But Indra took the form of a demon and drove the horse into the nether regions. Sagara ordered the sixty thousand sons, who had been given the task of guarding the horse, to search for it. Accordingly they began to dig deep into the earth. Each one dug a league deep, but even when they had penetrated the earth to the depth of sixty thousand leagues, they still could not find the horse. They bored still further until they reached the centre of the earth, which they found supported by elephants. Still they did not find the horse until, wandering into Patala, they caught sight of it grazing near the hermitage which the sage Kapila had set up there. Earth, wounded by the great crater which Sagara's sons had gouged out of her, and which was called Sagara, had already complained of their activities to her husband Vishnu; and this, combined with their previous misdeeds and their evident intention of seizing Kapila as the thief of the horse—and thereby disturbing his meditations—caused him to burn them all to ashes with his glance of sacred fire.

Sagara now sent his grandson Ansuman, son of Asamanjas, to see what had happened to the sixty thousand. Ansuman reached Patala and humbly approached Kapila, asking him if he knew anything of his uncles. Kapila was pleased by Ansuman's respectfulness and told him what had happened, but added that his uncles could be brought back to life if the sacred waters of Ganga could be made to descend to earth and to flow over their ashes in Patala. Kapila allowed Ansuman to return with the horse and the sacrifice was completed.

Though Sagara reigned for thirty thousand years and constantly sought to bring the Ganges down from heaven, he had no success. Ansuman succeeded to the throne and continued the effort, but neither he nor his son Dilipa were any more successful. The next king, Dilipa's son Bhagiratha, was a powerful ascetic and performed such extraordinary austerities that he persuaded Brahma to order Ganga to descend to earth.

She was very unwilling to leave heaven, and the gods realised that she would fall as heavily as she could. So Brahma warned Bhagiratha of this danger and advised him to propitiate Shiva, who would help him. Accordingly Bhagiratha underwent further penances, and Shiva agreed

to break the violence of Ganga's fall on to Mount Kailasa by catching her waters in his tangled hair. Thus, despite Ganga's fury and her wish to engulf the earth and carry it with her to Patala, she became confused and weakened on entering Shiva's hair, and emerged in seven separate streams. One of these sacred streams is the River Ganges as we know it. This followed Bhagiratha in his chariot towards the nether regions. But on his way Bhagiratha chanced to lead Ganga through the garden of the sage Jahnu, flooding it; and the sage in anger drank up all the water. However, Bhagiratha propitiated him, and Jahnu allowed Ganga to emerge and flow on from his ear. Ganga then flowed into the crater left by the sixty thousand, thus forming the ocean (Sagara). She then seeped down into Patala, where her waters moistened the ashes of Sagara's sons and, having purified them, released them for admission into Swarga.

Ever since she flowed from heaven, through earth and into the ocean and Patala, Ganga is said to water the three worlds. Later myths claim that her source is in Vishnu's toe. Though all seven sacred rivers are said to be branches of the original Ganga, other origins are attributed to the most important of them. Thus the Jumna (Yamuna) is identical with Yami, the twin sister of Yama and daughter of Surya and Saranyu; and Sarasvati, as we have seen, is given various origins. Apart from these, the best known of the holy rivers is Sutudri, the Sutlej.

Ganga is said at one time to have been married to Vishnu but he found that one wife was enough, and so gave Ganga to Shiva. As we have seen, she became the mother of Karttikeya, Shiva's son; and she also had a son by Agni, to whom she gave pure gold. She was also married to a mortal king, Santanu, for she had promised the Vasus, who had been cursed to be born as mortals, that she would be their mother in their rebirths and that immediately they were born she would kill them and so release them again to immortal life. In return for this favour each of the Vasus had to promise to give an eighth of his power to her last son. As each was born she duly killed him; but her husband Santanu, who was already an old man, was horrified by her behaviour and prevented her from killing the last and eighth one, who was to grow up as Bhishma, one of the heroes of the *Mahabharata*. After his death he resumed his position as a Vasu.

Holy pools

Many pools are considered to be holy, for each is presided over by its special deity or by a nymph (Apsara). These deities give boons, grant inspiration and confer wisdom on their worshippers. Most such deities are special to the pool they inhabit; but some are presided over by aspects of the greater deities, such as Sarasvati, originally a water goddess, and Vishnu. It is rare that such deities are other than benevolent; the great ocean is the true realm of the evil spirits, where they are watched over by Varuna.

Enemies of the gods

The demons, or asuras, as we have noted, were originally the gods of Iranian provenance, and included such mighty figures as the Vedic Varuna. But with the supremacy of the Aryan gods under Indra they were demoted to become demons and were driven from the heavens into the nether regions, usually considered to lie beneath the ocean. But their change of character did not entail a loss of power; one of the unusual features of Indian mythology is that gods and demons are of equal strength and constantly fight for dominion of the three worlds. In Hindu mythology, as we have seen, the gods are not always able to keep control of heaven. They owed their appearance of strength at first to their monopoly of amrita and in general to the sacrifices offered to them by men. The demons were ever-watchful for an opportunity to snatch the amrita but the gods, being already fortified with it, could fight them off. Alternatively the gods used ruses to keep it from them. The demons, for their part, and especially in later times, could acquire great power and force concessions out of the great gods, particularly Brahma, as a result of the austerities they performed. Many of them were extremely learned theologians and adept at obtaining boons in this

Above: *Sunda and Upasunda, asura brothers, fighting for possession of the Apsara Tilottama. The gods, wishing to destroy these asuras, had sent down Tilottama from heaven, and the brothers killed each other over her. Other asuras look on. Sandstone from Banteay Srey, tenth century.*

Below: *The churning of the milk ocean. Vishnu in his tortoise avatar is seen as the pivot for Mount Mandara, the churning stick. The deformed Daityas are at the head end of the serpent Vasuki, the churning rope, while the gods hold the tail end. Kangra painting, eighteenth century. Victoria and Albert Museum*

way; but again the gods usually outwitted them, by sheer trickery, by force of their own austerities, or by secret prayers and the like.

In the beginning, when the asuras were still considered to be gods, they took part in all the sacrifices performed. The devas, in order to gain the ascendancy, had a vision of silent praise; but the asuras were unaware of this and so became relatively weak. 'Silent praise' became a weapon against the asuras, who could not understand it. They further weakened themselves by taking the sacrificial offerings and putting them into their own mouths, while the gods fed each other and so acquired greater moral strength. The demons were excluded from drinking soma or amrita in the aftermath of the churning of the milk ocean. Both they and the gods had been weakened by the failure of amrita and other precious things to reappear in one of the periodic creations of the universe. The gods decided that the asuras would have to co-operate with them in churning the milk ocean in order to recover them, but the only way to induce the demons to join in was to offer them an equal share of the amrita. But they could never afford to honour their promise, for if the demons had been allowed to drink the amrita they would have become even stronger than the gods. Vishnu, however, promised to prevent such a disaster.

Hiranyakasipu meets his end. He defied the gods and tried to murder his son Prahlada for his devotion to Vishnu, whose lion avatar finally destroyed him. From a Pahari painting, nineteenth century.

Despite their suspicions the demons agreed to the proposal, and first helped the gods to tear up Mount Mandara for use as a churning stick. They then collected potent magical herbs and dropped them into the ocean, and found the serpent Vasuki in his underwater abode and brought

The asura Sumbha with his demon courtiers. He was another asura who gained great power by practising austerities, until he was finally destroyed by Durga. Jaipur painting, eighteenth century.

Kumbhakarna, the demon brother of Ravana, who was a giant as large as a mountain. Brahma subdued him by a trick but he was only destroyed when Rama met him in combat during the battle for Lanka. Trichinopoly painting, 1820.

only at her. Having smiled at them all sweetly and provocatively, the girl, whose name was Mohini, reminded them of the amrita by looking at it pointedly. One demon then hit upon the idea of asking Mohini to decide how they should apportion the amrita, and this the others approved. But Mohini archly expressed surprise that they should be willing to entrust such an important decision to a woman; her teasing entranced the demons, and reassured them that Mohini was to be trusted. They promised to abide by her decision unconditionally.

Mohini then pointed out that as gods and demons had laboured equally to produce the amrita, the gods were also entitled to a share of it. The demons were forced by their promise to agree, so Mohini summoned the gods and arranged gods and demons in two long rows facing each other. She then began to pass down the row of gods, giving each a draught of the amrita. But as she reached the end of the row, she suddenly vanished, and the cup of amrita vanished with her. Mohini was none other than Vishnu in a female incarnation!

A fight immediately broke out between the gods and the cheated demons. But the gods were already strengthened by the amrita they had drunk, and gained an easy victory over their furious enemies.

After this incident the demons were never again to have access to the source of amrita. As we have seen, the Naga serpent demons licked up a few drops spilt in Patala by Indra when he snatched away the amrita brought to them by Garuda, but this benefited only a few of the serpents. In general the serpents' only way of obtaining amrita was to watch at any sacrifice being performed, waiting for a slip in the correct ritual to be made—and if possible to cause it to be committed. If such a mistake were made the watchful demons could take possession of the amrita offered. In this role demons were called *devas yajnamusas*, 'sacrifice destroyers'; but though they ate the amrita, it lacked the potency that it would have acquired through proper performance of the ritual, and did not strengthen them as it would have fortified the gods. The force of their interference was more the negative one of depriving the gods of their sustenance.

Though the demons defeated the gods with increasing regularity by acquiring power through austerities, they were with equal regularity defeated by the gods, who counted on their becoming careless in their pride at universal dominion. Their full power is released only at the end of each age, when it takes part in the general destruction. This power is symbolised by the submarine fire in Patala, where it is fed by water. The fire was produced from the thigh of the sage Aurva, who had acquired such enormous powers through his austerities that he terrified the gods. Aurva was responsible for the existence of the ocean in which the demons dwelt, for he had prevented Sagara's mother from immolating herself on her husband's funeral pyre when she was pregnant with Sagara (Ocean).

him forth to use as a churning rope. Vasuki was wound round the mountain and had to be pulled from either end in order to twirl the massive churning instrument. Vishnu directed that the gods should take the head end and the demons the tail. But the demons mistrusted this arrangement and insisted on taking the head. This was really what Vishnu had foreseen; for as the churning progressed, Vasuki's breath blew hot and the demons were suffocated by it, while the gods at the tail end were refreshed by cool ocean breezes. Shiva was forced to rush round to the head in order to catch in his mouth the poison vomited forth by the unfortunate Vasuki. As we have mentioned, this gave Shiva his blue neck and also purified Vasuki, whom Vishnu thereafter wore as his girdle. As the churning progressed, Mount Mandara began to sink into the soft bed of the ocean and so, as we have already related, Vishnu assumed his tortoise avatar and dived to the bottom, where his back became a pivot for the churning stick.

In due course, one by one, the precious things appeared on the surface, and one after the other were given to or claimed by the various gods or rishis. The demons, however, were interested in only one thing, the amrita. At last it appeared, in a cup borne by Dhanwantari, the physician of the gods. Both gods and demons immediately dropped the churning rope and rushed to seize the amrita. The demons reached it first and made off with it; but they began to quarrel over which of them should be first to drink it. As they argued there appeared among them the most beautiful and appealing girl any of them had ever seen. At once they forgot about the amrita and gazed

The fire which he subsequently produced from his thigh declared immediately after its birth that it would consume the three worlds, and set about its work. But Brahma intervened to save his creation, and promised Aurva that his offspring would have free rein to consume the three worlds at the end of the age, but that meanwhile Brahma would provide the fire with a fitting abode in the waters from which he himself arose. At the end of the age the fire would consume everything, including the gods.

Different classes of asuras can be distinguished, beside the destroyers of sacrifice. The Daityas and Danavas, children of the sage Kasyapa by Diti and Danu, are ocean demons who were confined to the underwater realm of Patala by Indra, who also set Varuna to watch over them, thereby incidentally exiling his former rival. Hiranyakasipu and Hiranyaksha were famous Daityas, and the cause of two of Vishnu's incarnations. Daityas and Danavas are giants and their women wear jewels the size of boulders.

Other inhabitants of Patala are the serpent demons, Nagas, also sons of Kasyapa (by Kadru), some of whom, as we have seen, came to be worshipped as gods; the majority, however, personify evil, as they did in Vedic times when their prototype the drought demon Ahi or Vritra fought the epic battle against Indra. Their bodies are human to the waist, but end in serpents' tails. One such evil serpent was the monstrous cobra Kaliya, who inhabited the River Jumna and terrorised the herdsmen until he was overcome by the boy Krishna. Female Nagas sometimes look like nymphs and mortals fall in love with them.

Other sorts of demons are cannibals. One such was Baka, who demanded tribute in return for a promise that he would not eat the entire population of the towns near his abode. The tribute consisted of cartloads of vegetables and rice, and one man every day. On one occasion Bhima, the son of Vayu and a great opponent and slayer of asuras, also known as a glutton, offered to go as the human victim. On the way he felt hungry and ate all the vegetables; as he was just finishing Baka appeared. Despite Baka's mighty opposition, Bhima soon knocked his teeth out and dispatched him with a blow from his club. Such were Bhima's successes against the asuras that they had to promise henceforth not to molest human beings.

Asuras are able to assume any form they wish, as they amply demonstrated in their attacks on Krishna under the leadership of the arch-demon Kansa. The horse demon Kesin was one of these, and also an opponent of Indra.

Above: *Naga and Nagini, inhabitants of the nether regions of Patala, who sometimes haunt and terrorise rivers, but who here have emerged to do homage to Arjuna as a great ascetic. As descendants of the sage Kasyapa, the Nagas have considerable spiritual strength. Detail from the rock carvings at Mahabalipuram. Early seventh century.*

Left: *Ravana trying to lift Mt. Kailasa, the abode of Shiva and Parvati. The chief of the rakshasas, Ravana tried to pull up the mountain to make Shiva aware of his great powers but the god merely pressed down with his big toe and held the demon fast. Stone sculpture, thirteenth century.*

When Kesin led the asura forces against the gods he hurled a great mace against Indra and then a huge mass of rock, but Indra was always able to parry these attacks by breaking up the missile with his magic thunderbolt, and thus routed the asuras.

Some of the Daityas possess a special power; they can move their abode whenever they wish. Their city, named Hiranyapura, is sometimes situated beneath the ocean, but at other times it breaks out of the bounds set by Indra and moves under the earth or sails through the air.

Ketu and Rahu, earlier known as Svarbhanu, acquired special characteristics as a result of the churning of the milk ocean. When Mohini was passing down the line of gods and giving them amrita, one of the demons, a Daitya with four arms and a tail, had slipped between Surya and Chandra and received a portion of the amrita. Surya and Chandra discovered the fraud and called out to Vishnu, who immediately cut the demon in two with his discus. But the amrita had had its effect and both parts lived, the head becoming Rahu and the trunk Ketu. As immortal beings, they took their place in the stellar sphere. Ketu, represented by a dragon's tail, is conveyed about the sky in a chariot by eight swift red horses; while Rahu, represented by a dragon's head, travels in a chariot with eight black horses eternally yoked to it. He has never forgotten his hatred of the sun and the moon and, his mouth agape, he pursues them in turn through the sky. Sometimes he catches up with them and manages to swallow them, thus causing eclipses.

Enemies of men

Like the asuras, the rakshasas represent the forces of evil; but unlike the asuras, they do not confine themselves to a cosmic struggle with the gods but attack men directly. Rakshasas too are descended from the sage Kasyapa, by his wife Khasa, a daughter of Daksha. According to some, however, they sprang from Brahma's foot and were set to guard the waters. Another belief is that they are descended from the sage Pulastya like their leader, the celebrated Ravana.

The rakshasas are of grotesque appearance, many of them gorilla-like and hideous to behold, as is related by Hanuman, who spied them out in their camp before the battle of Lanka. But they often adopt disguises to hide their monstrosity – especially their womenfolk, who sometimes succeed in undermining the defences of mortal men by bewitching them, thereby achieving the status of domestic goddesses. Without disguise, however, they present a great variety of deformity. Some are dwarfs, others like beanstalks; some fat, others emaciated; some have over-long arms; some only one eye, or only one ear; some have monstrous bellies; some have crooked legs, some one leg, some three and some four; some have serpents' heads, others donkeys', horses' or elephants' heads.

Just as their appearance varies, so do their functions. There are the goblin-like pisachas and their near relatives the darbas, who haunt cemeteries and eat the bodies of the dead. There are the panis, aerial demons who inspire in men foolish actions, encourage slander and unbelief, and whose devious ways make them the special foes of Indra. There are the black dasyus, drought demons who steal the cloud cows from Vritra. There are the vartikas, fiends of evil omen. There are the grahas, evil spirits who often cluster about the god of war, Karttikeya, and who possess men's souls and make them insane. Finally there are the demons who specialise in attacking holy men. One such cooked his younger brother and gave the flesh to a saint to eat. When the saint had eaten he called his brother forth. The boy came to life and emerged, rending the body of the saint and killing him. The Bhutas are Shiva's attendants when he haunts cemeteries. They are the children of Anger; they animate dead bodies and delight in eating human flesh.

The leader of the rakshasas is most famous in his incarnation as Ravana, though he also appears in other guises, such as Sisupala and Hiranyakasipu. Ravana, the grandson of Pulastya, was the most wicked of them all, a breaker of all the laws and a ravisher of other men's wives. He had ten heads and twenty arms, copper-coloured eyes and a crescent of teeth like the young moon. He was as tall and as broad as a mountain, engulfing all, like the god of death with his mouth agape. The horror of his deeds was such that he stopped the sun and moon in their courses, the sun too frightened to give out heat, the wind to blow or the ocean to move. His physical strength was such that he could break the tops off mountains and churn up the seas; and his spiritual strength matched it, for he was a Brahmin on his father's side and austerities and learning were the source of his power. The gods had many encounters with him and the scars left by their weapons, including Indra's thunderbolt, Airavata's tusks and Vishnu's discus, marred his body, which otherwise wore the insignia of royalty, and made it repellent.

Ravana easily ousted his half-brother Kubera from his palace at Lanka and captured his magic chariot Pushpaka. Once in possession he reigned in splendour and pursued his career of wickedness. As we have seen, he was out-witted by the monkey king, Bali. But even after Bali had kept him captive Ravana did not heed his warning not to overreach himself again. As soon as he returned he embarked on a campaign against the gods, and owing to a curse which hampered them succeeded not only in capturing the celestial kingdom but also in making the gods his slaves and forcing all of them, including Brahma, Vishnu and Shiva, to perform menial, humiliating tasks in his palace. They eventually escaped from this bondage, but though they could do nothing immediately to curb Ravana, this was one of the many crimes for which he was finally punished by Vishnu in his Rama avatar.

Head of a yaksha, one of Kubera's attendants and guardians of hidden treasure in the Himalayas. Though of grotesque appearance, yakshas are not usually hostile to men. Sandstone from Choen Prei, tenth century.

An Apsara. Though originally water-nymphs, Apsaras became associated with Gandharvas as heavenly singers and dancers, and infatuated gods and men. Sandstone, Baphuon style, late eleventh century.

Sensing that retribution could not be long delayed, Ravana attempted to secure immortality for himself. Nikasha, his mother, was a devotee of Shiva and worshipped a lingam. One day Indra stole this lingam and Nikasha tried to regain it by undertaking a severe fast. Ravana told her not to torture herself in this way, for he would visit Shiva and bring her the Atmalingam (the true lingam). He therefore went to Mount Kailasa and began a course of austerities. He first stood on one of his heads in the midst of five fires for a thousand years; at the end of that time he cut the head off and threw it into the fire. Then he stood on a second head for another thousand years, and cut that off. Thus he continued with each of his ten heads; but as he was on the point of cutting off the last Shiva appeared and asked him to name the boons he desired. Ravana asked for three: immortality for himself; marriage to a woman as beautiful as Parvati; and the Atmalingam. He was immediately granted the Atmalingam and immortality, on condition that he should not use it to harm Shiva. But Shiva knew of no other woman to equal Parvati in beauty; Ravana threatened to perform more austerities and Shiva, fearing this—for such austerities generated a heat that could consume the world, was forced to yield up his own wife.

As Ravana prepared to return to Lanka, the sage Narada spoke to him and persuaded him that in fact Shiva had

no power to grant immortality and had been bluffing. Ravana, angry at being duped, tore off the top of Mount Kailasa and tossed it away; but he had thereby injured Shiva, whose home was there, and by infringing the condition he lost the boon of immortality.

But he still had Parvati and the Atmalingam; so he set off, carrying Parvati on his shoulders. She cried out to Vishnu to protect her, so he appeared in the guise of an old Brahmin and asked Ravana where he was going with the old hag on his shoulders. Ravana retorted that this was no hag but the most beautiful goddess of them all, Parvati. The Brahmin insisted, and invited Ravana to look for himself; so Parvati quickly transformed herself into a monstrous hag, and when Ravana beheld her he dropped her on the spot and proceeded south bearing only the Atmalingam.

When Ravana had journeyed some way further he wished to relieve himself but, mindful of Shiva's warning against putting the Atmalingam on the ground, he looked round for someone to hold it. The first person he caught sight of was Ganesa disguised as a cowherd, so he gave him the Atmalingam and warned him against putting it down, promising to be back within the hour. But Ravana failed to return before the hour was up, so the 'cowherd' could honourably put the lingam on the ground. It stuck fast to the earth and when Ravana returned he found it immovable, slowly sinking into the ground. He tried to pull it back but it then turned into a cow and continued to sink. Finally all that showed were the cow's two ears, which are still to be seen on the west coast on India.

His humiliation over this episode only served to increase Ravana's crimes, and the sum of them all led to Vishnu's incarnation as Rama and his eventual defeat.

Kumbhakarna was Ravana's brother. He was a giant with a body as large as a mountain, breath like a whirlwind and speech like thunder. Like Ravana, he performed austerities in the hope of gaining immortality; but he was more wary than his brother and demanded of Brahma that he be given immortality unconditionally. Several times Brahma refused his request and finally enlisted the help of Sarasvati in twisting the giant's tongue, so that on the next occasion when he intended to ask for eternal life he actually asked for 'eternal sleep'. Brahma immediately granted this request; but he later modified it so that Kumbhakarna woke for one day every six months. While he was awake Kumbhakarna had to eat enough food to nourish his vast body for the next six months, and his appetite was well-nigh insatiable.

During the battle of Lanka, Ravana became alarmed at the course of events and determined to wake his brother and enlist his aid. The rakshasas went to the cave where Kumbhakarna slept and set before him a dish of rice piled as high as Mount Meru and seasoned with hundreds of buffalo and deer. They then attempted to wake him up by throwing rocks and trees at him but his breath blew the missiles back. Finally they woke him up by driving thousands of elephants over him. He then ate the rice dish and some more animals, washed down with two thousand jars of liquor; after this he felt half fed, and determined to finish his meal in the battle. Kumbhakarna caused devastation in the armies of monkeys and bears, devouring them a hundred at a time. He captured Sugriva and took him prisoner into Lanka. But he met his match in Rama, who with divine weapons cut off all his limbs and finally decapitated him.

Other spirits

The yakshas are the attendant spirits of Kubera and live in the Himalayas, where they are the guardians of hidden treasure. Like their lord they are generally friendly towards men. When they show hostility it is usually in an effort to prevent them from gaining riches.

The Kinnaras also dwell in Kubera's heaven, where they are dancers, musicians and choristers. They have human bodies with horses' heads, and are said to have been born at the same time as the yakshas. More important are the Gandharvas, spirits who are half-man and half-bird, and usually friendly towards men. They are said to be descended from Brahma or from Kasyapa. The first Gandharva, who may have symbolised the fire of the sun,

had a great knowledge of divine truths and prepared and looked after the soma juice. His descendants also have amrita in their charge and are learned in medicine. They are said to have splendid cities of their own but they are usually found in Indra's heaven, where together with the Apsaras they sing and play their instruments, for they are skilled musicians. They are known to haunt the air, the forests and the mountains and many men have been deceived by the illusions that they work at twilight. Occasionally they actually fight men. Their only serious enemies, however, are the Nagas, whose kingdom in the nether regions they conquered and whose treasures they plundered. The Nagas called upon Vishnu to save them, and he descended to Patala in the form of Narmada (personification of a river) and routed the Gandharvas. The Gandharvas are celebrated for their fondness of women and for the power they exercise over them.

The Apsaras are the nymphs of Indra's heaven and partners of the Gandharvas in many of their love affairs. Though they are later known mostly for their dancing and singing, they began as water nymphs, and many still haunt rivers and holy pools. They are called the daughters of pleasure, for it is said that they were produced incidentally during the churning of the milk ocean and that despite their beauty neither gods nor asuras wanted them as wives; it was therefore decided that they should become the wives of all.

Nymphs of other sorts are also found in the heavens and in the foothills of Mount Meru. One of the most interesting of these is the beautiful Tapati, the chaste daughter of Surya and Chhaya, his substitute wife. After much consideration Surya decided to bestow his daughter on King Samvarana, his devout worshipper, so he arranged for Samvarana to get lost in the forest and to see and fall in love with his resplendent, golden daughter. But as soon as Samvarana spoke to Tapati of his love she vanished. Smitten with the arrows of Kama, the king followed, and in the end, half dead with love, he had another vision of the beautiful maiden, who revealed her identity to him and told him that she was not free to bestow her own heart, but that he should ask her father. Then Tapati again vanished. Samvarana worshipped the sun without pause for twelve days, at the end of which Surya made his final decision to give him his daughter's hand. A sage went up to the sun and led Tapati down to earth, where she was married to Samvarana; but Tapati would not descend into the valleys, so the couple spent the blissful years of their married life in the mountain forests. Meanwhile Samvarana's kingdom fell into anarchy; for twelve years no rain fell and no corn grew, and morality departed. At the end of twelve years, however, Samvarana and his celestial bride descended into his capital and restored peace and abundance. Tapati gave birth to a son, Kuru, who was the ancestor of both Pandavas and Kauravas, the protagonists of the *Mahabharata*.

Troops of minor deities

There exist many troops of minor gods who had their counterparts in the Vedas, or who are descendants of a single older god, or of a sage or Prajapati. A number of these are classed as Ganadevatas; they are attendant upon Shiva and live on Mount Kailasa, where they are commanded by Ganesa. The Ganadevatas include the Adityas (that is their late, minor form, representing the twelve annual phases of the sun); the Visvadevas, who are concerned with funeral offerings; the Vasus, who personify various natural phenomena and are attendants in Indra's heaven (they were reborn as Ganga's children, Bhishma being the youngest); the Sadhyas, the twelve sons of Dharma, who personify Vedic rites and prayers; and the forty-nine Rudras or Maruts, storm deities and children of Diti.

Other groups, which are sometimes said to be all manifestations of Vishnu, include the 88,000 Siddhas, holy beings of great occult power who inhabit the middle regions between earth and heaven; the Angirasas, descendants of the sage or Prajapati Angiras and of Agni, who personify light, fire and celestial phenomena and are ancient rivals of the Adityas; the Atharvans, similar to the Angirasas and specially connected with the Atharva Veda; the Bhrigus, 'roasters', descendants of Bhrigu, who are aerial deities connected with Agni, producing the fire, nourishing it, and making chariots; the Ribhus, descendants of Angiras and among the first men to obtain immortality through good works—they may personify the rays of the sun, are said to support the sky, and continue to be artisans as they were in the Vedas.

Demi-gods and rishis

Many figures in Indian mythology occupy an intermediate position between gods and mortals. Such are the Prajapatis, the ten beings created by Manu or by Brahma in order to carry out the detailed creation of the world; the Manus or world teachers; the Pitris or Manes, souls of the dead; and the rishis, or sages, whose spiritual prowess often gives them powers exceeding those of the gods, and whose very bones are said to have occult power, for late myths claim that Indra's thunderbolt owes its strength to being made from a rishi's bones. Some of the Prajapatis are better known as rishis.

The most important of the Prajapatis are Marichi, Atri, Angiras, Pulastya, Daksha, also known as Prachetas, Vasishta, Bhrigu and Narada. Marichi is father of the sun and founder of the solar dynasty, of which Rama was a scion. Atri is the founder of the lunar dynasty, to which Pandavas and Kauravas belonged. Pulastya is the father of Kubera and of Ravana and Kumbhakarna. Daksha is the ancestor of numerous deities and demons, for a number of his sixty daughters, including Diti, Kadru and Vinata, were married to Kasyapa; others were married to Chandra;

and one to Shiva, with whom he conducted a feud. Vasishta was the pupil of Agni, and passed on Agni's instruction in the twofold knowledge of Brahma to Vyasa. Bhrigu is famed for his learning, for he was the pupil of Varuna; he cursed Agni to consume everything, and supported Daksha in his feud with Shiva, whom he cursed to be worshipped as the lingam before going on to declare Vishnu to be the greatest of the gods. Narada is the son of Sarasvati, and therefore a gifted speaker and musician. His sense of humour led him to provoke many quarrels among the gods, for he is amused by misunderstandings and bored if things are too quiet. He caused Ravana to be captured by Bali by ingratiating himself with the demon king; but he also provokes disputes in heaven, acting on behalf of the demons out of mischief. A friend of Krishna, he was unable to avail himself of Krishna's offer of any one of his sixteen thousand and eight wives who was lonely; for when he went to visit their palaces to make his choice he found Krishna to be simultaneously with every single one of them.

The Manus are the world teachers who preside over the Manwantaras, or fourteen divisions of each Kalpa, and according to the Laws of Manu execute Brahma's re-creation at the beginning of each age by creating in turn deities, demons, spirits, nymphs and Pitris.

The Pitris or Manes are the souls of the dead forefathers. They are divided into innumerable classes according to their existence in life and also according to the length of time they have lived in Yama's abode. They gradually rise in the hierarchy until they are almost indistinguishable from gods as a result of the offerings made on their behalf by their descendants. The greatest misfortune is to be without a son, for without his offerings the dead man's soul is barred from the kingdom of the Pitris. The first Pitris are sometimes said to have been the sons of the gods; the gods offended Brahma by not worshipping him and were cursed by him to become fools; when they repented Brahma told them to seek instruction from their own sons and to address them humbly as Fathers or Pitris. The Prajapatis are sometimes referred to as the Pitris. Despite the general acceptance of the doctrine of reincarnation, belief in the Pitris has somehow survived.

The seven great rishis (Saptarshis) are Kasyapa, Atri, Vasishta, Visvamitra, Gautama, Jamadagni and Bharadwaja. Collectively they form the constellation of the Great Bear and were married to seven virtuous ladies. As already related, however, the daughter of Daksha, Swaha, disguised herself as six of them in order to seduce Agni. These encounters were seen by other gods, who began to spread slanders against the innocent rishis' wives. But the rishis believed the stories and drove away all the wives except Vasishta's, who was not suspected; she became the small star near the Great Bear, while the other six became the Pleiades (Krittikas) and nursed the son, Karttikeya, which Agni had fathered.

Kasyapa was married to thirteen of Daksha's daughters and had a huge progeny, which included the Adityas, the Daityas and Danavas, the Nagas and Garuda. Atri is more generally known as a Prajapati. Vasishta figures in the *Ramayana* as the priest of Rama's father Dasaratha and as the possessor of Nandini, the cow of plenty; in the *Mahabharata* and elsewhere emphasis is placed on his great rivalry with Visvamitra, who caused Vasishta's hundred sons to be devoured by a rakshasa and be reborn as outcastes for seven hundred births. Vasishta tried to kill himself but could not. Visvamitra was originally a Kshatriya king. One day he visited Vasishta in his hermitage and was surprised at the hermit's wealth; on discovering that the wealth was produced by Nandini, Visvamitra tried to seize the cow, but was overcome by Vasishta's occult powers. Seeing that a Brahmin was more powerful than a Kshatriya, Visvamitra determined to become a Brahmin, and by dint of the most awesome austerities forced Brahma to grant him this impossible boon. But Vasishta refused to recognise his new status and they became enemies. Gautama was Indra's preceptor; we have already seen how Indra seduced Gautama's wife Ahalya and was cursed for it. Gautama was tricked by the other six rishis

into striking Ganesa in the form of a cow and thus committing a crime which weakened his powers. Jamadagni, as we have seen, was the champion of Brahmins and father of Parasurama. Bharadwaja became a great friend of Rama; his son was Drona, who taught the military arts to the Pandava and Kaurava princes.

Beside the seven principal rishis there were many other sages, who play a great part in the epics, particularly the *Ramayana*. Chief among these was Agastya, who controlled the rakshasas in southern India and who sheltered Rama, Sita and Lakshmana in their exile. Vyasa was not only author of the *Mahabharata* but also ancestor of both princely houses in the epic struggle.

The Mahabharata

Many of the characters in the *Mahabharata* are of divine origin. Others attained the status of demi-god by their valour and were received as heroes in Indra's heaven. Others again were the bearers of divine weapons and so the agents of the gods. These, combined with the many rishis and demons who take part in the epic story, make the *Mahabharata* a great storehouse of myth. Furthermore

The performance of austerities was the way to gain the favour of the gods. Arjuna's was of such power that Shiva himself went to discover what was shaking the heavens. Detail from the rock carving at Mahabalipuram.

the epic took form over many centuries and therefore contains elements of Vedic mythology and, from later belief, an equal admixture of Vishnuism and Sivaism. The *Mahabharata* illustrates well both the conservatism of Indian thought and its seeming confusion. For example, while the heroes of the epic are considered as divine avatars surrounded by myth, or are miraculously fathered by gods, those of the gods who are direct protagonists, such as Krishna, seem to be no more powerful than the heroes, or at any rate the demi-gods, and intervene on behalf of their protégés as special warriors rather than as divine beings with invincible powers.

The epic opens with an explanation of its narrator's lineage. Vyasa was the son of the nymph Satyavati, who was seduced by the rishi Parasara. The sage, in gratitude for her favours, relieved her of the fishy smell which she had inherited from her mother, an Apsara cursed to turn into a fish, and also restored her virginity.

Vyasa was brought up secretly and in time Satyavati was seen by King Santanu, who fell in love with her. Santanu was formerly married to Ganga, who had become a mortal woman in order to bear the Vasus. She had killed all her children at birth except Bhishma, who was Santanu's heir apparent, and had then abandoned her husband. The king was now old, but when he saw Satyavati he could not rest until he had married her. Satyavati's father, however, would only consent to the match on condition that Satyavati's children should succeed to the throne. Bhishma, seeing the anguish of his father, renounced his claim, and swore that he would never marry and never father any children.

Santanu and Satyavati were therefore married, and in due course they had two sons. But the aged Santanu died before these sons reached their twentieth year. Chitrangada, the eldest, succeeded to the throne; but he had not reigned long before he embarked on rash military adventures, which led to his death at the hand of a Gandharva king also called Chitrangada. The second son, Vichitravirya, then ascended the throne and was married to Ambika and Ambalika, two girls found for him by Bhishma. But Vichitravirya suffered from consumption and soon died, leaving no heirs.

A time-honoured custom existed whereby if a man died childless it was incumbent on his nearest male relative to father a child on his widow, the child being considered that of the dead man; for, as mentioned earlier, without a son a man could not be admitted to the abode of the Pitris. Satyavati appealed to Bhishma to perform this office but he was bound to refuse, for he had sworn never to have children. Satyavati then thought of her firstborn, Vyasa, and summoned him to the palace. Vyasa agreed, so Satyavati tactfully prepared the widows to expect their husband's half-brother to visit them that night. Both expected to see the handsome Bhishma, and were horrified when they beheld instead the wild appearance and matted

Krishna demonstrates to the assembled princes how the fish target must be struck by aiming an arrow at its reflection in the cauldron. Arjuna steps forward to try his skill. Jaipur painting, eighteenth century.

hair of the hermit Vyasa. In her fright Ambika closed her eyes, and the son she conceived, Dhritarashtra, was born blind; Ambalika's reaction was to turn pale at the sight of Vyasa and her son was therefore born pale ('Pandu'). As neither of these attempts was really successful, Satyavati insisted that Ambika try again. But Ambika rebelled and substituted her maid; the third resultant son was Vidura, who was in fact an incarnation of Dharma.

The three sons were brought up by Bhishma, who acted as regent during their minority. When it was time for Pandu to assume the reins of office he married two women. The first was Kunti or Pritha, who was the daughter of a nymph and a Brahmin and sister of Vasudeva, father of Krishna. By virtue of a boon she had received from the sage Durvasas, Kunti was able to have five children by any god she chose. She had already availed herself of this boon once, and by worshipping Surya had received a son from him, Karna; however, she concealed his birth, casting him away on the River Aswa, whence he was passed to the Jumna (Yami) and so to the Ganges (Ganga). Ganga saw to it that he was found and looked after by Radha and her husband Adhiratha, who was to become Dhritarashtra's charioteer. Pandu's second wife was Madri, sister of the king of Madras.

But Pandu had committed the sin of Brahminicide:
one day while hunting he had mistaken a Brahmin rishi
and his wife for a pair of deer and had killed them. With
his dying breath the rishi had cursed him to be unable to
consort with his wives, prophesying that he would die
in the arms of one of them. Kunti, however, had recourse
to Durvasas' boon and bore three more children. By worshipping Dharma she had Yudhisthira; by Vayu she had
Bhima; and by Indra she had Arjuna. She allowed Madri to
make use of the fifth part of her boon; Madri worshipped
the Aswins and bore twins, Nakula and Sahadeva, who
were thus grandsons of Surya. One day, however, Pandu
was walking in the forest with Madri. The beauties of the
scene intoxicated him and he embraced his wife, ignoring
the Rishi's curse. No sooner had he done so than he fell to
the ground, dead.

The blind Dhritarashtra now acted as regent for his
brother's five sons, known as the Pandavas. They and his
own hundred sons, known as Kauravas from Kuru, the
common ancestor of both branches of the family, were
brought up together under the direction of Bhishma. As
guardian of the Pandavas, Dhritarashtra showed them
great kindness, but his sons, and particularly the eldest,
Duryodhana, soon showed jealousy of their cousins, especially after Dhritarashtra formally nominated Yudhisthira
as the heir apparent. As their education proceeded, the
rivalry between Pandavas and Kauravas became more pronounced. A Brahmin named Drona appeared at the court
and, after demonstrating his great skills, was appointed as
the boys' military instructor. Arjuna soon demonstrated
his talent in the use of weapons.

A tournament was held to mark the end of their education, and the Pandavas, particularly Arjuna, displayed
superior skill. This was followed by single combat with
clubs between Duryodhana and Bhima; but Drona had to
separate them, because the fight became too serious. One of
the spectators now stepped forward and challenged Arjuna
to single combat. This was Karna, whom Kunti alone knew
to be her son by Surya. He was a Kshatriya, but he had
disguised himself as a Brahmin and learned the military
arts from Parasurama, the avatar of Vishnu whose purpose was to humble the Kshatriyas. On discovering the
deception Parasurama cursed Karna to ultimate defeat
and death through wrong use of a weapon. As we have
seen, Karna's foster-father was a charioteer, so his challenge to Arjuna was at first rejected, for princes could
fight only princes. But Duryodhana, enraged at Arjuna's
public success, was determined to give Karna the chance
of defeating a Pandava. He therefore persuaded Dhritarashtra to confer on Karna the kingdom of Anga. Karna's
charioteer father then came forward to congratulate his
son, who publicly acknowledged and embraced him. Bhima
thereupon insulted Karna regarding his low lineage and
as Karna instinctively knew that he was the son of the
god Surya he was particularly wrathful. General fighting

now began, and the assembly broke up in disorder, but
not before Duryodhana came to Karna's defence, pointing
out that the lineage of heroes is always unknown (that
they may be gods and that their actions make them noble),
and challenging anyone to fight Karna.

The princes' instruction was now complete, and Drona
was entitled to claim some service from them as his fee.
Because of an old dispute with Drupada, King of the Pan-
chalas, who once had slighted him, Drona asked his pupils
to bring him Drupada in chains. The Kauravas failed to
defeat Drupada but, with the support of his brothers,
Arjuna captured him. Drona, triumphant, demanded half
his kingdom as the price of his release, and Drupada was
forced to agree. He returned home, filled with hatred of
Drona—but with admiration for his captor. He besought
from Brahma, and was granted, a son who would kill
Drona and a daughter who would marry Arjuna. These
were Dhrishtadyumna and Draupadi.

Meanwhile rivalry between the Pandavas and the Kauravas continued, and was brought to a head when Yudhisthira came of age to succeed to the throne of Hastinapur.
Duryodhana, always Dhritarashtra's favourite, persuaded
his father to allow him to succeed, and to agree to a plot to
kill the Pandavas by setting fire to their house. But the
Pandavas were warned in time by their uncle Vidura (third
son of Vyasa and incarnation of Dharma), and escaped to
the forest with their mother, Kunti, where they lived in
the guise of Brahmins. Duryodhana believed them to
have perished.

One day while in the forest the Pandavas heard that an
archery contest was to be held for the hand of Draupadi.
Drupada, her father, believed the story that Arjuna had
perished with the other Pandavas, but still wished her to
marry a good archer. The Pandavas decided to attend the
great assembly, and witnessed hundreds of princes from
near and far, including Duryodhana, submit themselves
to the test, which was to shoot five arrows through a
ring. One after the other the princes came forward, and
one after the other they failed. Finally Karna, now King
of Anga, stepped forward, and seemed fated to win; but
Draupadi intervened, saying that she would never marry
the son of a charioteer. Once again Karna could not prove
what he knew, that he was really the son of Surya, and
had to retire.

Now, to the astonishment of all, an unkempt Brahmin
hermit stepped from among the spectators and without
hesitation shot five arrows in succession through the ring.
Draupadi and her father acknowledged him the victor,
but the humiliated princes rebelled and, as at the tournament, the assembly broke up in confusion. The victorious
hermit now revealed his true identity, to the great delight
of Drupada; and the other Pandavas, also throwing off
their disguises, joined in the scuffle and put the angry
princes to flight.

Arjuna then returned to his mother in the forest and

announced to her that he had won a great prize; but before learning what is was, Kunti told him that he must share it with his brothers. Arjuna could not disobey his mother's command, nor could she withdraw it, so Draupadi became the shared wife of the five brothers and it was arranged that she should spend two days with each in turn.

In the mêlée at Drupada's court Karna and Duryodhana had recognised Arjuna and Bhima, and on their return home reported their discovery. Karna wished to dispose of the Pandavas in open warfare, while Duryodhana advocated a plot. But Drona rejected both plans and suggested a compromise: that the rights of the Pandavas should be partially acknowledged and the kingdom divided into two. Drona's advice was taken, and the Pandavas accepted the invitation to return home. Peace seemed re-established.

In their part of the kingdom, the Pandavas built a new

The battle of Kurukshetra, the great confrontation of good and evil which is the central event of the Mahabharata *and the epic clash for which the gods and the heroes whom they produced on earth had long been preparing, and to which dharma inexorably led them. Chamba wall hanging, eighteenth century.*

city, Indraprastha, and a marvellous palace, where the crystal floors were as clear as water, and invited the Kauravas to see it. Duryodhana, being shown round the palace, mistook a pool for a crystal floor and fell into the water. Draupadi laughed, and in his humiliation Duryodhana returned home to plot anew the destruction of the Pandavas and Draupadi. His anger was only heightened by Yudhisthira's performance of the horse-sacrifice, a symbol of universal power.

Duryodhana challenged Yudhisthira to a gambling match, and when this was accepted enlisted the help of his uncle Sakuni, a skilled cheater at dice. Yudhisthira lost steadily, and was provoked by Duryodhana's jeers to stake all. He lost the kingdom of the Pandavas, all his personal possessions, and finally himself, his brothers and Draupadi. Duryodhana now called upon his brother Dussasana to humiliate Draupadi in front of the assembled court. Calling her his slave, Dussasana pulled her by the hair and began to undress her. Draupadi called upon the gods to save her and in her fury looked like the goddess Durga; she cried out that she would not bind her hair up until it was anointed with the blood of Duryodhana and Dussasana. At this moment King Dhritarashtra heard the howl of a jackal and the braying of an ass and knew that the Kauravas were doomed. In his fear he asked Draupadi's mercy and offered to grant her any request. She demanded and was granted freedom for herself and her husbands.

But Duryodhana, scoffing at his father's scruples and fearful of the Pandavas at liberty, made a last challenge, again to be decided by dice. This time the loser was to retire to the forest with his people for twelve years and pass the thirteenth year unrecognised in a city; if he should be recognised in the thirteenth year he would have to pass another twelve years in the forest. Yudhisthira, refusing to owe his freedom to the generosity of a Kaurava, accepted the challenge—and again lost.

During the thirteen years of exile in the forest the Pandavas had many adventures, during which they formed alliances and made friends with Krishna, whose sister married Arjuna. They successfully passed the last of their thirteen years' exile in a city without being recognised, and then sent Krishna as their envoy to Duryodhana, re-

questing peace and a division of the kingdom. Duryodhana, who had also been making alliances and strengthening his armies, took the peace request as a sign of weakness and refused to make any concession at all. He even attacked Krishna, who fought the Kauravas and escaped.

War was declared. Krishna was claimed as an ally by both sides, as he was related to both. He offered the opponents the choice of himself unarmed or a large army. Arjuna chose his brother-in-law unarmed and Duryodhana chose the army. Meanwhile Kunti attempted to stop her oldest son, Karna, from fighting on the side of Duryodhana against her five other sons, the Pandavas. But Karna declared that the news of his true parentage had come too late, and that he owed allegiance to Duryodhana in gratitude for his worldly advancement and his kingdom; but he promised that he would only fight Arjuna. The armies met on the field of Kurukshetra.

Doubts about the war existed on both sides. Bhishma and Drona, together with Karna, fought on the side of Duryodhana and Dhritarashtra because, according to their duty, the laws of dharma, they owed him allegiance,

Bhishma, dying from the hundreds of arrows loosed by Arjuna, discourses to Yudhisthira on the duties of kings. Rajput painting, late seventeenth century.

though they recognised that his cause was unjust. On the other side Arjuna, reflecting on what was to come, quailed at the prospect of fighting his guardian and his tutor and shedding the blood of hundreds unknown. But Krishna, in the celebrated poem known as the *Bhagavad Gita*, gradually revealed his true identity as an incarnation of the Lord Vishnu, and explained to him the necessity to follow dharma. It is the duty of the soldier simply to fight, and personal feelings do not enter into it.

The Pandava forces were commanded by Dhrishtadyumna, Draupadi's brother, who was destined to kill Drona. The Kaurava forces were commanded by Bhishma, son of Ganga but cursed to be a mortal. Battle began but was inconclusive, for Bhishma was invincible. Yudhisthira and the Pandavas therefore visited the Kaurava camp and went to Bhishma, knowing that before the battle he had expressed sympathy for their cause, and asked him how they could overcome him. Bhishma revealed that he could not be overcome by god, man or beast and refused to fight a woman or a eunuch, but he hinted that he might allow himself to be challenged by Arjuna or Krishna. Krishna had taken a vow not to fight, and so restricted himself to acting as Arjuna's charioteer; the task of killing Bhishma therefore fell to Arjuna. While a eunuch challenged Bhishma in the field of battle and the great hero laughed, Arjuna shot a flight of arrows which brought him down. He was taken back to the camp of the Pandavas where, after predicting their victory and instructing Yudhisthira at great length in the art of government, he died of his wounds.

Drona then took over command of the Kaurava forces and fought for six days more. On the fifth day he killed Drupada, his old enemy. On the sixth day the Pandavas spread the rumour that Drona's son Aswathaman was dead. Aswathaman was the source of Drona's weakness; it had been prophesied that no harm would come to him so long as Drona lived. Drona would not believe the rumours at first, though one after another the Pandavas shouted that Aswathaman was dead. Drona said that he would believe the story only from the lips of Yudhisthira, who as the son of Dharma was incapable of telling a lie. Ac-

cordingly Bhima killed an elephant called Aswathaman and Yudhisthira, when asked by Drona if Aswathaman was dead, was able to say 'Yes', only adding inaudibly that he meant Aswathaman the elephant. At this Drona gave up the struggle and Dhrishtadyumna, Draupadi's brother, fulfilled his destiny by killing him.

Karna then became the third general of the Kaurava forces. As the son of Surya, he was capable of killing all the Pandavas, but he remembered his promise made to his mother and restrained himself. On the second day Arjuna came within range of Karna and the battle resolved itself into single combat between the two heroes. Both were armed with divine weapons. Arjuna had gone to the Himalayas as a supplicant and had returned with weapons from Indra, Varuna, Yama, Kubera and Shiva. Karna had been born with arms and armour, and though he had lost the armour to Indra, he had received in exchange a javelin charged with certain death for whomever it struck. Weapons of all sorts, like snakes and like birds, came whistling through the air from both directions but the contestants somehow withstood the onslaught. Finally Karna brought out Indra's javelin and hurled it at Arjuna. But he forgot that Indra was Arjuna's father and that the weapon had become possessed by a snake once injured by Arjuna. Driven by the snake's hatred, the javelin was therefore impelled at twice the speed intended by Karna, and missed Arjuna's throat. In fact it caught his diadem, for Krishna had meanwhile weighed down Arjuna's chariot. Karna now realised that the prophecy concerning his own death was being fulfilled—that he would die through the wrong use of a weapon. As he lost heart, his chariot began to sink into the earth, which opened to swallow it up. In a last spasm of hope, Karna jumped from the chariot and appealed to Arjuna in the name of honour and the rules of chivalry which forbid a warrior mounted on a chariot to attack another on foot. Arjuna retorted that honour had meant little to him when Draupadi was insulted, and killed Karna on the spot. At the death of his son Surya turned pale, and with the dimming of the sun all nature was grieved.

Despite Karna's death and the fear of the Kauravas, Duryodhana refused to concede defeat and, availing himself of a charm given him by demons which allowed him to remain under water, he fled to hide himself at the bottom of a lake. The Kaurava forces were meanwhile being killed one by one. Their new general was killed by Yudhisthira. Sakuni, the gambler, was killed by the youngest Pandava, Sahadeva, and those that remained of Duryodhana's ninety-nine brothers were killed by Bhima. Only four Kauravas now remained: Drona's son Aswathaman, Krita, Kritavarman, and Duryodhana.

Eventually Yudhisthira discovered Duryodhana's hiding place. But Duryodhana refused to emerge from the lake, saying that Yudhisthira might have his kingdom, for he himself wished to retire to meditate. As Yudhisthira steadfastly refused to accept anything from him not won in battle, Duryodhana agreed to fight in single combat with each of the Pandavas in turn. He fought first with Bhima, with maces as the weapons and Balarama acting as his second. After a fierce struggle, Bhima laid him low by smashing his thigh, the same thigh on which he had forced Draupadi to sit, thus insulting her. Bhima danced round the stricken Duryodhana, kicking him on the head, and thus incurring Yudhisthira's wrath, for this was an infringement of the rules of chivalry. Yudhisthira even felt it necessary to appeal to Duryodhana as their king and to offer to slay Bhima in punishment. The incident provoked a dispute between Balarama, who supported the Kauravas, and Krishna, who supported the Pandavas. Balarama pointed out that Bhima broke the laws of combat not only by kicking Duryodhana's head, but also by earlier striking him below the belt. Krishna replied that Duryodhana cheated at the game of dice, and that Bhima had vowed to smash Duryodhana's thigh.

Though Balarama was persuaded not to take revenge, Duryodhana, still alive, planned further treachery. He gave permission to Aswathaman, Drona's son, to avenge his father's death by killing the Pandavas while they were asleep. Aswathaman, together with Krita and Kritavarman, set off for the Pandava camp that night. They were intercepted by a fearsome figure, whom they fought until they realised that it was the god Shiva. But Aswathaman propitiated the god by lighting a sacrificial fire and casting himself on it. Shiva thus entered the body of Aswathaman, who proceeded to the Pandava camp, sought out and slew his father's killer, Dhrishtadyumna, and then all the other men in the camp, including Draupadi's five sons, one by each of her husbands. He cut off their heads, believing them to be the Pandavas themselves, and brought them to Duryodhana. But the Pandavas had been sleeping in the Kaurava camp that night and so escaped, and Duryodhana, horrified, died at the sight of their heads.

The Pandavas returned to Hastinapur and were reconciled with Dhritarashtra. Yudhisthira ascended the throne, performed the horse-sacrifice and reigned wisely and peacefully. But Dhritarashtra could not forget the loss of his sons and quarrelled constantly with Bhima, the slayer of his favourite. One day he sent for Bhima, pretending at last a reconciliation. But Krishna suspected his intentions and placed in iron statue before the blind king; Dhritarashtra made as if to embrace the figure before him and then crushed it in his arms. Eventually Dhritarashtra and his wife Gandhari, together with Kunti, retired into the forest where, two years later, they died in a forest fire.

The Pandavas were stricken with remorse at this disaster, and Yudhisthira renounced the throne. They set out, with Draupadi, on the long journey to Mount Meru, in the Himalayas. They were, in other words, making a pilgrimage towards death, for Indra's heaven is on Mount Meru. Their only companion was a dog, which followed them from Hastinapur. One by one the Pandavas died by the wayside, and each death was explained by Yudhisthira as the punishment for some weakness. Draupadi died first, because she loved Arjuna too much. Sahadeva died next, because he was too proud. The next victim was Nakula, who was too vain of his appearance. Arjuna fell after making the unfulfilled boast that he could destroy all his enemies in one day. Lastly Bhima fell, and as he lay dying Yudhisthira explained to him that his death was a punishment for the hatred he felt for his foes, which exceeded the needs of dharma or chivalric duty.

Yudhisthira alone reached the gates of Indra's heaven. His only companion now was the dog, which had followed him all the way from Hastinapur. Indra greeted the hero and bade him enter. But Yudhisthira refused to enter before being assured that heaven had a place for his brothers and Draupadi, the faithful wife. Indra told him that their spirits were already there. Yudhisthira still hesitated; he said he would not enter unless his dog could come too. Indra refused, declaring that dogs had no place in heaven. Yudhisthira insisted that his dog must be rewarded, and that while the faithful creature lived he would never abandon him. Thereupon the dog underwent a transformation and stood revealed as Dharma, the god of moral and religious duty and Yudhisthira's father. (Dharma was also identified with Yama, and Yama sends his watchdogs to fetch the dead.) Yudhisthira now passed beyond the gates of heaven, but was horrified not only to see no sign of his brothers and his wife—but Duryodhana installed on a throne, surrounded by all the Kauravas. Again he turned away, not wishing to remain in the same place as his enemies.

He was conducted to hell, where he witnessed all sorts of terrors, where the leaves were like weapons and the path covered with knives, where darkness prevailed and he stumbled over pools of blood and mutilated corpses upon which fed hideous birds of prey. He witnessed all the many hells and the tortures meted out in them, the smell of burning flesh and the screams of the damned. But among those screams he distinguished the voices of his brothers and his wife, and he resolved to stay and comfort them. As he voiced his decision, however, the whole scene was revealed to be the product of maya, or illusion, designed to test him.

Yudhisthira was now led to the Ganges to bathe and cast off his mortal body. He became an immortal and was welcomed to Swarga, Indra's celestial city, where he was joined by Krishna, his brothers and Draupadi. The true upholders of dharma on both sides of the struggle were present: Dhritarashtra, who was now king of the Gandharvas; Karna, son of Surya; Pandu and Kunti, father and mother of the Pandavas; Bhishma, son of Ganga, who had joined his seven brothers the Vasus, around Indra's throne; and Drona. They were surrounded by all the warriors who fell in battle and earned happiness for ever in Indra's heaven by virtue of their kind words and deeds and by patient endurance of suffering.

Bodhisattva Maitreya. Just as Gautama Buddha passed through over five hundred lives as a Bodhisattva (one who is irrevocably on the path to becoming a Buddha), so the next Buddha, Maitreya, who will be born five thousand years after the passing of Gautama, already exists as a Bodhisattva and was present when Gautama first turned the Wheel of the Law. Nepalese bronze, thirteenth century.

Queen Mahamaya, in her forty-fifth year, dreaming of a white elephant entering her womb, bearing a white lotus in his trunk. Sixty-four Brahmins, called by Suddhodana to interpret the dream, declared that it meant she had conceived a male child. Gandhara style relief, second century A.D.

Right: Manjusri, the Buddhist god of wisdom and grammatical knowledge. His sword is the symbol of enlightenment. Tibetan gilded bronze, seventeenth century. Victoria and Albert Museum

BUDDHIST MYTHOLOGY

Just as the teaching of Buddhism is a development of Upanishadic philosophy, so the mythology which grew up about Buddhism drew upon the traditions of the land in which the doctrine was first taught. It sought both to prove the historic Buddha's divine origin and to set him in the pattern of previous incarnations familiar to Indian believers and interesting enough to compete with the existing pantheon. As we have seen, Buddhism in turn provoked in early Hinduism a clarification of doctrine and further complication of the mythology.

Buddha's previous lives

Many stories of Buddha's previous lives are related in the collection of stories called the *Jatakas*, which show how he gradually acquired greater strength and moral stature as his soul passed from one incarnation to the other.

We first see him as the young Brahmin Megha, who while visiting the city of Dipavati spoke to a young girl carrying seven lotus flowers. He asked her what they were for and she replied that she wished to honour with them Lord Dipankara; that she had bought five of them for five hundred coins and was given the other two by a friend. Megha was interested in her description of Dipankara for he too wished to attain enlightenment, and offered her five hundred coins for the five lotus blooms. She accepted them only on condition that he would marry her. After seeing the glory of Dipankara, the Buddha of the age before ours, and hearing his sermons, Megha was strengthened in his resolve one day himself to become a Bodhisattva. His calling was predicted by Dipankara.

In one of Bodhisattva's lives he was a wise and holy hare. One day, while fasting, the hare thought to himself that if anyone were to come begging he would have no food to give him, and so he decided that should a beggar come he would give him his own flesh to eat. As the hare was meditating thus, Sakra's throne grew hot, and Sakra (Indra), curious to know what momentous spiritual event was taking place on earth, discovered the hare and decided to test his resolve. Accordingly Sakra took the form of a beggar and visited the hare, who without hesitation invited the beggar to make a fire and then, having shaken free the vermin in his coat so as not to harm them, threw himself into the fire. But Sakra now froze the flames and told the hare that he had only been testing him. In order to commemorate his self-sacrifice, the god squeezed a mountain and, drawing forth its juice, painted an image of a hare on the moon.

In another life Bodhisattva was Chadanta, a white elephant with six tusks who had two wives. One of the wives, who was jealous of the other, prayed to be reborn as a human princess. When she was grown up she was married to the King of Benares, and asked him to call together all the huntsmen of his kingdom. When he had done so she instructed them to hunt down an elephant with six tusks and bring her back the tusks. One of the huntsmen, Sonuttara, captured Chadanta in a pit and wounded him with arrows. Chadanta asked the huntsman why he wanted to kill him and was told about the queen of Benares. Now he understood the meaning of his fate and submitted to it. He helped Sonuttara to climb up to the root of his tusks, but the huntsman found that they were too hard to cut. So Chadanta took the saw in his trunk and himself cut off the tusks. He then collapsed in a pool of his own blood and died. On hearing the story the queen also died.

Bodhisattva in one of his many incarnations as a priest was a member of the household of King Yasapani of Benares. He aroused the enmity of the corrupt Kalaka, for he had given a fair judgment on a case where Kalaka had given unfair judgment. Kalaka aroused the fears of the king at Bodhisattva's popularity, and suggested that he should ask him to do something impossible—and then put him to death for not doing it. Yasapani therefore asked Bodhisattva to construct a pleasure garden in a single day.

That night, as Bodhisattva lay awake wondering what to do, Sakra appeared before him and assured him that the garden would be ready by the morning. Next day Sakra's promise was seen to be fulfilled, and so it was with the subsequent tests which the alarmed Yapasani set. Sakra created in turn a lake containing the seven precious stones, a palace to go with the lake, and a jewel to match the splendour of the palace. Finally Yasapani was convinced of Bodhisattva's divine support and adopted him as his friend. Kalaka was put to death.

In another life Bodhisattva was the son of a rich king, Maharatha, and was called Mahasattva. One day he and his two brothers were walking in the forest and came across a tigress with her cubs. The tigress was emaciated and too weak to stand up. At last Mahasattva began to reflect on the futility of physical existence and determined to sacrifice his own life so as to feed the tigress. He lay down before her, declaring that he wished to obtain release and enlightenment for the benefit of the world. But the tigress was too weak to kill him; so Mahasattva slit his throat, and the tigress, seeing the blood, began to eat.

Similarly, in one of his lives as an ascetic, he sacrificed his own life, this time in order to preach the virtue of patience. One day a king who had been an enemy of Bodhisattva in previous lives came to disport himself with his wives in the forest where the hermit lived. His wives, bored when the king fell asleep, wandered into Bodhisattva's hermitage, where many came to hear his words, including the gods. They too were entranced with his teaching, and hardly heard the king when he entered the hermitage looking for them. The king began to storm against them and the hermit, but Bodhisattva advised him to be patient. The king retorted that he would teach the hermit to practise what he preached, and drew his sword. Bodhisattva was cut to pieces, enduring his pain without complaint.

Buddha's birth

Mahamaya, the wife of King Suddhodana of Kapilavastu, dreamt one night of a white elephant entering her womb. She became pregnant and her womb became transparent like a crystal casket. She felt an urge to withdraw for meditation to the forest and there, while beneath a sal tree, she gave birth—from her side. The child was born in full awareness and looking like the young sun; he leapt on to the ground, and where he touched it there sprang up a lotus. He looked to the four cardinal points, to the four half points, above and below, and saw deities and men acknowledging his superiority. He made seven steps northwards, a lotus appearing at each footfall. His birth was greeted by Asita, a sage from the Himalayas, who likened him to Skanda, son of Agni. Astrologers made the prediction that either he would be a great emperor or he would renounce life and become a Buddha. He was named Siddhartha at a great ceremony attended by eighty thousand relatives and one hundred and eight Brahmins, and was given a hundred godmothers. Mahamaya, filled with joy, died two days after his birth. Her sister Prajapati, another of Suddhodana's wives, took charge of the infant.

Boyhood

Siddhartha was carefully educated for what his father hoped would be his destiny as a great king. He was a proficient pupil, but not interested in military exercises. His childhood companions were his cousin Devadatta and his half-brother Ananda. Ananda became his great friend but Devadatta was a rival, for the two boys were of opposed natures.

Devadatta never forgave Siddhartha for once nursing back to health a bird which he had shot for pleasure and for gaining the approval of the Elders for his action.

All through his childhood, Suddhodana took care to protect his son from exposure to the outside world for, remembering the astrologers' prediction at the child's birth, he wished above all to prevent him from renouncing life. He built him three palaces, barring them to the outside world and its cares.

Marriage

When Siddhartha came of age the bride chosen for him was Yasodhara, daughter of Dandapani. But Dandapani insisted that he show military competence before he would grant his daughter's hand, and so Siddhartha had to compete in a tournament against Devadatta and Sundarnand. But the first event of the day was no part of the formal tournament. Devadatta, on his arrival in the arena, killed a white elephant. The next arrival was Sundarnand who, discovering who had killed the elephant, threw it outside the city gate. Siddhartha then arrived, lifted the elephant with his toe and threw it two miles, over seven walls and seven moats. The tournament, composed of physical and intellectual tests, now began. Siddhartha won in the horse race, the chariot race, in music, recitation, mathematics and elocution. He and Devadatta tied in archery, then in wrestling; at last, in the fencing test, Devadatta won. He expected to be declared winner of the tournament on the basis of this, and so was doubly chagrined when Yasodhara passed him over and gave the garland to Siddhartha, for Yasodhara was his wife in previous lives and had promised to be his wife in all.

According to another version, five hundred princesses were assembled so that Siddhartha could make a choice of bride. His father gave him jewels to distribute among them according to his preferences. Siddhartha gave each one a jewel, and just as he had given out the last one, Yasodhara arrived. Having no more jewels, Siddhartha gave her his signet ring, and this was a sign of their betrothal.

Siddhartha and his young bride led an idyllic life, despite the fact that Suddhodana, becoming more fearful as the years went past that somehow his son would get to know of sickness and death, had confined him to the upper floors of the palace. Suddhodana made sure that they were ever filled with charming and voluptuous women so that Siddhartha could fully indulge all the pleasures of the senses. The Bodhisattva thus led a life of thoughtless pleasure and never dreamt of the outside world, for a necessary preliminary to enlightenment is full knowledge of the senses.

The Four Signs

Before long, however, the Devas decided that it was time for the Bodhisattva to begin his life's work, and so they filled the universe with the thought that it was time to go forth. Siddhartha became conscious of a wish to leave the palace and to see the city and persuaded his father to allow him to go forth accompanied by a charioteer, Chandaka. Suddhodana took elaborate precautions: he had the streets cleaned and decorated and issued orders that no old or sick men should be allowed near the route to be followed. But the Devas had other plans. On Siddhartha's first outing one of them took the form of a feeble broken-down old man and stood by the wayside. Siddhartha was astonished when he saw this figure, for no one had even spoken to him of old age, and he was more surprised when Chandaka, at his insistence, explained that all men were subject to aging. Siddhartha took three more chariot rides into the city, and on each occasion one of the gods stood by the route to teach him the true nature of life—lessons to which his previous ignorance made him especially receptive. Thus he saw in turn a helpless sick man, a dead man being carried on a bier, and a monk, calm and self-controlled. The prince came to learn that all that is born must die; that sickness comes to all; that he himself would one day die; and that renunciation was the path to peace of mind and honour and to salvation both for the man who withdraws from the world and for others. These revelations confirmed Siddhartha in his half-felt instincts, and he formed the idea that he too would withdraw from the grief of the world.

Soon after this, Yasodhara gave birth to a son, Rahula. Each Buddha has to have a son before renouncing the world, and so the birth of Rahula was a sign to Siddhartha that the moment had come for departure. He informed his father of his intention, but Suddhodana was horrified and locked him up in the palace. He lavished everything on his son, increasing the comfort and gaiety of his life. But this did nothing to weaken Siddhartha's resolution. On the night that he decided to make his escape there was great revelry in the palace; the Devas caused all the company to drink too much, and then to fall asleep suddenly in the midst of their pleasures.

Siddhartha alone was awake. He saw with disgust the mass of men and women, lying in immodest postures, their mouths hanging open and their clothes in disarray. He went to the apartments of Yasodhara, and looked for a while on his sleeping wife and son. Then he departed.

The search for enlightenment

The Devas aided Siddhartha in his firm resolve. As he approached the heavy gates of the palace their locks swung

Overleaf left: Buddha sits meditating. After his enlightenment he sat in thought for another four weeks seated under the pipal tree. In the fifth week Mara sent a violent storm, hoping to distract him, but the King of the Nagas, Mucilinda, coiled himself under Buddha and lifted him off the soaking ground. Then he spread his seven heads and made a canopy to keep him dry. Eleventh-century sandstone from Bayon.

Overleaf right: Sakra (Indra) commands the exchange of babies in the wombs of Devananda and Trisala. An illustration from a manuscript of the Kalpasutra, the Jain holy scriptures, of the fifteenth century. Victoria and Albert Museum

Prince Siddhartha goes forth in his chariot (left), and is made aware of the pain and unhappiness suffered by most of mankind. When he achieves enlightenment (right), Buddha's face bears the serenity of utter detach- *ment, while the forces of evil fall in disarray and men and animals look on in wonder. The leaves of the Bo-tree form a garland above Buddha. Gandhara style reliefs, second century* A.D.

open; they had lulled the guards to sleep, and they softened the footfalls of Siddhartha's horse, Kantaka. So he escaped from his father's vigilance, accompanied only by Chandaka. Shortly they reached the River Anoma (illustrious), and here Siddhartha instructed Chandaka to return to the palace. He divested himself of all his jewels, the symbols of his princely estate, cut off his long black hair, and gave them to the faithful charioteer, telling him to take back to Kapilavastu the message that either Siddhartha would extinguish old age and death and would return soon to Kapilavastu, or, lacking the strength, he would go to perdition and never be seen again. Chandaka, tears in his eyes, kissed his master's feet and then Kantaka licked them. Then, leading the horse, the charioteer returned unwillingly to the capital. But before he had gone many paces the faithful horse died. When he returned with Siddhartha's message there was great lamentation in Kapilavastu; but Yasodhara, faithful to her husband, cut off her hair and became a nun.

As Siddhartha continued on his journey in search of truth the Devas once more intervened. One appeared before him as a hunter, and exchanged clothes with him; the other appeared as a barber and shaved his head, so that Siddhartha now looked like a simple monk. After a few days he joined the three hundred pupils of Arara Kalama, a great sage, at Vaisali. He completed his studies with Kalama but still was not satisfied. He then attended the philosophy classes of Rudraka, but this was no better, and Siddhartha decided that knowledge cannot bring enlightenment. He and five other students left Rudraka and began to practise austerities. They continued, under Siddhartha's leadership, for some time and with such ardour that they were all reduced practically to skeletons. But once more

Siddhartha was disappointed, and decided that asceticism was no more the path to enlightenment than knowledge, for it so weakens the body that the physical shell encumbers the spirit. Siddhartha abandoned his five disciples, much to their scorn, and went to bathe in a river. There, in his weakness, he nearly drowned, but was saved by a Deva living in a tree, who stretched out his jewelled arm to save him. Then Siddhartha sought his first meal. The dish from which he ate was seized by a Naga and taken to the nether regions, but was afterwards snatched up to heaven by Sakra (Indra), taking the form of Garuda.

Siddhartha then spent seven fruitless years in search of enlightenment. Almost daily Suddhodana sent messengers to him imploring him to return, but Siddhartha steadfastly refused to come home until he had found enlightenment.

Enlightenment

Despite his refusals to go back to his home Siddhartha began to wonder whether after all enlightenment was attainable, or whether he had undergone seven years of privation for nothing. He was 35 years old. At length he passed through the country of Magadha, and decided that he would stake all in a last attempt. Near the town of Uruvela he seated himself in the lotus posture beneath a pipal tree born on the same day as himself, determined not to rise until he had achieved enlightenment.

As he settled himself for the great spiritual discovery the gods rejoiced in heaven and birds soared overhead in joyful anticipation. But the evil spirits were troubled, and their chief, Mara, attempted to distract him. First he informed him that his rival Devadatta had usurped the throne; but Siddhartha was unmoved. Then he raised a great storm which assailed the Bodhisattva with showers of rain, javelins, swords, arrows, rocks, hillocks and burning charcoal; but Siddhartha took no notice. Lastly he sent his three daughters, Discontent, Delight and Thirst, to seduce him; but the Bodhisattva addressed them and they were converted by his words. These temptations continued throughout the night, but Siddhartha resisted them all.

After four times seven days of fasting and deep meditation he obtained enlightenment, and became the Buddha. As he rose from his seat under the Bodhi tree (the tree of enlightenment), he declared that Mara was overcome, that all evil was destroyed and that he, Buddha, was the lord of the three worlds.

Preaching

Buddha now had to make the choice between preaching the truth to all mankind—and seeking only his own salvation. Brahma appeared before him and asked him to do the former; Mara, having failed to prevent Buddha's own enlightenment, now urged the latter course. But Buddha decided to remain and teach. Two merchants, with whom he had his first meal after enlightenment, became his first disciples. Then Buddha decided to seek out his old teachers. Trying to cross the Ganges, he had no money to pay the ferryman, who refused to take him over for the price of 'rowing him across the ocean of life'. So Buddha took flight and soared over the river.

He found his teachers dead, but his five disciples still deep in their asceticism in the Deer Park at Sarnath near Benares. As they saw him approaching they resolved not to rise and greet him, because he had abandoned his vows; but despite themselves they got up and showed him reverence. But they did not yet call him Buddha, and laughed when he explained to them that they should show him the proper respect. Nevertheless he had the patience to teach them the Four Holy Truths and the Holy Eightfold Path, the product of his enlightenment. Though the teaching of the Law (Dharma) came to Buddha by sudden revelation, we can see how it is the product of the experience of all his lives as a Bodhisattva. The Four Holy Truths are that birth, age, sickness and death are sorrow, and so is the clinging to earthly things; that the chain of reincarnation is the direct result of attachment to life and of desire; that the extinction of desire is essential for the attainment of detachment; and that the only way to extinguish desire is to follow the Eightfold Path. The Path consists of right belief (freedom from illusion, maya); right intention; right word—truth and openness; right conduct, peaceful and pure; right living, causing no injury; right effort towards self-control; right thinking—applying the mind to religious experience; and right meditation on all the mysteries of life.

Buddha's exposition of the Dharma in the Deer Park is referred to as the first turning of the Wheel of the Law. The Buddha revealed by this doctrine is clearly very different from that portrayed as the ninth avatar of Vishnu, for

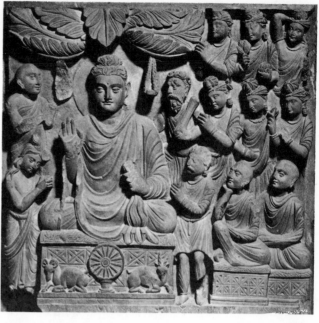

The sermon in the Deer Park at Sarnath near Benares. Buddha returned here after his enlightenment to preach to his five former disciples, who at first scorned him for abandoning asceticism but then were converted.

The Great Departure. Lying on a couch prepared beneath the Mallas' Sal trees at Kusinagra and surrounded by his monks and by kings and noblemen summoned to his side by Ananda, Buddha addressed his last words to his followers. Then he turned away and died, immediately entering Nirvana. Gandhara style reliefs.

his teaching is that neither asceticism nor indulgence is the path to enlightenment. But this part of Buddha's life hardly belongs to mythology; it is, however, the core round which the specifically Buddhist mythology was constructed.

Buddha's five disciples were joyfully converted, and after them many others. Buddha exhibited his miraculous powers as an aid to conversion. Among his converts were five hundred robbers, reclaimed in a mass conversion, who all became mendicants; thousands of people at Srivasti, who watched him walking on air and emitting light from his body; others before whom he multiplied his body; and King Bimbisara and his retinue of 'twelve myriads of men'.

At last, at the invitation of his son Rahula, Buddha went back as promised to his home at Kapilavastu. At first his return seemed hardly the triumph that Suddhodana had expected. Before seeing his family Buddha went begging for food in the streets of Kapilavastu; his father was horrified that his son should thus bring disgrace on his family. Buddha explained that he was no longer of the race of kings, but of the race of those who beg for their food; and that a man's station in life should depend on him and not upon his birth. He then preached the Dharma to his father and converted him. Next he went to seek his wife, who alone of the family had not greeted him. As soon as they were reunited she fell down and worshipped him and, upon her conversion, resolved together with Siddhartha's foster-mother Prajapati to found an order of nuns.

Two more important conversions were to follow. The first was of Ananda, to whom Buddha spoke on the eve of his wedding. The wedding, however, never took place; for Buddha, giving him a begging bowl, convinced Ananda that the greatest festival is the life of a monk who has attained Nirvana. Ananda, granted a vision of heaven and goddesses, was now to become Buddha's most faithful follower. The other conversion was of his own son Rahula, who came to his father asking for his patrimony and through Buddha's teaching was given an everlasting spiritual inheritance and became a monk. Finally Buddha ascended to the Heaven of the Thirty-three Divinities to convert his mother. He remained there for three months and accepted alms from the gods, who gained spiritual calm from his presence. On his return he was accompanied by Sakra (Indra) and the other gods and by a host of Brahmins, and was greeted on earth by all its kings, who bowed low to receive him.

The opposition to Buddha

The great success of Buddha's teaching created enemies for him and these were led by Devadatta, his rival from childhood. Devadatta's hatred of Buddha had steadily grown and now he sought to destroy him and his movement. His first tactic was to engineer a schism among Buddha's followers. Having weakened the movement from within, Devadatta removed one of its most powerful supporters, Ajasat, the son of King Bimbisara, Buddha's patron. He made an alliance with the king, and after gaining his confidence incited Ajasat to murder his own father. Next he planned an attack on Buddha himself. Enlisting the help of thirty-one of Ajasat's servants, he instructed one of them to murder Buddha. Then he arranged that another two would murder the first; another four would murder these two, a further eight would murder the previous four, and sixteen would murder the eight. Then he himself planned to murder the sixteen.

But the plan came to nothing, for as soon as Ajasat's servants heard Buddha preaching they became firm converts. Devadatta made a second attempt on Buddha's life; he had a great boulder rolled down a mountainside in the hope that it would crush Buddha; but before it reached him it split in two and fell to either side. The third plan was to set a drunken elephant, Malagiri, to crush Buddha as he was begging for alms. The people all around were terrified and fled; only Ananda, despite his fear, remained, admiring Buddha who advanced calmly, quite unmoved. As the elephant came nearer, Buddha's spiritual power overcame its spirit; the creature faltered, and finally came to Buddha and laid its head on the ground before him.

Following this incident all Devadatta's followers were converted and he, in despair, fell ill. When he recovered from his illness it was generally believed that he had repented. He went to visit Buddha in his monastery; but his true motives were revealed as he approached the gate, for flames shot out of the earth and consumed him.

The desire for death

Buddha's ministry continued for forty-five years, and one day Mara, the Evil One himself, approached him, again attempting to persuade him to accept Nirvana for himself and to forget about helping others to attain it through his preaching. To Mara's surprise, for Buddhas have the power to live to the end of the eon, Buddha replied that he would live for only three months more. As he spoke the earth trembled and Indra's thunderbolts flashed. Ananda came to him and asked why the universe was moved and filled with portents, and Buddha explained that he had given up his desire to live. He then adopted a position of yogic concentration and shook off the life remaining to him; thereafter his psychic power alone sustained him in a state where he was free from the bonds of Becoming.

When he knew that death was near Buddha made his last journey, to Kusinagara in the country of the Mallas. He reached a grove of sal trees which were flowering out of season and there lay down for his last rest on earth. He was visited by kings and noblemen and Brahmins, who had been summoned by Ananda from all the neighbouring countries. He spoke kindly to all who came, turning none away, and comforted Ananda and his other disciples, who despite some degree of holy detachment could not restrain their grief. Charging them to pursue their salvation diligently, Buddha fell unconscious and shortly died.

As Buddha's soul entered into Nirvana the earth trembled and was shrouded in darkness, while the heavens were lit up with a strange light and crossed by flashing thunderbolts. High winds swept over the earth and the rivers seemed to boil. The lesser spirits—Nagas, yakshas and Gandharvas—bowed in grief, but the higher gods who understood the meaning of these portents rejoiced. The body lay in state for six days and on the seventh was placed on a great funeral pile. There was great difficulty in igniting the pyre, but when the moment had come, divinely ordained, the fire lit of its own accord. When the fire had done its work Buddha's remains were seen, looking like a heap of pearls. They were divided into eight parts and taken reverently by eight princes into kingdoms near and far.

Buddhist cosmology and the Buddhist pantheon

Buddhism, with its strictly philosophical nature, was to the ordinary mind a distant and lofty creed. As time went by some of the age-old beliefs crept in and mingled with the new. Popular Buddhism is a strange mixture of Mahayana and the Hindu pantheon and cosmology.

The Buddhist universe is called Chakravala and there are three planes: above, around and below Mount Meru. The lower plane contains one hundred and thirty-six hells, each reserved for a particular type of sinner. Revilers of Buddha and the Law are sent to Avici, the lowest. Souls are reborn into the world after a period in one of these hells. These periods last at least five hundred hell years, each day of which equals fifty years on earth. The plane around Mount Meru contains the worlds of animals, ghosts (Pretas—beings consumed with hunger and thirst), demons and men. Around the peak of Mount Meru is the Heaven of the Four Great Kings: Dhritarashtra, guardian of the East; Virudhaka, guardian of the South; Virupaksha, guardian of the West; and Kubera, or Vaisravana, guardian of the North. Above this heaven is the Heaven of the Thirty-three Divinities or the Heaven of Sakra (Indra). Above these two heavens and the summit of Meru are twenty-four more heavens, one on top of the other, all lit with their own radiance. Six are inhabited by those who enjoy the pleasures of the senses. The other twenty heavens are the Chyana Lokas (regions of abstract meditation) and the Arupa Lokas (formless worlds), reserved for men of a high order such as Buddhas and Arhats.

Much of the Hindu pantheon has also been adapted to meet the needs of popular Buddhism, though the gods' functions are generally quite different. Indra (Sakra) is still King of the gods and Yama, called Dharmaraja, presides over the hells. But Shiva and Parvati, usually called Mahakala and Mahakali, are reduced to being Buddha's doorkeepers, while Kubera, called Jambhala, is his bodyguard. The goddesses of the Buddhist pantheon are reminiscent of the Sivaite shakti cults, though in their cruel aspects they often outdo Durga and Kali. The most revered of these goddesses is Tara, who is yellow, red or blue when she threatens and white or green when gentle and loving. Other terrifying goddesses are Kurukulla, and Cunda who, according to the spirit of the onlooker, appears to bear either arms or symbols of divine charity. Hariti, Kubera's wife, suckles five hundred demons and her principal feature is her inexhaustible fecundity. Ushas, the goddess of dawn, has her counterpart in Marishi but unlike Ushas she is frightening; she has a third eye on her brow like Shiva, three hideous faces and ten threatening arms. Gentler goddesses are Sarasvati, goddess of teaching, and the chief goddess, Prajna, goddess of knowledge. The gods exceed Shiva in his terrifying aspect. One, Yamantaka, accompanies Manjusri, the consort of Sarasvati, and like Shiva wears a necklace of skulls, has several heads and many arms. Another, Trailokyvavijaya, has four heads and four menacing arms and tramples Shiva underfoot.

The ruins of ancient Sarnath, near Benares. It was here, in the Deer Park, that Buddha preached his first sermon.

Trisala dreaming. Above her are the sixteen images of which she dreamed and which together foretold the coming birth of a great son, an emperor or a Tirthankara.

JAIN MYTHOLOGY

Mahavira, the great teacher of Jainism in the present age, lived at the same time as Buddha and like him was of the Kshatriya caste. He differed from Buddha, however, in that his parents were already Jains, worshipping the Lord Parshva, whose enlightenment resembles that of Buddha, though its message was different—for its core was the resistance to the urge to kill. Mahavira's parents therefore welcomed and encouraged his calling. His birth in Benares was heralded by miraculous portents. His mother Trisala, also called Priyakarini, had a series of sixteen dreams which foretold the birth of a son and his future greatness. In these dreams she saw in turn a white elephant, a white bull, a white lion, Sri or Lakshmi, fragrant Mandara flowers, the moon lighting the universe with silvery beams, the radiant sun, a jumping fish symbolising happiness, a golden pitcher, a lake filled with lotus flowers, the ocean of milk, a celestial palace, a vase as high as Meru, filled with gems,

a fire fed by sacrificial butter, a ruby and diamond throne, and a celestial king ruling on earth. These dreams were interpreted as portents of the coming birth of a great emperor or of a Tirthankara, a being higher than a god, who spends some time as a teacher on earth and whose soul is liberated by possession of the five kinds of knowledge.

Shortly thereafter the gods transferred the unborn child from the womb of Devananda, a Brahmin's wife, to that of Trisala, and in due course Vardhamana was born. The child was of exceptional beauty and developed great physical and spiritual strength. When he was only a boy he overcame a mad elephant by grasping its trunk, running up its head and riding on its back. On another occasion, when a god, to test his nerve, had lifted him up into the air, he tore the god's hair out and beat him until he was released.

Vardhamana obtained his enlightenment while sitting

under an Asoka tree after two and a half days of fasting. The gods had all gathered to watch the great event, and at the moment of Vardhamana's enlightenment they bore him up and carried him in a palanquin to a park, where they set him on a five-tiered throne and acknowledged him as Mahavira. Here he stripped himself of all his clothes and instead of shaving his head tore his hair out by the roots, for he was above pain. As he cast off his clothes, they were caught by the god Vaisravana (Kubera); one sect, the Digambaras (air-clad), believe that Mahavira wore no clothes thereafter, but the Swetambaras believe that Indra then presented him with a white robe, for white robes, unlike all other personal possessions, do not impede liberation of the soul by enmeshing it in the cycle of earthly life.

Mahavira's life was one of unexampled virtue and well illustrated his imperviousness to physical pain and his detachment from worldy concerns. After his enlightenment he gave away all his possessions and owned nothing beside the robe presented to him by Indra. A Brahmin, Somadatta, reminded him that he had received nothing when Mahavira distributed his wealth, and so the holy man gave him half the robe. Somadatta could not wear the garment without the other half, but he hesitated to ask for it and decided that he must steal it. The moment he chose was when Mahavira was engaged in penances while sitting on a thorny shrub; but Somadatta injured himself as he stealthily drew the robe away. Mahavira became aware of the theft only when he had risen from his deep meditation but he uttered no word of reproach, only making use of the incident as a lesson in his teaching. On another occasion while he was meditating some herdsmen drove nails into his ears and scorched his feet; but Mahavira maintained utter indifference to such pain. Another time, when Mahavira was meditating in a field, a farmer asked him to guard his bullocks. Mahavira took no notice of the farmer, who returned some time later to find the bullocks had strayed away, and Mahavira still sitting there, answering nothing to his complaints. The farmer went to search for his bullocks but returned empty-handed, only to find that the bullocks were once again back in the field. The farmer immediately assumed that Mahavira was trying to steal the animals, and began to twist his neck. But Mahavira still made no sign, and would have been killed had Indra not intervened and saved him. Ever after Indra assumed the role of Mahavira's bodyguard, and so saved mankind from the effects of such sacrilege.

When Mahavira felt that he was about to die he spent seven days preaching to all the rulers of the world, who had assembled to hear his holy words. They learnt of the complicated metaphysics of Jainism and above all of the absolute prohibition on killing, which led to the belief that the most virtuous life is spent sitting still and fasting, for then a man runs no risk of injuring life even involuntarily by swallowing or treading upon insects. On the seventh day of his preaching Mahavira ascended a diamond throne bathed in supernatural light. His death took place unseen by his assembled followers, for they all fell asleep. All the lights of the universe went out as the great Mahavira died, so his followers when they woke to darkness illuminated the city with torches. Some believe that Mahavira died surrounded only by a few of the faithful, but repeat that the moment of death was unseen.

With his death Mahavira became a Siddha, a freed soul of the greatest perfection, being both omniscient and detached from karma, the cycle of rebirth. In addition he was declared a Tirthankara (one who has forded the Samsara; escaped from the wheel of life), the very highest kind of Siddha, who has acquired the five kinds of knowledge, and has been a teacher on earth. Every Tirthankara has to have passed through the four stages through which a soul becomes free. Sadhus, ascetics, are at the lowest of these stages; above them come Upakhyayas, teachers; next come Acharyas, heads of orders; then Arhats, which are one stage higher and are freed souls which, though omniscient, are still attached to the mortal condition.

Mahavira enthroned, with auspicious objects above and below him. Above are a mirror, a throne, a vase and a water vessel; below are a fish, a srivatsa (said to represent a curl on Vishnu's breast) and a swastika. Miniatures from the Kalpasutras, fifteenth century.

A symbolic representation of a Jain holy place. Carved marble panel, nineteenth century.

The Jain universal cycle

The Jains imagine time as an eternally revolving wheel. Its upward course, Utsarpini, is under the influence of a good serpent, while its downward course, Avasarpini, is under the influence of an evil one. The Utsarpini consists of six progressively improving ages, while the Avasarpini consists of six periods of progressively greater degeneracy, rather like the Hindu Mahayugas. But the Avasarpini leads not to destruction but to the beginning of another Utsarpini.

Each Avasarpini and each Utsarpini produce twenty-four Tirthankaras, one of which was Mahavira. Tirthankaras cannot intercede on behalf of the faithful, for there is no ultimate god; their value to mankind is as objects of meditation. The world is at present near the end of an Avasarpini. Of the Tirthankaras which it has produced, many seem to have some connection with Hindu mythology. Thus the first, Rishabadeva, attained Nirvana on Mount Kailasa, the abode of Shiva; the seventh, Chandraprabha, was born after his mother drank the moon; the eleventh was born of parents who were both called Vishnu, and he attained Nirvana on Mount Kailasa; and the twenty-second, Neminatha, was born in Dwarka and was a cousin of Krishna. The other holy figures of Jainism would also seem from their names to be connected with Hindu belief. They are twelve Chakravartins, nine Narayanas or Vasudevas, nine Pratinarayanas or Prativasudevas, nine Balabhadras and, below them, nine Naradas, eleven Rudras and twenty-four Kamadevas. Jain gods and demons

are largely of Hindu inspiration, but there is one important difference: while demons can eventually work out their salvation, gods exist on a different plane and cannot attain liberation without first becoming human beings.

The Jain universe

The universe is symbolised by a headless man divided into three: trunk, waist and legs. The right leg contains seven hells where lesser gods are torturers of souls, each one specialising in a particular brand of physical torture. The left leg, Patala, contains ten kinds of minor deities and two groups of demons, each kind inhabiting a different kind of tree. The black Vyantara demons include the Pisachas, the Bhutas, the Yakshas, the Gandharvas and the Mahoragas. The white Vyantara demons include the Rakshasas and the Kimpurushas. The more fearsome of the two groups of demons are the Vana Vyantaras, which are subdivided into Anapanni, Panapanni, Isivayi, Bhutavayi, Kandiye, Mahakandiye, Kohanda and Pahanga.

The middle region of the universe is our world, and consists of eight ring-shaped continents separated by eight ring-shaped oceans. These surround Mount Meru.

The upper region contains in its lower part Kalpa, which is subdivided into sixteen heavens. Above these is the Kalpathitha, subdivided into fourteen regions. Gods of varying rank inhabit all these heavens, and they are divided both geographically and by caste, with Indra as their king. Some of the gods take pleasure in listening to the sermons of the sages, but not all are religious. Above the heavens of Kalpathitha is the home of the Siddhas, Siddha Sila.

Santinatha, the sixteenth Tirthankara, whose birth to a king of Hasti-napur brought peace to the land and respite from a plague. His height was forty bowshots and his sign is the deer. Stone sculpture, twelfth century. Victoria and Albert Museum

Further reading list

Archer, W. G. *The Loves of Krishna*. Allen & Unwin, London, 1957.

Basham, A. L. *The Wonder that was India*. Sidgwick & Jackson, London 1954.

Bhagavad Gita trans. by Juan Mascaro. Penguin Classics, Harmondsworth, 1962.

Buddhist Scriptures trans. by Edward Conze. Penguin Classics, Harmondsworth, 1959.

Dowson, John. *Classical Dict. of Hindu Mythology*. Kegan Paul, London, 1961.

Dubois, J. A. *Hindu Manners, Customs, and Ceremonies*. Clarendon Press, Oxford, 1906.

Elwin, Verrier. *The Myths of Middle India*. Oxford Univ. Press, 1949.
The Tribal Myths of Orissa. Oxford Univ. Press, 1954.

Garratt, G. T. *The Legacy of India*. Clarendon Press, Oxford, 1937.

Gray, J. E. B. *Indian Folk-Tales and Legends*. Oxford Univ. Press, 1961.

Grimal, P. (Ed.). *Larousse World Mythology*. Paul Hamlyn Ltd., London, 1965.

Hindu Scriptures trans. by Nicol MacNicol. Everyman Library (J. M. Dent), London, 1963.

Humphreys, C. *Buddhism*. Penguin Books, Harmondsworth, 1951.

Jaini, Jagnanderlal. *Outlines of Jainism*. Cambridge Univ. Press, 1940.

MacCulloch, John A. & Gray, Louis H. *The Mythology of all Races*. 13 vols. Cooper Square Pubs. Inc., New York, 1922.

Mahabharata & Ramayana condensed and rendered into English rhyming verse by Romesh C. Dutt. Everyman Library (J. M. Dent), London, 1963.

Marshall, Sir John. *Mohenjo Daro and the Indus Civilisation*. 3 vols. Arthur Probsthain, Ltd., on behalf of the Archaeological Survey of India, London, 1931.

Riencourt, Amaury de. *The Soul of India*. Jonathan Cape, London, 1961.

Smith, Vincent A. *The Oxford History of India*. Clarendon Press, Oxford, 1958.

Stevenson, S. *The Heart of Jainism*. Oxford Univ. Press, 1915.

Weber, Max. *The Religion of India*. Allen & Unwin, London, 1958.

Upanishads, The trans. by Juan Mascaro. Penguin Classics, Harmondsworth, 1965.

Woodward, F. L. *Some Sayings of the Buddha*. Oxford Univ. Press Worlds Classics, 1938.

Zaehner, R. C. *Hinduism*. Oxford Univ. Press H.U.L., 1962.

Acknowledgments

The publishers gratefully acknowledge the following for permission to reproduce the illustrations indicated.

Colour plates. Freer Gallery of Art, Washington: 53. Paul Hamlyn Library: 26, 30, 31, 35, 49, 56, 57, 74, 75, 98, 127, 131. Leonard von Matt: 34, 130, Indrajit Nalawala: 82, 83. Paul Popper: 6. Josephine Powell: 106, 107. Staatliche Museen zu Berlin: 99. Wim Swaan: 27, 52, 103.

Black and white. Paul Almasy: 13 *right*. Arch. Survey of India: 12 *upper seals*, 22, 36, 119, 134.

B. K. B. Benares Hindu University: 14 *left*, 50 *top*, 60 *top*, 63 *top*, 66 *bott.*, 72, 112 *top*. Museum of Fine Arts, Boston: *endpapers* 45, 66 *top*, 92 *right*, 94 *top right*, 100. Boudot-Lamotte: 12 *bott.*, 16, 43, 59 *top*, 79. Denis Brihat-Rapho: 50 *bott*. British Museum: 12 *swastika*, 37, 38 *right*, 64, 69, 94 *bott. left*, 126 *top*, 133 *right*. Bulloz: 58. J. Allan Cash: 10, 40, 47, 85, 136. District Gallery, Cent. Bohemian Cty., Prague: 24. Max Pol Fouchet: 80, 90 *top*, 115. Freer Gallery of Art, Washington: 132 *right*, 133 *left*, 134 *bott.*, 137. Giraudon: 14 right, 19, 21 *left*, 86 *bott.*, 94 *top left*, 108. Musée Guimet: 65, 97. Paul Hamlyn Library: 21 *right*, 32, 42, 45, 59 *bott.*, 60 *bott. left*, 73, 77, 78, 86 *top*, 104, 111, 113, 138. R. Lakshmi: 62, 70, 112 *bott.*, 114, 120, 139 *bott*. Lucknow State Museum: 71. Madras Govt. Museum: 92 *right*. Marburg Bildarchiv: 67, 129. Leonard von Matt: 25, 28, 38 *left*, 105, 110, 116, 117. Victoria & Albert Museum: 13 *left*, 55, 61, 63 *bott.*, 84, 90 *right*, 94 *bott. right*, 102, 118, 122, 124, 126 *left*, 132 *left*, 139 *top*. Vienna Bildarchiv: 89.

Index <small>Figures in italics refer to illustrations</small>

Acharyas 137
Adhiratha 120
Aditi 20, 51, 69, 80, 94
Adityas 15, 20, 33, 118
Agastya 59, 76, 79, 109, 119
Agni: Vedic 15, 17, 18, 19, 19, 20, 21, 28, 32; Hindu 38, 46, 60, 76, 79, 79, 87, 96, 101, 110
Ahalya 76
Ahi *see* Vritra
ahimsa 39
Airavata 17, 48, 66, 72, 73
Ajamila 77
Ajasat 134
Akrura 68, 108
Alaka 85
Amaravati 73
Ambalika 120
Ambika 120
amrita (soma) 15, 16, 28, 48, 76, 101, 112-3, 117
Amvika (Viraj) 28, 92
Ananda 128, 134
Ananta *see* Shesha
Andhaka 94
Angada 104
Angiras 79
Angirasas 118
Anjana 102
Anoma, River 132
Ansa 20
Ansuman 110
Apsaras 33, 88, 116, 117
Arhats 137
Arjuna 33, 42, 54, 70, 79, 107, 120, 121-5
Arun 80

Arupa Lokas 135
Aryaman 15, 20
Aryan invaders 12
Asamanjas 110
Asita 128
Asuras 42, 111-5
Aswa, River 120
Aswapati, King 78
Aswathaman 42, 124, 125
Aswini 21
Aswins 20, 21, 22, 80, 95
Atharvans 118
Atmalingam 116
Atri 118, 119
Aurva 110, 113, 114
Avasarpini (downward course) 138
Ayodhya 55, 60, 105

Baka 114
Bakasura 63
Balabhadras 138
Balarama 61, 62, 63, 64, 68, 69, 70, 71, 72, 108, 125
Bali 22, 48, 51, 76
Bali (Sugriva's half-brother) 58, 105, 108, 115
Behula 97
Bhaga 20, 46
Bhagavad Gita 71, 124
Bhagiratha 109, 110
Bhairavi *see* Kali
Bharadwaja 119
Bharata 54, 55, 58, 102, 104, 105
Bhima 70, 70, 80, 114, 121, 122, 124, 125
Bhishma 33, 54, 110, 120, 121, 123, 124, 124, 125

Bhrigu 19, 44, 118
Bhrigus 118
Bhubaneswar 53
Bhumi *see* Prithivi
Bhutas *see* Rakshasas
Bimbisara, King 134
Bodhi tree (pipal) 132, 133
Bodhisattvas 127, 128
Bo-tree *see* Bodhi tree
Brahma 20, 24, 25, 25, 28, 29, 33, 38, 38, 41, 42, 42, 45, 46, 48, 50, 58, 81, 86, 87, 89, 93, 96, 101, 110, 114, 115, 117
Brahman 25, 37, 38, 39
Brahmani *see* Sarasvati
Brahmanic developments 23
Brahmins 11, 12, 15, 28, 39
Brihaspati 19, 76
Budha 81
Buddha 39, 126-35, 129, 132
Buddha (as ninth avatar) 28, 72
Buddhi 101
Buddhism 39, 72, 126-35
Buddhist hell 135
Bull, Indus Valley 12, 13

Chadanta 128
Chaitraratha 84
Chakravala 135
Chakravartins 138
Chand 97
Chandaka 129, 132
Chandala 73
Chandi *see* Kali
Chandra 20, 46, 48

Chandragupta 77
Chandraprabha 138
Chanura 68
Chhaya 80
Chitragupta 33
Chitrangada 120
Chunda 93
Churning of the ocean 111, 112-3
Chyana Lokas 135
Chyavana 22
Cunda 135

Daityas 33, 76, 96, 114-5
Dakinis 94, 95
Daksha 41, 44, 46, 81, 96, 118
Danavas 16, 33, 114-5
Dandapani 129
Darbas *see* Rakshasas
Dasaratha 54, 55, 102
Dasra *see* Aswins
'Dasyus' 14
Dasyus *see* Rakshasas
Devadatta 128, 134
Devaka 62
Devaki 62, 68, 72
Devananda 136
Devas 129, 132
Devasena *see* Kaumari
Devi (Mahadevi) 44, 62, 90, 91-94, 97
Dhanus 48
Dhanwantari 48, 113
Dharani 91
dharma 33, 39, 47, 72
Dharma (Buddhist) 133, 134
Dharma (god) 24, 25, 88, 125
Dharmaraja *see* Yama
Dhenuka 63
Dhrishtadyumna 121, 124, 125

Dhritarashtra, King 120, 121, 123, 125
Dhumralochana 93
Digambaras 137
Dilipa 110
Dilwara 81
Dipankara, Lord 126
Dipavati 126
Diti 96
Draupadi 121, 122, 125
Dravidian peoples 12, 13, 38
Drona 121-5
Drumalika 61
Drupada, King 121, 122, 124
Durga 75, 91, 92, 93
Durga (demon) 93
Durvasas 60, 76, 120
Duryodhana 121-5
Dussasana 122, 123
Dwaparayuga 24
Dwarka 68, 71
Dyaus 15, 16, 18, 21, 95
Dyumatsena, King 78

Fertility goddesses:
Indus valley 12;
Bengal 13, 26
Four Holy Truths 133

Ganadevatas 100, 118
Gandhari 125
Gandharvas 20, 25, 33, 80, 117
Ganesa 12, 29, 100, 100, 101, 116
Ganga 54, 87, 89, 108, 108, 109-10, 120
Ganges, River 25, 29, 43, 44, 47, 86, 88, 110, 120
Garuda 24, 25, 80, 99,

101-2, 113
Gauri-Jagadgauri *see* Devi
Gautama 76, 119
Gayatri 89, 90
Govardhana, Mt. 66
grahas *see* Rakshasas

Hanuman 58, 60, 80, 102, 102, 104, 105, 115
Harappa 12, 13
Harihara 33, 34, 40
Hariti 135
Hastinapur 121, 125
Hayagriva 48
Heaven of the Four Great Kings 135
Heaven of the thirty-three divinities 134, 135
Himavan 91, 109
Hiranyakasipu 50, 50, 51, 112, 115
Hiranyaksha 50
Hiranyapura 115
Holy Eightfold Path 133

Indra: Vedic 15, 15, 16, 17, 18, 20, 28, 42; Hindu 46, 58, 64, 66, 70, 72, 73-5, 79, 81, 86, 87, 96, 102, 104, 110, 113, 115, 116, 125; Jain 137
Indrajit *see* Meghanada
Indrani 16, 17, 73
Indraprastha 88, 122
Indus Valley civilisation 13, 14

Jagadgauri 92
Jaganmata *see* Devi

Jahnu 110
Jain holy place *138*
Jain universe 138
Jainism 136-8
Jamadagni 51, 119
Jambavan 69, 105, 108
Jambavati 69, 71, 108
Jambhala 135
Janaka 55
Jarasandha 61, 68, 70, 70
Jatakas 126
Jatayu 58, 60
Jumna, River 62, 67, 110, 120

Kadru 97
Kaikeyi, Queen 54, 55, 102
Kailasa, Mt. 44, 109, 116
Kalaka 128
Kalama, Arara 132
Kalanemi 104
Kalaratri 93
Kalayavana 68
Kali 91, 93, 94, *95*
Kalichi 77
Kalindi 69
Kaliya *55*, 63, 114
Kaliyuga 25, 72
Kalki (tenth avatar) 25, *25*, 72, *72*
Kalpa 24, 138
Kalpasutras 129, 136
Kalpathitha 138
Kama 29, 44, 86, 87, 88, 91, 96, 99, 117
Kamadevas 138
Kamadhenu 51, 87
Kamala *see* Lakshmi
Kansa 61, 62, 68, 114
Kantaka 132
Kapila 110
Kapilavastu 128, 132, 134
karma 37, 137
Karna 80, 120, 121, 122, 123, 125
Kartavirya 51
Karttikeya 29, 44, 84-88, *84*, 91 101, 110, 115
Kasyapa 51, 80, 96, 97, 101, 115, 119
Kaumari 86, 87
Kauravas 54, 71, 121-5
Kausalya 54
Kaustubha 48
Kesin 86, 87, 114, 115
Kesini 110
Ketu 115
Khajuraho *90*
Khara 55
Khasa 115
Kinnaras 84, 117
Konarak *80*
Kond mother goddess *26*
Kravyads 18
Krishna (eighth avatar) 47, 48, 55, 61-72, *63*, 64, 66, 79, 96, 105, 108, *120*, 123, 124, 125
Krita 124, 125
Kritavarman 124, 125
Kritayuga 24, 47
Krittikas 87, 88
Kshatriyas 15, 28, 51
Kubera 58, 76, *84*, 84, 87, 115, 117
Kubja 68
Kumara *see* Karttikeya
Kumbhakarna 59, 108, *113*, 117
Kunti 80, 120, 121, 122, 123, 125
Kurma (second avatar) 48
Kuru 117, 121

Kurukshetra, Battle of 122, 123
Kurukulla 135
Kusa 60
Kusanabha, King 80
Kusinagara 134

Lakshmana 54, 55, 58, 60, 76, 104
Lakshmi 46, 47, 48, 72, 81, 89, 90, 90-91
Lakshmindra 97
Lanka 54, 58, 80, 88
Lava 60
Lingam symbol *see* Phallic worship
Lord of the Beasts 12, 23, 39, 46
Lord of the Universe 25

Madri 120, 121
Magadha 132
Mahabharata 33, 39, 42, 46, 48, 54, 71, 79, 100, 119-25
Mahakala 135
Mahakali 135
Mahamaya, Queen *126*, 126, 128
Mahapralya 24
Maharatha, King 128
Mahasattva 128
Mahavira 136, 137, *137*
Mahayugas 24
Mahendra, Mt. 104
Mahisha 92, 93
Maitreya 126
Makara 79, 88
Malagiri 134
Manasa 97
Mandara, Mt. 48, 109, 112, 113
Manes *see* Pitris
Manjusri *126*, 135
Manu 29, 39, 95
Manus 118
Manwantaras 118
Mara 132, 133, 134
Marica 59
Marichi 118
Marishi 135
Markandeya 29, 78
Marttanda *see* Vivasvat
Maruts 17, 23, 28, 33, 79, 96, 118
Matarisvan 19
Matsya (first avatar) 48
maya (illusion) 14, 44
Mayavati *see* Rati
Megha 126
Meghanada 58, 76, 77
Mena 91
Meru, Mt. 25, 33, 47, 109, 125
Mitra 15, 20, 32, 46, 79
Mohenjodaro *11*, *12*, 13
Mohini 113, 115
Munda 93
Muru 70

Nagas 33, *105*, 108, 113, *114*, 114, 117
Naginis *114*
Nahusha, King 76
Nakula 121, 125
Nala 88
Nalasotu (Nala's bridge) 58
Nanda 62, 66
Nandi *41*, 43, *46*, 92
Nandini *see* Surabhi
Nara, waters of 25, 28, 29
Narada 78, 80, 96, 108, 116, 118
Naradas (Jain) 138
Naraka 69, 70
Narasinha (fourth avatar) *50*, 50

Narayana 28, 29, 46
Narayanas (Jain) 138
Narmada 117
Nasatya *see* Aswins
Neminatha 138
Nidhis 84
Nikasha 116
Nirrita *32*
Nirvana 134
Nisumbha 93

Padma *see* Lakshmi
Pandavas 71, 121-5
Pandu 120, 121, 125
Panis *see* Rakshasas
Parasara 120
Parasurama (sixth avatar) 51-54, *55*, 101, 121
Paravani 84
Parijata 48
Parijata tree 70
Parshva, Lord 136
Parvati 29, 43, 44, 44, 46, 81, 86, 87, 88, 91, *92*, 92, 96, 100, 101, 116
Patala 51, 108, 110, 113
Patala (Jain) 138
Pavanarekha 61
Phallic worship 13, 42, 43
Pinaka 43
pipal tree *see* Bodhi tree
Pisachas *see* Rakshasas
Pitamaya *see* Brahma
Pitripati *see* Yama
Pitris 73, 77, 79, 118
Prabhasa 71
Pradyumna *see* Kama
Pragjyotisha 69
Prahlada 51
Prajapati 23, 29
Prajapati (sister of Mahamaya) 128
Prajapatis 79, 118
Prajna 135
Pralamba 64
Prasena 105
Pratinarayanas 138
Prithivi 15, 16, 18, *25*, *33*, 95, 96
Prithu 96
Priyakarini *see* Trisala
Pulastya 115, 118
Puloman 76
Purusha 17, 25, 28, 29
Pushan 20, 46
Pushpagiri 79
Pushpaka (chariot) 84, 88
Put 33
Putana 62, 64

Radha *55*, 66, 68, 91
Radha (*Mahabharata*) 120
Rahu 115
Rahula 129, 134
Raji 76
Rakshasas 29, 115-7
Raktavira 93
Rama *see* Ramachandra
Ramachandra (seventh avatar) 54-60, *55*, 58, 60, 102, 104, 105, 108, 115, 117
Ramayana 54, 79
Rambha 48
Rasalia (Krishna's dance) 66
Rati 86, 88, 96
Ratri 22
Ravana *53*, 54, 55, 58, 76, 77, 104, 105, 108, 114, 115-7
Revanta 80
Revati 96
Ribhus 18, 118
Rig Veda 17, 40
Rishabadeva 138
Rishis, Seven 118-9

Rohini 62, 72, 81
rta 15, 33
Rudra 17, 22, 23, 29, 37, 39, 42, 79
Rudraka 132
Rudras 118
Rudras (Jain) 138
Rukma 69
Rukmini 68, 69, 70, 91, 96

Sabahu 59
Sadhyas 118
Sagara, King 109, 110
Sagara (Ocean) 110, 113
Sages *see* Rishis
Sahadeva 121, 124, 125
Sakra 128, *129*, 132, 134, 135
Saktasura 62
Sakuni 122, 124
Samba 61
Sampati 104
samsara 37, 47, 72
Samsara (Jain) 137
Samvarana, King 117
Sanchi 107
Sandhya 41
Sani 100
Sanjna 80, 88, 95
Sankha 48
Sankhasura 68
Santanu, King 110, 120
Santinatha *139*
Saptarshis *see* Rishis
Saranyu 18, 20, 32, 80, 88, 95
Sarasvati 20, 41, 46, 81, *83*, 89, 89-90, 117
Sarasvati (Buddhist) 135
Sarayu, River 60
Sarnath 135
Sashona 93
Satarupa *see* Sarasvati
Sati 44, 46, 87, 91
Satrajit 69, 105, 108
Satrughna 54
Satyabhama 69, 70, 108
Satyavan 78
Satyavati 120
Saurasa 104
Savitri 77, 78
Savitri (goddess) 20
Savitri (son of Aditi) 20
Sermon in the Deer Park *133*, 133
Shambhara 96
Shasti 97
Shesha 25, *25*, 44, 46, 62, 71, 97
Shitala 97, *97*
Shiva: 12, 13, 23, *25*, *33*, 44, 51, 77, 78, 79, 81, 86, 87, 88, 91, 93, 94, 96, 100, 101, 110, 113, 115, 116, 125;
    Ardhanarisvara *46*;
    Bhairava 37, 42, *43*, 43; Bhuteswara 29, 43; Hindu 39, 42-6; Lingodbhava *38*, 41; Lord of the Beasts 12; Mahadeva 26, 42; Nataraja 29; Natesa 42
Shiva's weapons 43
Siddhartha 128, 129, 132, *132*, 133
Siddhas 118, 137, 138
Siddha Sila 138
Siddhi 101
Sisupala 48, 69, 70, 70, 115
Sita 55, 58, 59, 60, *62*, 91, 104
Skanda *see* Karttikeya

Skanda (son of Agni) 128
Soma: Vedic 19, *19*, 20; Hindu 81
Soma *see* amrita
Somadatta 137
Somnath, shrine of 101
Sonuttara 128
Sraddha 88
Sri *see* Lakshmi
Srirangam 102
Subrahmanya *see* Karttikeya
Sudarsana 70
Suddhodana, King 128, 129, 134
Sudras 28
Sugriva 58, 80, *105*, 108, 117
Sukanya 22
Sukra 20
Sumati 110
Sumbha 93, *112*
Sumitra 54
Sunda *111*
Sundarnand 129
Sura 48
Surabhi 48, 66, 119
Surpanakha 55, *59*
Surya: Vedic 15, 18, 20, 21; Hindu 38, 75, 79-80, 88, 95
Sutlej, River 110
Swaha 87
Swarga (Indra's heaven) *endpapers*, 17, 22, 33, 58, 73, 110, 125
Swastika *12*
Swetambaras 137
Syamantaka 105

Tandava (Shiva's dance) 44
Tapati 117
Tara (Buddhist) 135
Tara (Wife of Brihaspati) 81
Taraka 87, 88
Tilottama *111*
Tirthankaras 136, 137, 138
Trailokyvavijaya 135
Tretayuga 24, 51
Triad of gods 40, 41
Triad of goddesses 94
Trinavarta 62
Trisala *136*, 136
Trisiras 93
Tvashtri 15, 17, 18, 33, 88

Uchchaisravas 48, 73, 87, 101
Ugrasena 61, 68, 71, 72
Ugrasura 63
Uma 91, *92*, 92
Universal spirit 25
Upakhyayas 137
Upanishads 39
Upasunda *111*
Urvasi 79
Uruvela 132
Usanas 81
Ushas 15, 21, *21*, 22, 23, 95
Utathya 89
Utsarpini (upward course) 128

Vach *see* Sarasvati
Vaijayanta 88
Vaikuntha 47
Vaisravana 137
Vaisyas 28
Vaivaswata 48, 80
Vajra (Indra's sceptre) *15*, 16, 17
Vajranabha *see* Sudarsana
Valmiki 60
Vamana (fifth avatar) *50*, 51

Varaha (third avatar) *33*, 48-49
Vardhamana *see* Mahavira
Vartikas *see* Rakshasas
Varuna: Vedic *14*, 14, 15, 16, 17, 20, 23, 28, 32, 33, 111; Hindu 76, 78-79
Vasanta 88
Vasishta 118, 119
Vasudeva 62, 68, 72
Vasuki 43, 48, 108, *111*, 112, 113
Vasus 17, 33, 110, 118
Vatsasura 63
Vayu: Vedic 15, 17, 18, 28; Hindu 76, 80-81, 87, 102
Vedas 12, 14, 28
Vena 95, 96
Vichitravirya 120
Vidharba 110
Vidura 120, 121
Vinata 101, 108
Vindhya 109
Virabhadra 46
Viraj (female half) *see* Amvika
Viraj (creator of Manu) 29
Visha 48
Vishnu: Vedic 20, 22, 23; Hindu *25*, 28, 37, 39, 44, 46-8, 49, 51, 76, 77, 86, 89, 91, 101, 110, *111*, *112*, 113, 115, 116
Vishnu's avatars: *see separate entries*
    Matsya, Kurma, Varaha, Narasinha, Vamana, Parasurama, Ramachandra (Rama), Krishna, Buddha, Kalki
Vishnu's weapons 46, 47
Visvadevas 118
Visvakarma 17, 58, 68, 80, 88, 95
Visvamitra 119
Visvarupa 18
Vivasvat 20, 32, 80, 95
Vritra 15, 16, 17, 42, 73
Vyantara demons 138
Vyasa 100, 119, 120

Yadavas 61, 68, 71, 72
Yakshas 29, *116*, 117
Yama (son of Vivasvat) 20, 32, 33, 37, 80; Hindu 46, 77-78, 77, 95, 135

Yamantaka 135
Yami 20, 32, 80, 95, 120
Yasapani, King 128
Yasoda 62, *63*
Yasodhara 129, 132
Yoga 48
Yoni symbol 44, 76, 91
Yudhisthira 37, 70, 121, 122, 124, 125